# Genealogical Abstracts

# of

# Orphans Court Records,

# Northampton County,

# Pennsylvania

# Volumes A-E,

# 1752-1795

# Volume 1

************************************

by
Candace E. Anderson

Published by
Closson Press
Apollo, PA

Published by
Closson Press
257 Delilah St, Apollo, PA 15613-1933
www.clossonpress.com
First Edition - Reprint
ISBN 978-1-55856-280-6
Library of Congress No. 2009926071

My search to find my ancestors in eastern Pennsylvania led me to prepare this work. After searching church records, family histories prepared by many able researchers, and, of course, the many bits and pieces of history left behind by those ancestors, I felt a more in-depth study of the times during which my early family members lived would help me understand the rich heritage they left me. I am grateful to the suggestion made to me long ago to consider the importance of the records of the Orphans Court in my efforts to find my ancestors. Not only have I found many of my family names in these records, I have also gained a clearer picture of life during the 1700s. I dedicate this book to the memory of my eastern Pennsylvania ancestors who bravely left their homelands in Europe to come to America to provide for the immediate needs of their young families and, in the process, to prepare the way for their many descendants (including me and my family) to enjoy the rich blessings that this country provides.

CEA
1998

## TABLE OF CONTENTS

**SECTION** **PAGE**

## INTRODUCTION

Northampton County, Pennsylvania, was created in 1752 but, at that time, included considerably more area than the present-day county. It was created from the northern part of Bucks County (taking from Bucks County the area now included in present-day Lehigh and Northampton Counties) plus the entire northeastern corner of Pennsylvania, until then considered unsettled lands. Its boundaries went north from the northern border of Bucks County to the southern New York border, and east from the Delaware River to as far west as the middle of present-day Lycoming County. The county held these 1752 boundaries until 1772, when Northumberland County was formed. It continued to lose area as new counties were formed, taking its present-day borders in 1843. It is important for the reader to realize that these border changes took place. Even though an ancestor may have lived in the same area for a number of years, he could have lived within the borders of several different counties during those years. The researcher, then, should study a good history of Pennsylvania to learn when these changes took place so that he can search the appropriate county records during the various time periods. Records are generally kept in the county archives where the particular area was located when the records were made, and not in the county archives where the area in now located.

One might hear the term "Orphans Court" and think that it would involve only matters concerning orphans, children without fathers and mothers. However, while the Orphans Court did deal with the concerns of orphans, it involved a lot more than that. First, it should be mentioned that "orphan" did not mean "parentless." It simply meant "fatherless." The mother was often still very much alive. At that time, there seemed to be no concept of joint ownership of property between spouses. If a man left a will, he could determine how his estate would be handled. However, if he died intestate (that is, without a will), while the widow was always provided for, the estate was divided among all of his heirs. The eldest son had preference over all other heirs in taking over the property and, if he refused to accept it, the preference was handed down, son by son, until one of them chose the honor. If no son accepted the land or if there were no sons, then the daughters had the opportunity, though, usually, only through their husbands. There are a few exceptions to this procedure found in these records, however, where a daughter in her own right inherited the property.

Types of records one can find kept by the Orphans Court, in addition to the concerns of orphans, are many. When a man died intestate, the distribution of his estate was taken to this court for consideration. Often, the names of all his heirs were listed in the records of the proceedings. The administrator of the estate could petition the court for an inquest into the estate to see if it could be conveniently partitioned among the heirs without ruining the whole. Once the administrators settled their accounts for the estate with the Registrar's Office in Easton (these accounts do not appear in the Orphans Court records), if they found that there were insufficient funds on hand to pay off the debts of the deceased and to provide for the care and education of the minor children left behind, they could petition the court for permission to sell the property. Even if a man did leave a will, sometimes an heir just was not happy with the administration account and he could petition the court for an audit to review the account. There are also records concerning wounded soldiers, or their widows, petitioning the court for money for support. Within the records are many hints of family situations which make one curious for more information—family quarrels and complaints, family hardships, disappearances of loved ones, the horrors of war, missionary work in Jamaica, even a mention of treason. All the entries have something to do with matters within Northampton County but there are entries involving the estates of men from other counties, states, or even other countries, whose heirs lived in Northampton or when they also owned property in this county.

Genealogical information one can find in these court records include the following: names of widows and children; the names of grandchildren, brothers, uncles, aunts, grandfathers, friends, and neighbors; the names of the husbands of the daughters of the deceased; the place of residence of a family and the property they held; ages, death dates, war service; the location of relatives in other counties, states, and countries; occupations. While no record includes all of this information, almost every record does give some valuable piece of genealogical data.

These court records usually state the township where the deceased lived or owned property. However, at times, the township is not specified but, rather, the deceased is said to have been from Northampton County. In some instances, he was not from the county at all but, owning property within county borders, his affairs were brought to this court. In the genealogical abstracts in this book, when the township was specified in the record or when another county was named as residence of the deceased, note is made of that fact in the abstract. If the original record simply stated that the deceased was from the county, no comment of that fact is made in this work.

Northampton County Orphans Court was generally held at Easton, the county seat. When it was not held there, note has been made in this work as to the site (this situation occurred very rarely). With one exception, every record in Volumes A to E are written in English. That one exception occurred on 26 March 1789 when the report of inquest into the valuation of an estate was written and signed in German, though the court session itself was written in English. Usually, several justices were present at each court; a minimum of three appears to have been a requirement until 1791, though as many as ten have been present at a court session. (Beginning in 1791, many court sessions met with only two justices present.) There are a number of court dates when the justices were not named, usually on consecutive days. Note has been made when this situation occurs in the records. It is probable, in these instances, that the same justices met on those days as had met on the preceding day and, so, were not re-listed. On 14 August 1777, the first court held after the Declaration of Independence, the phrase, "in the Commonwealth of Pennsylvania," was added to the heading, written in large letters. This entry was the only one where the author saw this phrase used. During the following court session, held on 17 September 1777, ten men sat as justices, more than ever before. For a very brief time, the registrar of the court recorded his name at the end of the court session.

An interesting note: In 1776, the last court held for the year was on June 18. There were several blank pages left in the record book after this date. No more entries were made until 14 August 1777—over a year between sessions. Quite probably, there was some confusion in the new country of the United States as to how to proceed, who could serve as justices in the courts, and what laws should now be followed. Very few men who had served as justices before the Declaration of Independence appear as justices after that historic day. Once court was back in session, there were quite a number of requests for guardians for orphaned children, perhaps the aftermath of war.

Following are brief explanations of the types of records brought to the Orphans Court and the meaning of certain words used:

**Administration account**: These accounts do not appear in the Orphans Court records but are often mentioned. The administrator of an estate had the duty to list all the assets and liabilities of the estate, from money on hand to how many and what type of possessions the deceased held at the time of his death (everything was listed, too, from barrels of flour and types of tools to how many items of clothing the deceased had). The account was then filed with the registrar's office at the county seat. When there was a dispute with this account by an heir (perhaps an heir felt something was omitted from the list or questioned the honesty of the administrator), the court would order an audit of the account, appointing three men to do so (at least two of whom were required to perform the audit). Even if a man left a will, the administration account of his estate could be audited under the authority of the Orphans Court if someone questioned its accuracy.

**Audit**: At least two of the three men appointed by the court were to review the administration account of the administrators of the estate in question to check for accuracy and errors. They were usually given a date to report back to the court to state their findings.

**Auditors' report**: The auditors would return to court and report what they had discovered about the administration account. Usually, during that same court session, a distribution of the estate would be made. "In pursuance of an Order of this Worshipful Court directed to us the subscribers_______, Auditors appointed to Examine the administration account of ___________...we have carefully examined the same and do find as here under stated...." Sometimes the auditors found that the administration account was just fine; at other times, though, errors were found and corrections were made.

**Distribution**: Without a will being left behind by the deceased, the court had no way of knowing what the deceased wished concerning the handling of his estate. A distribution would be made by the Orphans Court of these "will-less" estates among all the heirs, which usually included the widow and children. However, grandchildren were also included as heirs when a child of the deceased was also deceased and had left issue (children). The widow usually received one-third of the value of the estate (which would eventually go to the other heirs upon her death) and the remaining two-thirds were divided among the other heirs, the eldest son generally receiving two of the shares, all other heirs receiving one share (any grandchildren involved dividing their deceased parent's share among them). The eldest son had preference when it came to any land left in the estate if it could not be properly partitioned and distributed among the heirs. If he accepted the land, he would then be required to pay the other heirs their shares according to a certain time schedule set down by the court.

**Request sale**: When the administrator (who was often the widow, called the administratrix), after settling the estate, found that she did not have sufficient funds on hand to pay the debts of the deceased or to maintain and educate the children left behind, she would petition the court for the right to sell the property. Without permission from the court, the administrator could not sell the property of an intestate man. The court usually approved the sale, sometimes requiring an audit first, and would give the administrator a set length of time to advertize the sale. "That your Petitioner administered to her said Husbands Estate and has since settled her administration account in the Registers Office at Easton whereby it appears that the Personal Estate of the said dec'd is not sufficient to pay his just debts and bring up the children. Praying the court grant her an order to make sale of the said Tract of Land in order to pay the Just Debts of the said dec'd and bring up the children." The court would grant the petition if the administrator "...do make sale of the said Tract of Land aforesaid first giving due and publick notice of the time when and places where the same sale is to be held and also the Quantity and Quality thereof and the place where the same is situate to be fixed up at the most publick places at least ten days before the sale...."

**Return of sale**: After the land was sold, the administrator would return to court to report the sale. "That in obedience to the within order of court on the _____ I did expose to sale by publick vendue or out cry first having given due and legal Notice of the Time and place of sale agreeable to the within order and that I did then and there sell the said Land and premises with the Appurtenances to ____ for ____ Lawful Money of Pennsylvania he being the highest bidder for the same."

**Partition (request inquest)**: Often there was no need for the administrator to make a sale of the property to pay debts. The heirs would simply want to have the estate partitioned if possible and, if not possible, for each heir to get his share. Mention has already been made (see, "distribution") on how shares were determined. The court would be petitioned for an inquest into the estate to determine wether or not the partition could be made (generally it could not be made). The court would order the sheriff of the county to chose twelve men to go to the property and make an assessment and valuation. The sheriff would then return to court with an affidavit signed by all twelve men stating what their valuation was. "...which said Tract as the Petitioner apprehends cannot be divided without prejudice to and spoiling the whole and as the Petitioner is desirous that the said Tract should be viewed and valued agreeable to the Acts of Assembly in that case made and provided he humbly prays that the court be pleased to award an Inquest for the purpose and the Intent that he may on the Return of the said Inquest pay the rest of the children the value of their shares of the said Tract as by the said Act of Assembly is directed and appointed. Wherefore it is considered and ordered by the court that a writ of our Lord the King do Issue out of the said Court commanding the sheriff of the said County that taking with him twelve honest and lawful men of his Baliwick by whom the truth of the matter may be better known...." Of course, after 1776, the phrase, "our Lord and King," was not included in this writ.

**Twelve men**: They were assigned when a valuation of property was needed to determine if it could be partitioned among the heirs. The court instructed the county sheriff to select these men who would sign the resulting valuation either by oath or by affirmation (probably determined by religious affiliation, since some sects did not permit the swearing of an oath). Their names appear twice in the report of inquest—first, as the sheriff told the court who they were, and second, in a list of those who signed the report. Often, the names of these men were spelled differently in each list (note of these differences are made in this work). These records, then, are a good source for identifying how men, particularly the non-English, actually spelled their names and how the clerk, probably of English heritage, heard the names and then spelled them. When deciding which spelling to use, the reader should probably choose the name given in parentheses, which is the way the name was written on the inquest by the juror (if he could write—some men signed with their marks). These men, apparently, had to be citizens, as indicated in the following comment taken from one report, "Some of the Jurors named in the foregoing Inquest were born aliens and not yet naturalized. The court Quash the said inquest and a new writ...." In later records, these men were referred to as the jury.

**Report of inquest**: After an inquest was made on the property of the deceased by the twelve-man jury, the sheriff of the county would come into court to make a report of their findings. Often they would report that the land "...cannot be justly divided and partitioned unto and among the children of the said dec'd without prejudice to and spoiling the whole wherefore the Inquest do value and appraise the same at ____." If the land could not be partitioned, the eldest son usually agreed to accept it, paying the other heirs as outlined earlier (see "distribution"). He would then be required to provide the names of one or two men who would act as securities (or sureties) for him.

**Securities/sureties**: Men, chosen by the heir who had agreed to accept the land of the deceased, who promised to guarantee that the heirs would be paid their shares as outlined by the court. In early records, these men were usually referred to as "securities" but occasionally as "sureties." In later records found in Volume E, the word "sureties" was generally used when referring to these men.

**Adjoining or bounded by**: In later records, the deceased's real estate was identified by noting the township in which it was located, stating the acreage, and naming the neighboring (adjoining) property owners. Sometimes the records use the word "adjoining" and at other times, the words "bounded by." The author does not know if the use of either words has significance and, thus, copied the appropriate term as used in the record. In the very latest records of Volume E, mention is also made, for some of the estates, of the history of the tracts—when it was bought and from whom or when it was granted by patent or warrant. Occasionally, reference is made to the land being part of a larger tract of land, such as "Dry Land Tract" or "Indian Land Tract."

**Guardians**: Guardians were required for any orphaned children under the age of 21 years, even if she was a married daughter. If the child was 14 or older, he had the right choose his own guardian. If the child was less than 14, the court appointed a guardian. Very rarely was the child's mother appointed as guardian. The guardian was usually a family friend or relative, but could be a local lawyer. Usually, the record stated which age category the minor orphan was in—over 14 or under 14. In a few instances, the actual age of each child is given, a great plus for the researcher. If a guardian abstract in this book does not include a note about the age of the child, then that information was not included in the record. Occasionally a new guardian was needed, possibly because the former one was moving out of the county, had died, or decided he just didn't want the responsibility anymore. Occasionally, the request for a new guardian was made because he was not trusted by the administrator. Sometimes, when the child reached the age of 14, he decided he wanted a new guardian and, at that age, he had the right to chose his own and could petition the court for a change. Sometimes the minor child was referred to as an **infant**, but that designation did not necessarily mean a baby. It was simply another way to refer to a minor child, though it appears to mean the child was still under age 14.

**Next friend**: Someone who would petition the court on behalf of a minor was called the next friend. He was often someone who was close to the family—an older brother, uncle, grandfather, or friend.

**About these abstracts:**

**These records were abstracted without adding assumed information. If a relationship is given in the record, it is stated in the abstract. In no relationship is given in the record, the author did not assume one in the abstract. However, at times, the author has placed information, contained in later court sessions, into earlier records involving the same estate, to help clarify a situation (the information placed within parentheses).

**There are a few obvious errors in the records. For example sometimes a person is referred to by one name and, later, by another, within the same record. Also, there are a few instances where a record failed to list a particular child in every list, sometimes from one record to another and, at times, within the same record. Note has been made of these discrepancies, when discovered by the author, after the abstract for that entry is given. Such obvious errors, though, were not frequent.

**Names of people were copied as written in the records. At times a person would have his name spelled differently within the same entry. Note was made of this difference by placing the alternate spellings used in parentheses. Umlauts are used in the abstracts only when they were used in the actual records. However, even though county and township names were often misspelled in the records, the spelling of all Northampton County townships has been corrected in these abstracts. Words within quotes, however, are spelled as they appear in the records, except that surnames have been capitalized.

**The words "the late" and "late of" are frequently used. It appears that "late of" refers to someone who had left the area and not to someone who was deceased. The term "the late" was used both to indicate a deceased person and to indicate someone who had changed positions (i.e. "the late sheriff" referred to someone who was serving as the county sheriff but was no longer in that position).

**Often, when the widow had remarried, the name of her new spouse was given. At times, though, the new spouse is not named but the widow is referred to as "first name, new surname, the late former surname." When this situation occurs in the records, the abstract will contain the title, "Mr.," even though that title was not used in the records. Occasionally, the widow is mentioned, but not by name. Rather, she is listed as, "the widow now intermarried with," or "since deceased," or just, "the widow."

**Every name mentioned in the court records has been copied in these abstracts, noting its role in the proceedings, except for a few instances where an extensive list of creditors or debtors was included. In these situations, the author has noted that the names were not copied and indicates approximately how many were listed.

**When the record mentions the number of children, it is noted. Otherwise, they are listed without note of how many are listed in the entry. Therefore, if the abstract states that the deceased had a certain number of children, that information was recorded in the original record.

**The amount of each heir's inheritance has not been included in this work. Also, the findings given in the auditors' reports are generally not given in these abstracts.

**At times, the dates of the court sessions are out of order. These abstracts keep the date-order as found in the records. However, the author, in trying to keep each abstract entirely on the same page has taken the liberty to rearrange some abstracts within the same court session to make this feature possible without leaving too many large empty areas at the bottom of a page.

**Usually, when a woman is named as the administrator ("administratrix"), she is the widow of the deceased and the record states that fact. Sometimes, however, her relationship is not given. When the record does not state that the administratrix was the widow, the abstract does not list her as such.

**Sometimes, to denote a father and son by the same name, or to denote two men by the same name, not necessarily father and son, "junior" and "senior" are used in the record. At other times, "the elder" and "the younger" are used. The author has kept the terms used in the records. The reader should be aware, though, that the men might not be father and son. There are a few instances in these records where this relationship is obviously not so. If the relationship is given, it is included in the abstract.

**Some records do not mention nor list all the children of the deceased, only those who were minors in need of a guardian. In many records, reference is made to the fact that there were other children. In these cases, note is made in the abstracts that there were other children. Often there were several court sessions dealing with a particular estate. Though one record might not have listed all the children, a later record might list them all.

**Since the eldest son had preference in accepting the land of the deceased, he is usually listed in records involving his interests. Just remember that he could have had older sisters.

**In many of the earlier records, the children are listed with the sons first, then the daughters. It appears that the sons are listed in birth-order then the daughters, in birth-order. This method of listing the children does not mean that the sons were all born before the daughters. Later records more often listed the sons and daughters mixed together, again, probably in birth-order.

**Some estates reviewed by the Orphans Court were brought before the court many times, sometimes spanning several years, as requests were presented, complaints heard, and decisions made. If the reader suspects a relationship to a family mentioned in an early court record but does not find it mentioned, he should search later records concerning the same estate. Often, new pieces of the family puzzle were added each time the court reviewed an estate.

**If the reader finds an ancestor in these abstracts, he should review the original court records himself. There might be more in those records of importance to him than was abstracted by the author. The records can be found in Easton as well as on microfilm.

**Volume A: 20 December 1752—18 September 1755:**

**Court on 20 December 1752**
**Justices, the Esquires: Thomas CRAIG, Hugh WILLSON, James MARTIN, John VANATTA**

Guardians for minor children of George LITTLE JOHN (also distribution):

| | |
|---|---|
| widow: | Dorothy, administratrix, now wife of Mr. ROTENHOFFER, |
| 3 children: | George Frederick LITTLE JOHN, eldest son, under age 14 |
| | George Henry LITTLE JOHN, under age 14 |
| | Katherine LITTLE JOHN |
| guardians: | for two sons—their mother and William PARSONS |

Guardians for minor children of Jacob ROTENHOFFER (also distribution):

| | |
|---|---|
| widow: | Dorothy ROTENHOFFER, administratrix |
| 2 daughters: | Margaret, under age 14 |
| | Dorothy, under age 14 |
| guardians: | for both daughters—their mother & Sebastian NOFF |

**Court on 4 April 1753**
**Justices, the Esquires: Thomas CRAIG, Aaron DUPUI, William PARSONS**

Guardians for minor children of Ludwich MEYER (had a will) (also distribution):

| | |
|---|---|
| executors: | Christopher HAYMAKER and Henry KECK |
| widow: | Susannah, now wife of Conrad GEESY |
| children: | Martin, the eldest |
| | Hans Michael |
| | Sebastian |
| | Catharine |
| guardians: | for all 4 children—children's grandfather, Johannes SHALTER of Upper Milford; children's uncle, Martin MEYER; children's mother, Susannah GEESY |

**Court on 29 May 1753**
**Justices, the Esquires: Thomas CONIG, Hugh WILSON, William PARSONS**

Guardian for Samuel, minor over age 14, orphan son of Samuel MANN:

| | |
|---|---|
| guardian: | James McCOLLASTER |

Guardians for minor children of George MARSTELLER, Upper Saucon Township:

| | |
|---|---|
| widow: | Margaret MARSTELLER, administratrix, has or soon will marry Jacob LUDWIG |
| children: | George, eldest son |
| | Mathias |
| | Elizabeth, wife of John GONN |
| | Margaret, wife of Nicholas FRANTS (FRANCE) |
| | Catharine |
| | Frederick, minor over age 14..................guardians: his brothers, George and Mathias |
| | Mary Elizabeth, minor over age 14..........guardian: Mathias OPPS |
| | Nicholas, under age 14 |
| | Henry, under age 14 |
| | John, under age 14 |
| guardians: | for last 3 children—Mathias OPPS and Christian RINKER |
| | Eve, infant..............................................guardian: Nicholas FRANTS |

**Court on 21 June 1753**
**Justices, the Esquires: Thomas CRAIG, Hugh WILSON, Aaron DUPUI**

Guardians for Mary Regina, under age 14, orphan daughter of Jacob BECKLER:
guardians: Joseph FULHARD and Jacob ERNHARDT

Estate of Carrel KEIPER, Milford Township—complaint of Michael KEIPER, eldest son, that the administrators for Carrel had included 175 acres Michael had bought from Peter CRYLING; he requested a correction of the account:
administrators: Michael ALLER and Daniel ALLER
attorney: Lewis GORDON
other children: not named

Guardians for Charles Ludwig, over age 14, son of Carrell (Charles) KEIPER
guardians: Joseph FULHARD and Simon HELLER

Guardians for minor children of Lawrence ERB (had a will) (also distribution):
widow: Margaret, sole executrix, now wife of John RYSEWIGH
children: Casper, eldest son
Margaret, minor over age 14....................guardian: Michael REEDER
Ludwig, minor over age 14......................guardian: older brother, Casper ERB
Barbara, infant.........................................guardian: Felix BRUNNER

**Court on 8 August 1753**
**Justices, the Esquires: Thomas CRAIG, Hugh WILSON, Aaron DUPUI, James MARTIN**

Estate of Carrell (Charles) KEIPER, Milford Township (2 sons & 3 daughters)—request for valuation:
land: 50 acres and adjoining dwelling, granted by warrant to eldest son Michael in trust for Carrell
children: Michael, eldest son—wants to purchase the estate
Catherine, wife of Michael ALLER
Elizabeth, wife of Daniel ALLER
Mary, wife of Christopher ALLER
Charles Ludwig, infant
auditors: Frederick SCHOLL, Joseph GROWF, Joseph EVERHARD, Jacob WETZELL

Estate of George MARSTELLER—complaint of several children and guardians of the children that their dwelling was in need of repair; court orders that it be rented:
daughter Margaret, wife of Nicholas FRANTZ—agrees to rent it for 5 years at _12/year & make repairs

**Court on 20 September 1753**
**Justices, the Esquires: Thomas CRAIG, Hugh WILSON, Aaron DUPUI**

Estate of John PEARCE:
administrator: Joseph SAWEN—to give better security

Guardians for minor children of Jacob PAINTER—motion by Nathaniel VERNON:
children: Daniel, minor over age 14
Malachi, minor over age 14
Elias, under age 14
guardian: for all 3 children—Anthony LERCH

**Court on 8 August 1753 (out-of-order)**
**Justices not named**

Estate of Charles KEIPER: lists children, guardians, and auditors as earlier entry
court orders that son Michael shall have preference in purchasing the estate

**Court on 21 September 1753**
**Justices, the Esquires: Thomas CRAIG, Hugh WILSON, John EVERAT**

Estate of Charles KEIPER, Milford Township, 250 acres and warrant land—report on assessment:
children: eldest son, Michael KEIPER, eldest son—to accept the land
others as listed earlier

**Court on 20 December 1753**
**Justices, the Esquires: James MARTIN, Aaron DUPUI, John ATKINS**

Guardian for 3 minor children of Adam KOCK (7 children, 3 under age 14):
petitioner: George BOYER on behalf of orphan children
widow: Mary, now wife of Frederick ROYER, "who lately absconded being indebted to sundry persons in divers sums of money who are about to seize on the estate...."
minor children: Henry
Christian
Elizabeth
guardian: for all three children—Frederick SEITS

**Court on 21 December 1753**
**Justices, the Esquires: James MARTIN, John VAN ETTEN, John ATKINS**

Estate of Moses DUPREI, late of Lower Smithfield—request audit:
administrators: Mr. PRICE and Aaron DUPREI, Esq.
widow: Ann, now wife of Daniel SHOEMAKER
auditors: John ATKINS, Esq., Matheis ROWE, Ephraim CULVERT

New guardians for minor children of Ludwig MEYER:
guardian: former—Martin MOYER, appointed 4 April 1752, has left area
new—John JONES of Bethlehem

**Court on 21 January 1754**
**Justices, the Esquires: James MARTIN, Peter TRAXLER, William PARSON**

Guardians for minor children of George HAHN (had a will) (all over age 14) :
executor: George HOFFMAN—about to leave the province
children: Sebastian
George Adam
Margareth
guardians: John TRAXLER and Jacob ERNHARD

Estate of Charles KEIPER:
Michael KEIPER withdrew his plea of 20 December last—now content with the valuation

**Court on 23 January 1754**
**Justices, the Esquires: Aaron DUPUI, Peter TRAXLER, William PARSON**

Estate of George MARSTELLER—request for valuation:
guardians and heirs as listed earlier
eldest son: George—wants to purchase estate
appraisers: Joseph GROFFE, Joseph EVERHART, Frederick SCHOLL, Jacob BACKMAN

**Court on 21 March 1754**
**Justices, the Esquires: Thomas CRAIG, Aaron DUPUI, John EVERAT**

Estate of George MARSTELLER—request inquest:
petitioner: son George
heirs: names of heirs as listed before
auditor: Frederick SCHOLL, now dead

**Court on 21 January 1754**
**Justices, the Esquires: James MARTIN, Peter TRAXLER, William PARSONS**

Estate of Jacob BECKLER—distribution:
widow: Anna Maria, administratrix
only child: Mary Regina

**Court on 16 January 1754 (out-of-order)**
**Held at home of Daniel BROADHEAD, Esq., in Lower Smithfield Township, before**
**Justices: Daniel BROADHEAD, John VAN ETTEN, John ATKINS**

Estate of Moses DEPUI—request sale and guardians; refers to an award to Ann for maintenance of children by the court held 12 September 1750 in Newtown, Bucks County:
widow: Ann, now wife of Daniel SHOEMAKER
children: Winnefred, over age 14.........................guardian: her uncle, Daniel DEPUI
Nicholas, under age 14
Elizabeth, under age 14
Mary, under age 14
guardians: for 3 younger children—Daniel SHOEMAKER and Daniel DEPUI
auditors: John ATKINS, Mathew ROE, Ephraim COLVER (appointed 21 Dec. 1753)

**Court on 20 June 1754**
**Justices, the Esquires: James MARTIN, Aaron DUPUI, John ATKINS**

Guardians for minor children of Abraham MILLER:
children: Abraham, minor over age 14..................guardian: John McDOWELL
Joseph, under age 14
Catharine, under age 14
Salome, under age 14
Elisabeth, under age 14
guardians: for 4 younger children—Joseph and Isaac MILLER

**Court on 20 June 1754, continued:**

Estate of George MARSTELLER, Upper Saucon Township: inquest report by Sheriff Nicholas SCULL, Esq.:
10 children, including:
George, the eldest—agreed to sell rights and shares to Nicholas FRANCE
Frederick
Mary Elizabeth
Eve
Nicholas
Henry
John
securities: Nicholas FRANCE, Joseph GROVE, Henry BACHMAN, and Paul FRANCE
12 men: Solomon JENNINGS, Joseph FULLER. Henry WEAVER (WEBER), Paulsor PILE (Balthasar BEIL), Henry (Heinrich) BAUGHMAN, Christian NEWCOMER, Jacob BAUGHMAN, Jacob SAVITZ (ZEWITZ), Joseph GROVE (GRAFF), Leonard BIDLEMAN (BEIDELMAN), John REDROCK, and John (Johannes) KOOKEN

**Court on 19 December 1754**
**Justices, the Esquires: Thomas CRAIG, Daniel BROADHEAD, James MARTIN, John ATKINS, Aaron DUPUI**

Guardian for infant Mary, child of Jacob SHEAVER:
guardian: Henry SHEAVER

**Court on 20 March 1755**
**Justices, the Esquires: John ATKINS, Aaron DUPUI, James MARTIN, John EVERAT**

Estate of Peter ROUP, of Williamton Township—request audit:
4 children: Michael, eldest son
Sophia, wife of Peter MOLICK
Margaret, wife of John KOOK
Jacob, under age 21
auditors: Michael MOORE, Jacob SCHYMER, Nicholas BEST, Anthony LERCH

**Court on 18 June 1755**
**Justices, the Esquires: Thomas CRAIG, Timothy HORSFIELD, John VAN ETTEN, John EVERAT**

Estate of George MARSTELLER—motion by Mr. JOHNSTON, attorney of Mathais OX:
Nicholas FRANCE, one guardian of children, as surety for estate, cited to appear in court

Estate of Christian ISHBACH—motion by attorney Mr. JOHNSTON requesting sale:
administrator: Philip KISSINGER

**Court on 5 May 1755**
**Justices, the Esquires: Hugh WILSON, James MARTIN, Peter TRAXLER**

Estate of Jacob SHEAVER (had a will)—motion by Henry SHEAVER:
executors: Jacob BAUGHMAN and Thomas OWENS—executors had exhibited an account at Philadelphia which was imperfect
guardian: of daughter Mary, Henry SHEAVER—states that she is now living with Thomas OWENS

**Court on 17 September 1755**
**Justices, the Esquires: Thomas CRAIG, Hugh WILSON, James MARTIN, John ATKINS**

Estate of Christian ECHBACH, Upper Saucon Township, 164 acres warranted land (left 2 sons and 5 daughters)—request sale:

| | |
|---|---|
| petitioner: | Philip GEISSINGER |
| children: | Christian, under 21 |
| | John, under 21 |
| | Barbara |
| | Maria |
| | Susannah |
| | Christina, under 21 |
| | Elisabeth, under 21 |
| auditors: | Jasper SCULL, Thomas OWENS, Henry SHEENER |

**Court on 18 September 1755**
**Justices, the Esquires: Thomas CRAIG, Hugh WILSON, James MARTIN, John ATKINS**

Estate of Jacob SHEAVER—motion by James BIDDLE, attorney for Henry SHEAVER, guardian:

| | |
|---|---|
| executors: | as listed earlier |
| auditors: | Timothy HORSFIELD, Esq., John OKELY, William EDMUND |

Estate of Jacob PAINTER—request to order administrator to appear and report to court and give security:

| | |
|---|---|
| petitioner: | Mr. GORDON |
| administrator: | John PAINTER |
| guardian: | Anthony LERCH |

Estate of Christian ISHBACH, 164 acres warranted land—auditors' report; permission to sell:

| | |
|---|---|
| administrator: | Philip KISSINGER |
| auditors: | as listed earlier |

**End Volume A: gap of several years**

**Volume B: 22 March 1758—17 March 1762:**

**Court on 22 March 1758**
**Justices, the Esquires: Thomas CRAIG, Hugh WILSON, Timothy HORSEFIELD, Lewis KLOTZ, Conrad HESS, James MARTIN, ____ ARMSTRONG**
**Registrar: Charles SWAIN**

Guardian for Nathaniel MANN, a minor over age 14:
guardian: James CRAIG, Allen Township

**Court on 20 June 1758**
**Justices, the Esquires: Lewis KLOTZ, Conrad HESS, Thomas ARMSTRONG**
**Registrar: Charles SWAIN**

Estate of Abraham WOTRING—request for distribution:
administrators: Peter WOTRING and Paul POLLIET
widow: Anna
children: Peter
Margaret SNYDER
Mary POLLIET
Elizabeth ANDREWS
Barbara Ana
William
Abraham, under 21
Ephraim or Eve, under 21
[listed as both in separate courts—here as Ephraim but, on 20 September 1758, as Eve. Child is left out of children's list twice.]
auditors: George REX, Nicholas SNYDER, Jacob MICHLEY, Wolrich FLIECHINGER

Estate of Lawrence KUNGEL—request an accounting:
petitioner: John KUNGEL, oldest brother of Lawrence, and next of kin
administrators: Nicholas GOWER and the widow
widow: Katharine, administratrix, now wife of George STEYTINGER
two children: now dead
[error in record: This record makes it appear that Katharine is the widow of Nicholas GOWER, "That Katharine the widow of the said Nicholas GOWER...remarried to George STEYTINGER...." However, a later record makes clear that Nicholas was an administrator and Katherine was the widow of John KUNGEL, not of Nicholas GOWER. See court on 6 May 1761.]

**Court on 20 September 1758**
**Justices, the Esquires: Timothy HORSEFIELD, James MARTIN, Peter TREXLER, Conrad HESS**
**Registrar: Charles SWAIN**

Estate of Abraham WOTRING, Whitehall Township—auditors' report:

widow: Anna Margaret
children: Peter, eldest son
Margaret, wife of Johannes SNYDER
Mary, wife of Paul POLLIET
Elizabeth, wife of Martin ANDREWS (ANDREAS)
Barbara Ann
William
Abraham, now age 14, chose Paul POLLIET as guardian
Eve
Adam?*
auditors: as listed earlier

[*note: An Adam is listed once among the heirs as accepting the division, "so that we are all satisfied with it....Martin ANDREAS Adam and Abraham WOTRING...." Adam is not listed, though, in the distribution list nor on the list of payees of the administrators.]

Estate of George MARSTELLER—petition of Nicholas FRANCE in answer to 1754 citation to appear:
Nicholas said, because of, "troubles of the times," he could not appear earlier but he has since satisfied the heirs, Frederick and Mary Elizabeth. For remaining heirs, Henry BACHMAN and Paul FRANCE were admitted as sureties.

**Court on 19 December 1758**
**Justices, the Esquires: William PLUMSTEAD, Peter TREXLER, James MARTIN, Lewis KLOTZ, Timothy HORSEFIELD, Thomas ARMSTRONG**
**Registrar: Charles SWAIN**

New guardians for daughters of Peter SHEAVER—petition of Christian SHOOK*, guardian and grandfather, on mother's side; Christian now advanced in years and infirm, declines guardians:

children: Elizabeth, minor now over age 14
Mary, under age 14
guardian: Nicholas BEST, of Williams Township, whose wife is aunt of girls

[*possible error in record—the first mention of Christian is as the petitioner, Christian SHOOK; twice, later in the record, he is listed as Christian KEIFER]

Guardians of minor BEAR children:

children: John, minor over age 14..........................guardian: Peter GROVE
Barbara, now both over age 14................guardian: Daniel KNAWS, Weisenberg Twp.
Jacob, under age 14
Ann (Adam?)*, under age 14
guardian: for two younger children—Daniel KNAWS

[*possible error in record: Ann's name is listed three times but the first time it is written in the record, the name is crossed out and "Adam" is written in.]

Guardians for minors, George Jacob CROW and Anna Amelia CROW, both over age 14:

guardian: their mother Magdalena CROW

**Court on 21 December 1758, afternoon**
**Justices, the Esquires: Timothy HORSEFIELD, Conrad HESS, Charles SWAIN**
**Registrar: Charles SWAIN**

Estate of Peter ROUP*—request for an appraisal and guardians:
children: Michael, eldest son, the petitioner
Jacob
Margaret wife of Jacob ZOOK
grandchildren, children of deceased daughter Sophia:
Margaret EBILE, minor over age 14........guardian: Jacob KOHIOR
Jacob EBILE, minor over age 14.............guardian: George ROUP
John MELICH, under age 14..................guardian: father, Johns MELICH
appraisers: Michael MOOR, Anthony LERCH, Michael SHOEMAKER, Nicholas BEST
[*error in record: in the court response to the petition, Peter is mistakenly called Michael]

**Court on 20 March 1759**
**Justices, the Esquires: Peter TREXLER, Thomas ARMSTRONG, James MARTIN, Timothy HORSEFIELD, Lewis KLOTZ, Conrad HESS**

Estate of Philip SCHLOUGH—request for distribution:
widow: Margaret, administratrix, now wife of Philip GROSS
children, all under age 21 except the oldest:
George, eldest
Margaret
Catherina
Jacob
Clara
Rosina
Philip
auditors: Anthony LERCH, Jacob MOREY, Stophel WAGGONER

Estate of Peter GROW—request for distribution:
widow: Magdalena
children: Simon, administrator
Peter
George Adam
Anna Margaret, wife of Michael HUMBLE
George Jacob, under age 14
Anna Amelia, under age 14
auditors: Nicholas MOYER, Melchior SMITH, Daniel KNOWS

Estate of John BEAR—request for distribution:
widow: Regina, administratrix, now wife of Peter GROVE, Jr.
children, all under age 14:
John
Barbara
Jacob
Adam
auditors: George KNOWS, John LITTENWALTOR, Jeremiah TREXLER

## Court on 21 March 1759
## Justices, the Esquires: Jeremiah TREXLER, Thomas ARMSTRONG, James MARTIN, Thomas CRAIG, Hugh WILSON, Timothy HORSEFIELD, Lewis KLOTZ, Conrad HESS

Estate of Philip SCHLOUGH, Lower Saucon Township—request audit:

| | |
|---|---|
| widow: | Margaret, now wife of Philip GROSS |
| children: | George, eldest son |
| | Margaret, minor over age 14....................guardian: Rudolph OBERLEY |
| | Catherine, minor over age 14...................guardian: Rudolph OBERLEY |
| | Jacob, minor over age 14.........................guardian: Philip GROSS |
| | Clara, under age 14 |
| | Rosina, under age 14 |
| | Philip, under age 14 |
| guardians: | for younger 3 children—George HEARTSWELL, brother of their mother |
| auditors: | George SHULE, Christian RINKER, Stophel WAGGONER, George HEARTSWELL |

## Court on 20 March 1759 (out-of-order; possibly mis-dated)

Guardians for Anton HAGEN, under age 14—Anton's, "father died some years since and his mother on or about the 24th September last whereby he is left an orphan...."

| | |
|---|---|
| guardians: | Timothy HORSEFIELD and John OHOLY, the petitioners, of Bethlehem, next friends |

Estate of Philip SCHLOUGH—petition of son George for distribution:

widow and issue as listed earlier

| | |
|---|---|
| appraisers: | George SHULE, Xian RINKER, Stophel WAGGONER, George HEARTZEL |

## Court on 21 March 1759: (as before)

Guardians for 2 minor children of the deceased husband of Mary SNYDER—(left widow and 2 children):

| | |
|---|---|
| widow: | Mary |
| 2 children: | David SNYDER, under age 14 |
| | Elizabeth SNYDER, under age 14 |
| guardians: | John TOOL and Jacob MOREY |

## Court on 22 March 1759
## Justices, the Esquires: Peter TREXLER, Thomas ARMSTRONG, Thomas CRAIG, Hugh WILSON, Lewis KLOTZ, Conrad HESS

Estate of Peter ROUP, valuation at _190, motion by Mr. HENDERSON that son Michael agrees to purchase the land at valuation and give security to other heirs:

| | |
|---|---|
| security: | Peter KICKLINE of Eastern Tavern |

Estate of John SENSINGER—John was killed by, "Indians and that the place he lived on was afterwards almost a waste, the House in bad condition, Barns and Stables burnt, Fences almost all down...Gasper SNER is desirous of going to settle on the said plantation...." The plantation had been valued at _75 before it had been destroyed and is not worth as much now but Gasper is willing to take the land at that valuation. Court allows the purchase:

| | |
|---|---|
| widow: | Magdalena, administratrix, now wife of (John) Gasper SNER |
| children: | Margaret, age 9 |
| | Magdalena, age 8 |
| | Andrew, age 6 |
| | Barbara, age 4 [possible error—child is listed as a "boy" and is not listed in later text] |

## Court on 26 March 1759
## Justices, the Esquires: James MARTIN, Conrad HESS, Charles SWAIN

Estate of Frederich MENGELL—request for distribution:

| | |
|---|---|
| administrators: | George LEMBERT and George KUNGELL, |
| widow: | Mary Elizabeth, now wife of Mr. SHOEMAKER |
| only issue: | "Margaret and another child" [later in the text: "to Margaret and the other child of the said dec-d," and, "...the said Margaret and such other child." Perhaps the mother was pregnant? See later entries.] |
| auditors: | John TREXLER, George REX, Jacob REX |

## Court on 20 June 1759
## Justices, the Esquires: Peter TREXLER, Thomas ARMSTRONG, James MARTIN, Timothy HORSEFIELD, Lewis KLOTZ, Conrad HESS

Guardian for Ann Maria LAR, age 8 months:

| | |
|---|---|
| petitioner: | Frederick KERN, her grandfather and next friend |
| guardian: | Maudlen LAR, her mother |

Guardians for minor children of John SENSINGER (all under age 14):

| | |
|---|---|
| children: | Margaret |
| | Magdalen |
| | Andrew |
| | Barbara |
| guardian: | their uncle and next friend, John KUNGEL |

## Court on 4 August 1759
## Justices, the Esquires: James MARTIN, Timothy HORSEFIELD, Conrad HESS

Petition of Thomas SCHAAF of Bethlehem, weaver—he and his late wife have "some little Estate coming to them in Germany, some time since sent a Power of Attorney to recover the Same, that soon after your Petitioner's wife departed this life leaving issue an only Daughter named Anna, now two years old and your Petitioner being now informed that the persons from whom the monies is due refuse to pay....":

| | |
|---|---|
| Only issue: | Anna, age 2 |
| guardians: | Andreas Anton LAWATSCH and Matthew SCHROPP |

Guardians of minor children of Frederick MENGELE:

| | |
|---|---|
| children: | Margaret, under age 14 |
| | Magdalen, under age 14 |
| guardian: | for both children—John KLICH, their first cousin |

Estate of Frederick MENGELE—auditors' report, mentions that Jost VOLLER is to get 5 shillings, "for his trouble":

| | |
|---|---|
| executors: | George LEMBERT and George CONEKEL (KUNGEL) |
| widow: | Margaret [possible error: later she is referred to as Mary Elizabeth SHOEMAKER] |

Guardian for minor child, Peter SHEAFFER, under age 14:

| | |
|---|---|
| guardian: | his mother and next friend, Catherina SHEAFFER |

**Court on 4 August 1759, continued:**

Estate of Peter SHEAVER (SHEAFFER)—request for distribution:
administrator: John LeFEVRE
children: Peter
Elizabeth
Mary
auditors: Jost VOLLERT, Peter KICHLINE, Adam YEO (YOHE)

Guardians for minor child of Patrick DEVENY:
widow: Margaret, now Mrs. MACARDEY
child: Margaret, under age 14
The mother, "hath been twice married since the death of Patrick DEVENY...." and now lives in the Province of the Jerseys. The court appointed John MOOR, Esq., High Sheriff of the County, as guardian. Margaret could still live with her mother who said she would not charge anything for Margaret's maintenance.
auditors: Jost VOLLERT, Abraham LeFEVRE, John CRAWFORD

**Court on 19 September 1759**
**Justices, the Esquires: William CRAIG, Hugh WILSON, Peter TREXLER, James MARTIN, Timothy HORSEFIELD, Aaron DUPUI, Thomas ARMSTRONG, Lewis KLOTZ**

Guardian for only son of John Frederich OTTO, practitioner in "Physick" of Bethlehem Township, by his wife, the deceased Anna Maria:
His late wife: Anna Maria, "late weaver, some years since departed," had lands in "Franchfort," Germany. John Frederich requested that a guardian be appointed for Anna Maria's only son by John Frederich so that he could execute his power of attorney, with the guardian, to sell the estate.
Only son: Joseph, age 15........................................guardian: John OAKLEY, Esq. of Bethlehem

Estate of Peter SHEAVER—auditors' report:
widow: Catherina
children: Peter, eldest son, under age 14................guardian: his mother, Catherina
Elizabeth
Mary
guardians: for two daughters, Nicholas BEST

Estate of Jacob HERMAN, died about 1741—request sale:
administrator: Jacob FRALEY of Rockamion, administrator de bonis non
widow: Mary Elizabeth (had been the administrator)
4 children: Jacob
Matthias
Mary, wife of Valentine HOUSSWERT
Elizabeth, wife of Henry SHAFER
Widow Mary Elizabeth had remarried, to Jacob SHAFER (SHEVER), but she died in 1758. She had failed to administer Jacob HERMAN's estate, including 244 acres of land surveyed 6 December 1739 and warranted 10 May 1740. Jacob SHAFER, her second husband, was now also dead. His executors were Jacob ACKMAN (BACHMAN) and Thomas OWEN. (Reference is made back to courts held 5 May 1755 and 18 September 1755.)
auditors: John JONNINGS, Anthony LARCH, Jacob MOREY

**Court on 19 September 1759, continued:**

Estate of Philip SLOUGH—auditors' report and distribution:

| | |
|---|---|
| widow: | Margaret, now wife of Philip GROSS (GROCE) |
| children: | George, of Lower Saucon Township, yeoman—accepted the land |
| | Margaret..........guardian: Rudolph OBERLEY |
| | Catrena (Catherine)..........guardian: Rudolph OBERLEY |
| | Jacob..........guardian: Philip GROSS |
| | Clara..........guardian: George HEARTSELL |
| | Philip..........guardian: George HEARTSELL |
| | Rosina..........guardian: George HEARTSELL |
| auditors: | Anthony LERCH, Jacob MOREY, Stophel WAGGONER |

**Court on 25 March 1761**
**Justices, the Esquires: Hugh WILSON, Timothy HORSEFIELD, Lewis KLOTZ, Conrad HESS, Jacob ARNDT**

Estate of Samuel NEWCOMER, died about 1755, 224 acres in Upper Saucon Township—request partition:

| | |
|---|---|
| widow: | Elizabeth |
| 3 children: | John, eldest son |
| | Samuel |
| | Mary |

Minor children of Michael WOLFGANG, petition of guardian, Lewis GORDON:

| | |
|---|---|
| children: | Mary Margaret |
| | John |

Both their parents were now dead and John KNOWS had been caring for them. However, Lewis was their guardian. "John KNOWS is detaining them in his custody for a considerable sum which he charges them with for their maintenance." The court ordered them to be turned over to Lewis immediately.

Minor children of Peter SHAFFER, petition of Nicholas BEST, guardian:

| | |
|---|---|
| children: | Elizabeth |
| | Marrillis |

Peter, "was supposed to be murdered by the Indians but is yet alive and is returned to his Plantation in Plainfield Township...." BEST had settled with the father and wanted to be discharged as the guardian.

Estate of Daniel YUNCHER (JUNCHER), Lowhill Township—auditors' report and distribution:

| | |
|---|---|
| administrator: | Nicholas PRETER—ordered to pay the heirs |
| widow: | Anna Elizabeth |
| children: | George, eldest son |
| | Jost |
| | Simon |
| | Elizabeth |
| | Henry |
| other heir: | Peter GROSS |
| auditors: | Jacob HELVEY, Dewalt (Theobold) MOYER, Christian RISE, Andreas REESE |

The auditors, sent out by the court on 18 September 1759, wrote a report on 15 January 1760. Nicholas BRODER, of Weisenberg Township, had called them together in, "the Name of the Justices."

**Court on 25 March 1761, continued:**

Estate of Jacob HERMAN, died in 1741, Lower Saucon Township—request sale:
administrator: Jacob FRALEY
widow and 4 children

Estate of Christian STAHL, Heidelberg Township, died about 1756—request sale and guardians:
administrators: Peter MESSEMER and Jacob PETER
widow: Anles
4 children, all under age 14:
Ann Elizabeth
Ann Katherine
Gertrude
Paul
guardians: for all 4 children—Michael OHL and Henry SMITH

Estate of Michael DINCKE, Heidelberg Township, died about 1756—request sale and guardians:
widow: Katherine now wife of John WASSUM
three children, all under age 14:
Mary
Margaret
Jacob
guardians: for all 3 children—Frederick KERN and Leonard HOOR

Guardian for Margaret DEWINNY, now age 16, daughter of Katherine McCURDY:
petitioners: Samuel McCURDY and his wife Katherine
guardian: William MACK

Estate of William YELD, Lynn Township—request sale:
administrator: Philip ANTHONY

Estate of John AIRHART, Lower Smithfield Township—request sale:
widow Lovess, administratrix

Guardians for minor children of Michael HELFRICH, Macungie Township (all under age 14):
next friend: Christian STEININGER:
children: Margaret
John
George
Michael
guardians: George STEININGER, Jr., Matthias OX, George PLANK

Guardian for minor children of Michael WOLFGANG (both under age 14):
children: Mary Margaret
John Michael
guardian: Lewis GORDON

**Court on 25 March 1761, continued:**

Estate of Peter WALBERT, died about 1758:

| | |
|---|---|
| widow: | Elizabeth, administratrix, now wife of Matthias LUDWIG |
| 8 children: | George, minor over age 14 |
| | Ann Mary, minor over age 14 |
| | Katherine, minor over age 14 |
| | Anna Sibilla, under age 14 |
| | Elizabeth, under age 14 |
| | Juliana, under age 14 |
| | Gertrude, under age 14 |
| | Sophia, under age 14 |
| guardian: | for older 3 children—Peter TROXLER |
| guardians: | for younger 5 children—their mother and uncle, George KLEIN |

Guardians for 5 minor children of Christian SHOPPART, Whitehall Township, died about one year ago. Children's grandfather, Christian SHOPPART, the elder, was also deceased without living issue and also left an estate for the children (all under age 14):

| | |
|---|---|
| widow: | Elizabeth, next friend |
| 5 children: | John |
| | Christian |
| | Mary Katharine |
| | Elizabeth Barbara |
| | Ann Eve |
| | Anna Mary |
| guardians: | Lawrence GOOD, Adam HAVERSLEY, Stophel BAR |

Guardians for NEWCOMER children, minors, Upper Saucon Township, father died about 1754:

| | |
|---|---|
| 3 children: | John, eldest son, over age 21 |
| | Samuel, now 18.....................................guardian: Philip BALE |
| | Mary, under age 14................................guardian: her cousin, John NEWCOMER |

Guardians for minor children of Francis ROTH, died about 1757:

| | |
|---|---|
| widow: | Elizabeth, administratrix, 2nd wife |
| child by first marriage: | |
| | Francis, now age 15................................guardian: Henry GRIM |
| 5 children by 2nd wife, all under age 14: | |
| | Henry |
| | Katherine |
| | Magdalene |
| | Elizabeth |
| | Margaret |
| guardians: | for younger 5 children—Philip SAILER, John MERTLE, Elizabeth ROTH |

Guardians for minor child, Henry, under age 14, of Daniel JANEKER (were other children):

| | |
|---|---|
| guardians: | Abraham BERLIN, of Easton, and Elizabeth JANEKER |

**Court on 25 March 1761, continued:**

Guardians for minor KEEMERER children (all under age 14):

children: Rachina Margaret
Mary Elizabeth
Jacob

guardian: their mother, Anna Margaret KEEMER

Guardians for minor children of Jacob STEPHENS, died about 1760 (the children were all under age 14 except Susannah, "who is incapable of choosing guardian by reason of her lunacy...."):

petitioner: Christian RUTH, next friend of children

2 children, by former wife: "have been very ill used since," father's decease by Mary their step-mother
John Jacob
Susannah Katherine

widow: Mary, now wife of John BEAR, "who is likely to squander the said Estate as his wife is administratrix...." The court issued a citation for Mary BEAR to appear in court and give an account.

children by Mary:
John Adam
Mary Elizabeth
Elizabeth Katherine
Mary Katherine

Guardians: for all but Susannah—Melchior SMITH and Peter HAAS

Guardian: for Susannah Katherine—Christian RUTH

[note: at times it appears that Susannah Katherine was really two daughters, but the way the guardians were appointed makes it probable that she was just one girl]

## Court on 6 May 1761
## Justices, the Esquires: Lewis KLOTZ, Conrad HESS, Jacob ARNDT

Estate of Balzer LOHR, Lower Saucon, died about 1757, left plantation in Lower Saucon and Williams Township—request inquest:

5 children: Henry
Martin
Balzer
John
Margaret

grandchild: Mary LOHR

Guardians for minor children of Michael WOLFGANG, Upper Milford Township (both under age 14) (were other children):

children: Mary Katherine
Anna Mary

guardians: Michael KIEPER and Jacob HAUN, next friends

Guardians for 3 minor children, of John AIRHART, Lower Smithfield Township (all under age 14):

widow: Lovess

3 children: Barbara
George
John

guardian: for all 3 children—John MOOR, Esq.

**Court on 6 May 1761, continued:**

Estate of Thomas QUICK, died about 1756, Upper Smithfield, plantation of 200 acres—request sale:
administrator: William ENNIS
wife and 10 children

Estate of Lawrence KUNGEL, died 1755, left estate, "over the mountains," in Lower Smithfield Township—request sale:
administrators: Nicholas GOWER and the widow
widow: Katherine, now wife of Mr. STEITINGER
left two children, both now dead, who lived two years after their father's death (children of Katherine)

Estate of George GRUNDT, Weisenberg Township—request sale:
administrator: Peter GRUNDT
5 living children, all over age 15

Estate of Peter REESER:
administrators: Peter GIFFIN and his wife Margaret—they were about to remove from the county and give the estate over to other administrator, Adam REESER. They requested a settlement and guardians for the minor children or, "order them to be put out apprentices to Trades or Husbandry...." They were ordered to return to court in June with children.
auditors: John JONES, Anthony LERCH, Blass BOYER

**Court on 16 June 1761 (on loose paper)**
**Justices, the Esquires: not named**

Estate of John AIRHART, Lower Smithfield Township, 195 acres—return of sale:
widow: Lowess AIRHART, administratrix
sold to: John MIXELL, yeoman

**Court on 6 May 1761, continued**

Guardian for Maudlin, over age 14, minor daughter of Jacob BRICKER, Lehigh Township:
guardian: Felte WALTMAN

Guardians for minor children of William YETT, Lynn Township (both under age 14):
children: William
Mary
next friends: Philip and Paul ANTHONY
guardian: for both children—Thomas EVERETT

Guardians for minor children of Jacob SWARTZ, Macungie Township:
petitioner: Leonard KRONIGER, next friend
children: George, minor over age 14......................guardian: Lewis KLOTZ, Esq.
John, minor over age 14.........................guardian: Lewis KLOTZ, Esq.
Katherine Mary, under age 14.................guardian: Samuel JOHNSTON
Philip, under age 14...............................guardian: Melchor SMITH

Guardian for minor child named John TETTER, over age 14:

guardian: Henry KECK

**Court on 6 May 1761, continued:**

Guardians for minor children of Peter REESER, Lower Saucon Township:

children: Anthony, minor over age 14....................guardian: Paul REESER of Easton
Katherine, minor over age 14..................guardian: George LAWBAUGH
Conrad, under age 14
Paul, under age 14
Philip, under age 14
Peter, under age 14
guardians: for younger 4 children—Adam REESER and Nicholas BEST

Complaint of Stophel WAGGONER, Lower Saucon Township, concerning Jacob FRALEY, administrator of estate of Jacob HERMAN:

Stophel was the highest bidder at the sale of the HERMAN property, but, "by the deceit and collusion of the said Jacob FRALEY, the Cryer did not cry it off..." and the land was now inhabited by Henry SHAVER. Stophel wanted court to straighten it out. Several witness were questioned and the court determined that the sale of the land to Henry SHAVER was unjust and, therefore, was set aside.

Complaint that John KNOWS charged 15 pounds for the maintenance of Michael and Anna Margaret WOLFGANG, children of Michael WOLFGANG, but the court had allowed only 9 pounds.

Estate of Samuel NEWCOMER, Upper Saucon Township—inquest report by Sherif John MOORE, Esq.:

widow
children: John, eldest son—to accept land and pay the heirs
Samuel
Mary
security: John MOORE
12 men:by oaths—Balzer BOIL, Henry (Heinrich) BACHMAN
by affirmation—Jacob MOREY (MORRY), Henry (Heinrich) BRUNNER, Andrew (Andreas) ARTMAN, Henry (Heinrich) WEAVER, Philip SELLER (SÖLLER), George BACHMAN, Jacob GROVE (GROFF), John (Hanes) MOSULMAN, Michael SIDER (SEIDER), and John (Johannes) BACHMAN

**Court of 16 June 1761**
**Justices, the Esquires: Hugh WILSON, Aaron DUPUI, Lewis KLOTZ, Robert LYLE, Jacob ARNDT**

Estate of John BARE, died about 6 years ago—report by guardian, Lewis KLOTZ, Esq. that Richina and Peter GROW had sold the land without the approval of the court; the children wanted their inheritance:

widow: Richina, administratrix, now wife of Peter GROW
children: John
Barbara
Jacob
Adam

Guardians for Luke, over age 14, minor child of Daniel BRODHEAD, Lower Smithfield:

guardian: his brother, Daniel BRODHEAD

Estate of Lawrence KUNCKLE—return of sale:

administrators: Katherine KUNCKLE and Nicholas GOWER

sold to: Lawrence KUNCKLE, son of John [possible error: were the names switched?]

**Court of 16 June 1761, continued:**

Complaint of John SHATE in right of his wife Elizabeth, daughter of George GRUB, deceased:
said widow and administrator did not give just inventory—court ordered them to report

Complaint of Henry LOHR and Martin LOHR, children of Balzer LOHR:
said accounting of administrator, William WAGGONER, recorded by him in the Registrar's Office at Philadelphia, was erroneous and defective—resettlement ordered at Easton

Report on complaint concerning sale of estate of Jacob HARMAN by Jacob FRALEY to Henry SHAFER:
Jacob FRALEY, administrator, sold 244 acres in Lower Saucon Township to Henry SHAFFER. At desire of Stophel WAGGONER, John JONES, clerk at the vendue, was examined under oath. It was found that the sale was unfair and Stophel WAGGONER was the last fair and highest bidder.

**Court on 24 September 1761**
**Justices, the Esquires: Hugh WILSON, Lewis KLOTZ, Thomas ARMSTRONG**

Guardians for minor children of Philip SCHMYER, Macungie Township:
children: Michael, over age 14
John, under age 14
guardian: for both—Lewis KLOTZ, Esq.

Estate of Balzer LOHR, tracts of land in Williams and Lower Saucon Townships—report on resettlement by High Sheriff John MOOR, Esq.:
administrator: William WAGGONER
5 children: Henry, eldest son—took only one share by consent and refused land
Martin—accepted the property
Balzer
John
Margaret wife of William WAGGONER
grandchild: heir of son Peter LOHR, deceased
securities: Valentine OPP, Abraham BERLIN
12 men: for Williams Township tract—by oath: Lawrence MERKEL, Jacob BEST, Nicholas BEST, Michel SHOEMAKER, Leonard HARTZEL, Michael COOK, Melchor HAY, Paul REESER
by affirmation: Balzer HESS, William FULLBRECHT (FULLBRIGHT), William KEYL, Michael MYER
for Lower Saucon Township tract—by oath: Melchior HAY, Jacob SCHYMER, Rudolph OBERLEY, Adam REESER, Peter KNIGHT, Philip GROSS, Paul FRANS, Tobias SHULE
by affirmation: Edward BECK, Anthony LERGH, Michael HELLER, Gratius LERGH

Estate of George GRUB—request audit:
petitioner: Mr. JOHNSTON on behalf of John SHATE and wife Elizabeth, daughter of deceased
auditors: Samuel SEGAR, George REX, Andreas MAIS

## Court on 2 December 1761

## Justices, the Esquires: Thomas CRAIG, Timothy HORSFIELD, Lewis KLOTZ, Jacob ARNDT, Henry GEIGAR, Robert LYLE

Estate of Jacob SWARTZ, Sr., died 1759, two tracts in Macungie Township, 150 acres & 80 acres—request for partition:

| | |
|---|---|
| widow: | Katherine |
| 11 children: | Jacob, Jr. |
| | Sophia, wife of David MARSH |
| | Elizabeth, wife of Leonard CRONINGER |
| | Susannah, wife of Henry VON POOL |
| | Margaret |
| | Abraham, the petitioner |
| | the rest under age 21: |
| | George |
| | John |
| | Katherine |
| | Mary |
| | Philip |

Estate of Catherine (Katherine) FIREBACH, died about 2 years ago, land in Lowhill Township—request sale:

| | |
|---|---|
| administrator: | George HARTMAN |
| 7 children: | eldest, not named |
| | Christina |
| | Maria |
| | Catherina |
| | Elizabeth |
| | Adam |
| | Philip |
| guardians: | George HARTMAN and Michael TYBER |

Estate of Peter REESER, died some years ago, plantation in Lower Saucon Township:

| | |
|---|---|
| widow: | since married to Peter GIFFIN |
| 7 children: | Jacob, the petitioner |
| | other six are minors, under age 14, not named |

Estate of Jacob SWARTZ, land in Macungie Township, 150 acres and 80 acres—request for partition

Guardians for Christian, over age 14, minor child of Adam KOCH:

| | |
|---|---|
| petitioner: | Frederich SEITZ of Macungie Twp., next friend |
| guardian: | Jacob SLOUGH of Macungie Township |

## Court on 17 March 1762

## Justices, the Esquires: Hugh WILSON, Aaron DUPUI, Lewis KLOTZ, Thomas ARMSTRONG

Estate of Henry FIREBACH, Lowhill Township—return of sale:

administrator: George HARTMAN—bought the land

Estate of Christian STAHL, Heidelberg Township—return of sale:

administrators: Peter MESSEMER and Jacob PETER

buyer not named [Report has many blanks throughout]

**Court on 17 March 1762, continued:**

Estate of Jacob BILTSHOUSE, died about 2 years ago, Upper Milford Township—request sale and guardians:
administrator: John ORT
widow: Ann Margaret
3 children, all under age 14:
Jacob
John
Catherina (Katherine)
guardians: for all 3 children—Jacob SCHMITT and Andrew INGLEMAN

Estate of Jacob SWARTZ, Macungie Township, two tracts, 150 acres and 80 acres—inquest report by High Sheriff John JENNINGS:
widow: Katherine
11 children: Jacob, eldest son—accepted the property
Margaret
Abraham
George
John
Katherine
Mary
Philip
Sophia, wife of David MARSH
Elizabeth, wife of Leonard CRONINGER
Susannah, wife of Henry VAN POOL
securities: Frederich NUNEASTER of Easton, shopkeeper, and Melchior SMITH
12 men:by oath—Peter HAAS, George KERR, Herman MOOR (MOHR), George STININGER, Christian ROOT, Nicholas MOYER, Adam SMITH, Nicholas WETTERHOLT, Thomas KOOTZ, William HANTZ
by affirmation—Frederich ROMICH and Jacob SLOUGH

Estate of Adam SHAFER, died about 7 years ago, Salisbury Township—request sale:
widow: Margaret, administratrix, now wife of Adam BLANK
one child: Valentine
[error in record: Margaret is listed as Katherine in one place]

Guardians for 5 minor children of Conrad FRY, Lynn Township (all under age 14)—also request sale:
widow: Hester, administratrix (Ester)
5 children
guardians: Frederich ROUSENBERGER, Thomas EVERETT, and Andrew FULK.

Guardians for minor STEININGER children, both "very young":
widow: Agad, now wife of Burget MOSER
children: Henry STEININGER
Catherine STEININGER
guardians: Michael TYBER and Daniel KNOWS

Guardians for minor children of Hans Teter BAUMAN—petition by best friend, George KLEIN:
children: Bernard, under age 14
Henry, under age 14

guardians: Lewis KLOTZ, Esq., and George KLEIN

**Court on 17 March 1762, continued:**

Guardians for minor children of Conrad FRY, Lynn Township:
children: Jacob, over age 14
Sarah, over age 14
Esther, over age 14
Moses, over age 14
Aaron, under age 14
Hannah, under age 14
Joshua, under age 14
Katherine, under age 14
Elizabeth, under age 14
guardian: for older 4 children—Frederich ROUSEBERGER
guardians: for younger 5 children—Andreas FOULK and Thomas EVERETT

New guardian for Katherine, under age 14, minor child of Jacob SWARTZ (were other children):
guardian: former—Samuel JOHNSTON, Esq.
new—Lewis KLOTZ, Esq.

Estate of Christopher HENSEY—report of administration account:
administrator: Conrad JACOBI
Said that Christopher, "had no known Kindred or Relations within this Province, at the time of his Death, nor hath any one appeared since to claim the same...." Balance of the estate was paid to the, "Registrar of the Court for use of Proprietary and Governor according to the law."

New guardian for Margaret WOLFGANG, under age 14:
guardian: former—Lewis GORDON
new—Lewis KLOTZ, Esq.

Estate of George GROB—request audit:
Mr. Samuel JOHNSTON, attorney for John SHATE, stated that Mary Margaret GROB, administratrix, had concealed a large part of estate fraudulently from the appraisement. Requests an examiner to inspect her accounts.
auditors: George KLEIN, John OKELY, George REX

Estate of Peter REESER, Lower Saucon Township—inquest report by Sheriff John JENNINGS, Esq.:
12 men:by oath—Philip GROSS, Joseph RICHARDS, Jacob SCHEINMER, Ludwig EAGENDER, Benedict LUTZ, Jacob BEST, George LABACH, George MOYSH
by affirmation—Anthony LERCH, Rudolph OBERLEY, Edward BECK, Nicholas RIPPELL

**End of Volume B**

**Volume C: 23 June 1762—19 September 1765:**

**Court on 23 June 1762**
**Justices, the Esquires: Hugh WILSON, Timothy HORSFIELD, Lewis KLOTZ, and others, their fellow justices**

Estate of Elias DIETRICK, died 1760, Mt. Bethel Township, 119 acres, 38 perches—request inquest:
widow
5 children: Elias, the eldest
John
Judah
Christina
Jacob

Estate of Melchior FETTER, died about 15 months ago, Salisbury Township—request inquest:
widow
3 children: Henry, eldest son
Gertrude
John

Estate of Thomas NEIL, died 1761, Allen Township, 96 acres—request sale:
administrator: Joseph NEIL
widow: Susannah
7 children

Estate of Nicholas WALBERT, land beyond Blue Mountain, Lower Smithfield Township—request sale:
administrator: David SHEIB

Estate of Michael KNAPPENBERGHER—request audit:
widow: Katherine, administratrix, now wife of Jacob TONNER, who has used land since Michael's death
administrator: Barnard BISBING
children
auditors: John TOOL, John JARRETT, and Sebastian TRUCKMILLER (to evaluate the rent Jacob TONNER is paying)

Estate of John BARE, died about 1755—request audit:
petitioner: guardians, Lewis KLOTZ and Daniel KNOWS:
widow: has since married Peter GROW
children: Barbara
John
Jacob
Adam
auditors: Herman MOOR, William HAYS, James RALSTON

Estate of Jacob BRICKER, died 1761, Lehigh Township—request audit:
widow: Mary Godlieb, administratrix, now wife of George SHOEDER
children: Adam, late of Lehigh Township
others not named
auditors: John WALKER, John HAYS, Michael RUCH

**Court on 23 June 1762, continued:**

Guardians for George, under age 12, eldest son, one of the children of Christopher BENDER, Plainfield Twp.:
guardian: Casper DOHL

New guardians for children of Katherine FIREBACH:
guardians: former—Michael TYBER with George HARTMAN
new—Adam KLEIN, in place of Michael TYBER

Guardians for minor children of Michael KNAPPENBURGHER:
children: Henry, over age 14.................................guardian: Jacob WAGGONER
George, over age 14................................guardian: Frederich SHAFER
Conrad, over age 14................................guardian: John EGENER
Katherine, under age 14..........................guardian: Frederich ROMICH

Estate of Conrad FRY, Lynn Township—return of sale:
widow: Esther FRY, administratrix
sold to: George Adam GROWCH

**Court on 23 September 1762**
**Justices, the Esquires: John MOOR, Conrad HESS, Lewis GORDON**

Guardians for 2 minor children of Frederick PROTZMAN, yeoman, Williams Township:
widow: Barbara, next friend
2 children: John, over age 14...................................guardian: Peter KECKLIN
Nicholas, over age 14..............................guardian: Nicholas BEST

Estate of Adam BETZ, died in 1759, Robeson Township, Berks County, PA, 150 acres in Lower Smithfield Township—request sale:
widow: Susannah, administratrix
9 children: Abram
John
Mary
Adam
Katherine
David
Susannah
Solomon
Elizabeth

Estate of Jacob BILTHOUSE, died 1759—request audit and that the administration account be produced—the estate was granted to the widow and John ORT, "who have not paid into the Hands of the said Petitioners, said Guardians....":
administrators: John ORT and wife
widow: Margaret now wife of Jacob SERFING
3 children, all minors:
Jacob, the eldest
John
Katherine
guardians: for all 3 children—Andreas INGLEMAN and Jacob SMITH

auditors: not named

**Court on 23 September 1762, continued:**

Estate of William GASTON, died 1755, Mt. Bethel Township, 192 acres—partition ordered and guardians approved:

widow: now deceased
5 children: John, eldest son, minor over age 14.......guardian not named
William, over age 14..............................guardian: Thomas SULLIMAN
Hugh, over age 14................................guardian: William McFARREN
Jennet, over age 14................................guardian: Hugh PATTERSON
James, under age 14...............................guardian: Robert LYLE, Esq.
auditors: Alexander GALBREATH, David ALLEN, Alexander MILLER, John MILLER

Estate of Michael ROUP, died 1758, Lower Smithfield Township, 142 acres—request inquest:

widow: Maudlin
5 children: Michael, eldest son
Peter
Christian
Eve
Lewis

Estate of Thomas NEAL—return of sale:

administrator: Joseph NEAL
sold to: George SHARP

Guardians for minor children of Leonard STEIN:

widow: Anna Maria, administratrix
children: Jacob, over age 14..................................guardian: Michael OHL
Lewis, over age 14
Leonard, under age 14
Magdalena, under age 14
Albertina, under age 14
guardian: for 4 younger children—George REX

Estate of Conrad FRY, Lynn Township—request audit:

administrators: Esther FRY and Andreas FOULK
auditors: John EVERET, Charles FOULK, Frederich ROMICH

Guardians for 5 minor children of Nicholas HYLE:

widow: Mary Margaret, now wife of Nicholas LEVERMAN
5 children: John, over age 14...................................guardian: Peter DAHL
Jonathan, over age 14............................guardian: step-father, Nicholas LEVERMAN
Mary Margaret, under age 14
Susannah, under age 14
Mary Elizabeth, under age 14
guardian: for 3 younger children—Casper DAHL

[error in record: Nicholas LEVERMAN is listed as the father-in-law of the child Jonathan rather that his step-father]

**Court on 23 September 1762, continued:**

Guardians for minor children of Martin KOCHER:
petition by: Anna Mary KOCHER
children: Nicholas, over age 14..............................guardian: Paul POLLIET
Elizabeth, over age 14.............................guardian: Henry GEIGER, Esq.
Martin, under age 14...............................guardian: George REX
Adam, under age 14................................guardian: George REX

Guardians for minor children of Elias TETRICK:
widow: Elizabeth, next friend
children: Christina, over age 14
Jacob, under age 14
guardian: for both—Jacob KROTZ

Estate of Bendiwine VANDERLIP, Lower Smithfield Township, 50 acres—request sale:
administrator: Samuel DUPUI, petitioner

Estate of John BEAR—auditors' report:
widow
children: John, eldest son
Barbara
Jacob
Adam
auditors: Herman MOHR and William HAYS

Estate of Elias DETRICH, Mt. Bethel Township, 119 acres—inquest report by High Sheriff John JENNINGS:
children: Elias, eldest son—accepted the property
John
Judley
Christina
Jacob
securities: Frederich NUNEASTER of Easton, tavern keeper; John LONG, of Mt. Bethel
12 men:all by oath—John DURHAM, William MACK, Derick (Direk) ATEN, Henry (Hendrick) ATEN, Moses EVERETT, Alexander CAMPBELL, Henry DILDINE, James HAMILTON, Jacob MINER (not listed with signers), Jacob WOOD (not list with signers), Henry WIDEMAN, Henry VOLLERT

Estate of Melchior FETTER—distribution:
administrators: Appollonia FETTER and Henry FETTER
widow
children: eldest son, not named
Gertrude
John......................................................guardian, Henry GECK

**Court on 23 September 1762, continued:**

Estate of Michael KNAPPENBERGER—report of valuation:

widow: Katherine, administratrix, now wife of Jacob TONNER
children: Henry (his labors thought to be a full equivalent for maintenance)
George
Conrad
Katherine
Hannah's funeral charges and maintenance for one year (perhaps this means she died a year after her father)
appraisers: John TOOL, John JERRAT, Sebastian TRUCKMILLER

Estate of Jacob BRICKER. Lehigh Township—auditors' report and distribution:

widow: Anna Mary, now wife of George SHRADER
children: Adam, eldest son—two shares
Katherine, wife of Valentine WELTMAN
Magdalena
auditors: John WALKER, John HAY, Michael RUCH

Estate of Melchor FETTER, Salisbury Township, 89 acres and 25 acres—inquest report by High Sheriff John JENNINGS, Esq.:

children: Henry, eldest son—accepted the land
Gertrude
John
sureties: George KNOWS and Peter BOCHER, yeoman
12 men: by oaths—George KNOWS, Christian CASEL (CASSEL), John CREASMORE, Philip CUNIUS, Peter HARR, Conrad CRUMBACH, Peter BOGART, George DUTE, Leonard HEIGLE, Jacob SNAR, Henry (Heinrich) JACOBI
by affirmation—George LYBART (LAMBORD)

**Court on 23 December 1762**
**Justices, the Esquires: Timothy HORSEFIELD, Lewis KLOTZ, Aaron DUPUI, Thomas ARMSTRONG, and others**

Estate of William GASTON, Mt. Bethel Township, 192 acres—report of partition:

children: eldest son—refused to accept land
William, second son—accepted the land
John
Hugh
Jennet
James
sureties: Robert McCRACKON, and Thomas SILLIMAN, both of Mt. Bethel Township
auditors: David ALLEN, Alexander MILLER, John MILLER

**Court on 23 December 1762, continued:**

Estate of Michael ROUP, Lower Smithfield Township, 142 acre—inquest report by Sheriff John JENNINGS:

| | |
|---|---|
| widow | |
| children: | Michael ROUP, eldest son—accepted the land<br>others not named |
| 12 men: | by oath—John McDOULL, Philip BUSSARD (Filib BOSSER), Lawrence REMEY, George HARTLIEP, (Johan) Jacob STERNER, Nicholas GOWER, Peter BOZARD (BOSSART), Christian MILLER, Abraham MILLER (MULLER), John MIXALE<br>by affirmation—Jacob SEVITZ (ZEVITZ), Bartil SHIVELY |

Guardians for 4 minor children of Michael ROUP (were other children):

| | |
|---|---|
| widow: | Maudlin |
| 4 children: | Michael, eldest son—accepted the land<br>Peter, over age 14....................................guardian: Michael ROUP<br>Christian, over age 14..............................guardian: Michael ROUP<br>Eve, under age 14....................................guardian: John MOOR, Esq.<br>Lewis, under age 14.................................guardian: Mathias KERN |

Guardians for minor children of Conrad BITTENBENDER:

| | |
|---|---|
| petitioner: | next friend of children, Christopher (Stophel) BITTENBENDER |
| children: | Stophel, the petitioner, under age 14.......guardian: John MOOR, Esq.<br>George, under age 14................................guardian: John MOOR, Esq.<br>Jacob, under age 14..................................guardian: John MOOR, Esq.<br>Conrad, under age 14................................guardian: Christian BITTENBENDER |

New guardian for minor children of Michael WOLFGANG (both under age 14):

| | |
|---|---|
| children: | Katherine<br>Anna Maria |
| guardians: | former—Jacob HAWN and Michael KEIPER, Michael moved out of county<br>new—John MOOR, Esq. |

Guardians for minor children of Henry BOYER, Towamensing Township (left 7 children):

| | |
|---|---|
| children: | Frederick, over age 14.............................guardian: Henry GIEGER<br>Margaret, over age 14.............................guardian: not given<br>Elizabeth, over age 14.............................guardian: not given<br>John, under age 14..................................guardian: George REX<br>Mary, under age 14..................................guardian: George REX<br>Henry, under age 14................................guardian: Joseph PELLY<br>Ann, under age 14...................................guardian: Joseph PELLY |

**Court on 23 December 1762, continued:**

Estate of Michael ZIMMERMAN, the younger, Upper Milford Township—request sale:
administrator: Jacob KURR
Michael ZIMMERMAN, the elder, also deceased, Upper Milford Township, made a will and bequeathed 330 acres in Upper Milford Township and Upper Hanover Township in Philadelphia County to be equally divided with 2 sons, they paying his 3 daughters 40 pounds each.
children of Michael, Sr.:
Michael, Jr.
George
Elizabeth
Feronica
Katherine
Michael, Jr., left widow and 2 children:
widow: Elizabeth
children: Michael
Elizabeth

Estate of Philip KARCHER, Weisenberg Township (mis-dated as 1763 but in 1762 records)—request sale:
widow: Margaret, administratrix

Estate of Jacob SWARTZ, Macungie Township—request for valuation (mis-dated as 1763 but in 1762 records):
administrator: Jacob, eldest son—accepted the land
auditors: Lewis GORDON, Esq., and John MOORE, Esq.

Estate of Leonard STEIN, Heidelberg Township—request for audit (mis-dated as 1763 but in 1762 records):
administrator: Anna Mary SHRADER
auditors: Peter KECHLIN, Nicholas SNYDER, Valentine UPP

Estate of Jacob SWARTZ—auditors' report and distribution:
widow: Katherine
children: Jacob, eldest son—accepted the property
Sophia, wife of David MARSH
Elizabeth, wife of D-d CONNINGER
Susannah, wife of Henry VAN POOLE
Margaret
Abraham
George
John
Katherine
Mary
Philip
auditors: John MOOR and Lewis GORDON

Estate of Bandawine VANDERLIP—return of sale:
administrator: Samuel DUPUI
sold to: Nicholas DUPUI

**Court of 24 March 1763**
**Justices, the Esquires: Timothy HORSEFIELD, Lewis KLOTZ, Aaron DUPUI, Thomas ARMSTRONG, and others**

Estate of Michael ZIMMERMAN, the younger, Up. Milford Township, 103 ½ acres & 207 acres—return of sale:
- administrator: Jacob KURR
- sold to: John YOND

**Court on 23 June 1763**
**Justices, the Esquires: Lewis KLOTZ, Aaron DUPUI, Thomas ARMSTRONG**

Estate of Peter MILLER, Upper Milford Township, died about 13 years ago—request sale:
- widow: Catherine, administratrix, now wife of Herman NEESE
- 3 children: one died as minor, intestate
  - Peter, under age 21
  - Margaret, under age 21

Estate of Frederich GERMANTOWN, died about 1756, Plainfield Township, 100 acres warranted land—request partition:
- widow: Catherine
- 4 children: Conrad, over age 21, eldest son—other 3 are minors:
  - Margaret
  - Barbara
  - Elizabeth

Guardians of Bernard BOWMAN, now over age 14, eldest son and minor child of Hans Dieter BOWMAN:
- guardian: John MOOR, Esq.

Guardians of minor children of Henry FREEDLY, Heidelberg Township (left 3 children):
- administrator: Elizabeth FREEDLY
- children:
  - Henry, age 7............guardian: George BRINNING
  - Elizabeth, age 4............guardian: George BRINNING
  - David, age 2 ½............guardian: Martin ROMICH

Guardians of minor children of Andrew MYER, Heidelberg Township (left 8 children):
- widow: Mary, administrator
- children:
  - Christina............married
  - Peter, age 16............guardian: not named
  - Mary, age 14............guardian: not named
  - Catherine, age 13............guardian: Frederich SNYDER
  - Elizabeth, age 12............guardian: Frederich SNYDER
  - Jacob, age 8 ½............guardian: Adam DISHLER
  - Andrew, age 4............guardian: Adam DISHLER
  - Paul, age 2 ½............guardian: Adam DISHLER

Estate of Jacob STERNER—request sale (left children, all under age 21):
- administrator: Elizabeth STERNER

Estate of Jacob STEFFEN—auditors appointed (left children):
- widow: Mary, administratrix, now wife of John BARE

auditors: Lewis KLOTZ, William EDMONDS, George GOOD

**Court on 20 September 1763**

**Justices, the Esquires: Aaron DUPUI, Lewis KLOTZ, John MOOR, Jacob ARNDT, Robert LYLE**

Guardians for minor children of Frederick GERMANTOWN, Plainfield Township (all under age 14):
widow: Katherine
children: Margaret
Barbara
Elizabeth
guardian: their mother, Katherine

Estate of Andrew MOYER, died 3 years ago, Heidelberg—request sale:
land: 25 acres, land adjoining Rev. Mr. Richard PETERS
widow: Mary, administratrix
8 children
Andrew mistakenly made "considerable improvements" on the Reverend's land. Mr. PETERS, "Hath allowed your Petition leave to Dispose of to the best advantage for the sake of the children being unwilling to deprive them of the Labour of their dec-d father."

Estate of ________MILLER, died about 11 years ago, Lower Smithfield Township, 280 acres—request inquest:
widow
5 children: Abraham (Abram), eldest
Joseph, over age 21, the rest are minors:
Catherine
Salome
Elizabeth

Estate of Frederich GERMANTOWN, Plainfield Township, 200 acres—inquest report by High Sheriff John JENNINGS:
children: Margaret
Barbara
Elizabeth
Conrad, eldest son, two shares—accepted the land
securities: Peter KECKLEIN of Easton, and Peter METZ of Plainfield
12 men: by oath—Casper DULL (DOLL), Peter METZ, Jacob SORBER, Peter MELICK, George DEETS (DIETZ), Deal BOWER, Leonard ERB, Ludwig ERB, Peter (Peter Phillip) HAN, Nicholas SNYDER, Leonard BOYER
by affirmation—Jacob HUBLER

Estate of Jacob STERNER, Towamensing Township—return of sale:
administratrix: Elizabeth STERNER
sold to: Peter HUBER

Estate of Frederich SHOLL, Lower Saucon Township—return of sale:
widow: Barbara SHOLL, administratrix:
sold to: Christian BACHMAN

Estate of Adam MARKLE, Williams Township—return of sale:
land: 175 acres, adjoining Jacob and Nicholas BEST
widow: Elizabeth MARKLE, administratrix
sold to: Michael MEYER

**Court of 20 March 1764**
**Justices, the Esquires: Hugh WILSON, Lewis KLOTZ, Henry GEIGER, Robert LYLE**

Estate of Abraham MILLER, Hamilton Township, 280 acres—inquest report by Sheriff John JENNINGS, Esq.:
12 men: by oath—Jacob STROUD, Jacob STERNER, Lawrence REMICK (REMY), Lawrence KUNKLE, Adam STECKER, Michael ROUP (RUPE), Abram SNELL
by affirmation—Phillip BUGERT, George MINNER, John MINNER, George FREDERICH, Jacob SEWITZ

Guardians of minor children of Abraham (Abram) MILLER, Sr., Lower Smithfield Township:
petitioner: Abraham MILLER, Jr.:
children: Elizabeth, over age 14.............................guardian: George HUBER
Salome, over age 14...............................guardian: Jacob MILLER

Guardian for minor child of George LEITLOFF, Lynn Township (left 2 children):
administrator: Peter TREXLER
children: Erhart, now married
George, about age 12...............................guardian: Frederich ROMICH

Guardians for 7 minor children of Frederich REITZ, Whitehall Township (left 7 children):
administrator: John WYAND, petitioner
children: Henry, over age 14
Anna Margaret, over age 14
Elizabeth, over age 14
Anna
Eva Elizabeth
Jacob
Lawrence
guardian: for 3 older children—Adam GABLE
guardian: for 4 younger children—David BERRINGER

Guardians for minor children of Jacob CHRISTMAN, died about three years ago:
widow: Eve Margaret
7 children: Eve, wife of Melchior BEAR
George, over age 21
Jacob, over age 14...................................guardian: Hans Nicholas STAYLOR
Susannah, over age 14.............................guardian: Melchior BARE
John
Phillip
Henry
guardians: for younger 3 children—their mother and Nicholas STAYLOR

Guardians for minor children of Peter MILLER, Upper Milford Township (left 2 children):
widow: Katherine, administratrix, now wife of Herman NEIS
children: Margaret, over age 14
Peter, under age 14
guardian: for both—George KLEIN

**Court of 20 March 1764, continued:**

Request for new guardian for children of George MARSTELLER, Upper Saucon:

petition of Matthias OX, one guardian—stated that other guardian, Christian RINKER, might abuse funds and requested a new guardian be appointed in his stead. "...but the said RINKER keeps the childrens money in his own Hands...the said RINKER'S circumstances are very low...afraid the money will be lost."

Court issues citation for Christian RINKER to appear in court and report.

Guardian for George, over age 14, minor child of George YERIG:

petitioner: Adam SHULER, of Upper Milford Township, a relation of deceased
guardian: Adam SHULER, the petitioner

New guardian for Margaret DEWINNIG:

Some years ago she chose William MACK as guardian but she was now suspicious of him and desired a new guardian. "But being very suspicious that the said William MACK hath not Disposed of the said Estate to the best advantage nor taken care of her Person."
new guardian: John JENNINGS, Esq.

Guardians for minor children of Jacob MARKLE (left 5 children):

widow: Catherine, administratrix
children: Mary Elizabeth, now married
Jacob, age 15, over age 14.......................guardian: George Adam LYLELSPECHER
John, under age 14
Catherine Elizabeth, under age 14
John George, under age 14
guardians: for younger 3 children—their mother and John MARKLE

Guardians for minor children of Jacob SAME, Williams Township (left 4 children):

administrator: Bernard MILLER
children: Anna Magdalena, over age 14.................guardian: Rudolph OBERLY
Eve Margaret
Anna Margaret
Anna Mary
guardian: for younger 3 children—Conrad RAMLY

Estate of William LABAR, died 1761, Mount Bethel Township—request partition:

land: 270 acres adjoining William CRAIG, and William McALLROY, near Blue Mountains
widow: Dorothy
6 children by former wife:
William, eldest son
Esther, wife of Christopher SIZMAN
Elizabeth, wife of Joseph LONG
Mary, wife of Simon HEARSH
Charles
Barbara, wife of Casper ROMMAGE

**Court of 20 March 1764, continued:**

Estate of Jacob CHRISTMAN, died about 3 years ago, Upper Milford Township, 150 acres—request partition:
- widow: Eve Margaret
- 7 children: George, eldest son
  - Eve, wife of Melchior BARE—other five under age 21:
  - Jacob
  - Susannah
  - John
  - Phillip
  - Henry

Estate of Leonard STEIN, Heidelberg Township—request sale:
- widow: Anna Maria, administratrix, now wife of George SHRADER
- children: several, five of whom are under age 21

Auditors' report on William MACK, former guardian of Margaret DOWINNEY:
- auditors: Daniel BRODHEAD, Henry ALLSHOUSE, Adam YOHE—MACK is to pay the balance of the estate to the present guardian, John JENNINGS.

**Court on 19 June 1764**
**Justices, the Esquires: Aaron DUPUI, Timothy HORSEFIELD, Lewis KLOTZ, John MOOR, Jacob ARNDT**

Estate of Peter REESER, Lower Saucon Township—request audit:
- administrators: Margaret GIFFIN (late REESER), and Adam REESER
- widow and children
- auditors: Anthony LERCH, Edward BECK, Rudolph OBERLY

Estate of William LABAR, Mt. Bethel Township, 170 acres—inquest report by Sheriff John JENNINGS, Esq.:
- children: William, the eldest son
  - others not named
- surety: John LONG
- 12 men:all by oath—John LONG, John DURHAM, Henry DILDINE, Henry WIDEMAN, Nicholas FUNSTON, Jacob SNYDER, Ludwig HENRY, George YOUNG, Jacob WOOD, Elias DETRICH, John DETRICH, David ALLEN

New guardian for minor REESER children, all under age 14:
- Children: Conrad
  - Paul
  - Phillip
  - Peter
- guardian: former—Nicholas BEST (with Adam REESER)—Nicholas, "finds it very Inconvenient to his Private Business to act or Discharge the Duty of a Guardian...."
  - new—Matthias BROOCH of Williams Township

Estate of Peter WALBERT, Macungie Township—request partition:
- widow: Ann Elizabeth, administratrix, now Mrs. LUDWIG
- auditors: Sebastian TRUCKMILLER, William HENTZ, John ROMICH

Estate of Jacob CHRISTMAN, Upper Milford Township, 150 acres—inquest report by Sheriff John JENNINGS, Esq.:

children: George, eldest son—accepted the land
Eve, wife of Melchior BEAR
Jacob
Susannah
John
Philip
Henry

12 men:all by oath—Martin KINKINGER, Adam KROMMAS, Phillip HARTSHOUGH, Baltzer FETTERMAN, Jacob WETZEL, Frederich KERN, Adam KALE, Nicholas STALLER, Christian FISHER, Francis WESCHO, George REINHARD, Christian REINHARD

Guardians for 4 minor children of William MORY, Upper Saucon (all under age 14):

widow: Mary Catherine, administratrix
4 children: Godhard
Anne
Elizabeth
William
guardians: for all 4 children—appointed Henry BRUNER and John APPLE

Estate of Peter VICKART, Upper Milford Township, 100 acres—request sale; auditors appointed:

widow: Maria Margaret, now widow of John LINDT, deceased
auditors: Nicholas SNYDER, Valentine UPP, Ludwig KNOWS

Estate of Phillip LIPPENCUT—request partition:

widow: Margaret, administratrix
children: not named

Estate of Jacob MARKLE, died 1763, Weisenberg Township, 130 acres—request sale:

administrator: Jacob BAKER
widow: Katherine, administratrix
5 children: Mary Elizabeth
Jacob
John
Katherine Elizabeth
John George

Guardians for minor children of Abraham MILLER, Lower Smithfield Township:

children: Abraham, of age
Elizabeth, over age 14............................guardian: George HUBER
Salome, over age 14...............................guardian: Jacob MILLER

Guardians for minor children of Henry FRANCE, Heidelberg Township:

children: Barbara, age 16
Peter, age 12, the petitioner
guardian: for both children—Abraham FRANCE of Lehigh Township

Estate of Leonard STEIN, Heidelberg Township—return of sale:
widow: Anna Maria, now wife of George SHRADER
sold to: Nicholas HAREDWORK

**Court on 19 September 1764**
**Justices, the Esquires: not named**

Estate of John JARRET, died about 9 years ago, Macungie Township—had a will which was proved in Easton but he had revoked it. It was declared null and void—request for partition:
widow
13 children: John, eldest son
Edward
Junae
Samuel
Phillip
William
Sebastian
Daniel
Mary, wife of Adam EVERTY
Elizabeth, wife of Daniel TURNY
Joan, wife of John WETSEL
Margaret, wife of Frederick STACKLER
Sarah, wife of Martin SPIEGEL

Guardians for minor children of John JARRET, Macungie Township:
children: Edward, the petitioner, of age
Sebastian, age 20....................................guardian: John WETZEL
Daniel, age 17........................................guardian: Daniel TURNEY

Estate of Christian STALL, Heidelberg Township—request audit:
administrator: Peter MESSIEMER
widow and children
auditors: George REX, Michael ROCH, Paul POLLIET

Estate of Jacob MARKLE, yeoman, Weisenberg Township, 130 acres—return of sale:
administrators: Katherine MARKLE and John BAKER
sold to: Philip ARNOLD

**Court on 17 December 1764**
**Justices, the Esquires: not named**

Estate of John JERRET, Macungie Township, 514 acres—report of inquest by High Sheriff Peter KEICHLAN (KEICHLIN, KECKLIN), Esq.:
widow
children: John, eldest son—accepted the land
sureties: John REISS and Melchior BEAR
12 men:all by oath—Martain (Martin) KINKINER, Christian STINNINER, Tewalt MEGLIN, John RICE, Melger BEAR, John BEHR, Phillip WALDEN, Gotfrit DIFFINDERFER, Jacob TANNER, Christopher SMITH, Lewis FORSH, Andrew EISENHART

**Court on 17 December 1764, continued:**

Guardians for minor RICE children:

| | | |
|---|---|---|
| children: | George, over age 14.................................guardian: | John OLLEWINE, Esq. |
| | Andrew, over age 14................................guardian: | Jacob WETZEL |
| | Elizabeth, under age 14...........................guardian: | John WETZEL |

## Court on 22 March 1765
## Justices, the Esquires: Aaron DUPUI, John JENNINGS, Henry GEIGER

Estate of Abraham MILLER—valuation and distribution:

children: Abraham, the younger, eldest son—accepted the land
Joseph
Catherine
Salome
Elizabeth

securities: John MOORE, Esq., John McDORSELL

Estate of Michael REIKEL, died about 5 years ago, Macungie Township, 4 tracts—request inquest:

land: one in Macungie Township
two in Upper Milford Township
one in Salisbury Township

widow: now married to Adam CROMMOS

10 children: Ludwig, eldest son
Catherine, wife of Phillip HAGAR
Maria, wife of Henry KEMRER—remaining 7 children under age 21:
George
Jacob
Martin
John
Michael
Barbara
Rosina

auditors: Anthony LERCH, Edward BECK, Rudolph OBERLE

Estate of Henry REES, died about a year ago, Upper Milford Township, 250 acres—request inquest:

8 children: John, eldest son
Catherine, wife of Christian RINER
Barbara, wife of George STAHL
Mary Elizabeth, wife of Jacob HICKINGER—the remaining children under age 21:
Henry
John George
Andrew
Elizabeth

Guardians for minor children of Michael REIKEL, died about 5 years ago, Macungie Township (were other children):

| | | |
|---|---|---|
| children: | Ludwig, eldest son, the petitioner, of age | |
| | George, age 19.......................................guardian: | Dewalt MECKLIN |
| | Jacob, age 18..........................................guardian: | John WETZEL |

**Court on 22 March 1765, continued:**

Guardians for Leonard BURGART—petition by Christian FEICHTNER and his wife Margaret (late Margaret BURGART), next friend of Leonard:

Leonard had for sometime past been non compas mentis (lunatic) and unable to care for himself or his fortune. The Overseers of the Poor of Whitehall Township were appointed as guardians.

Estate of Henry MILLER, Lynn Township—request for sale and guardians for 3 minor children:

administrators: John SMITH and wife, Elizabeth (the late MILLER)
children: Christian
Andrew
Anna Mary
guardian: for all 3 children—Christian MILLER

Guardians for minor children of Michael REIKEL (left "five children still alive") (all under age 14):

widow: Catherine now wife of Adam KRAMMER
children: Barbara..................................................guardian: Frederich ROMICH
Rosina....................................................guardian: Frederich ROMICH
Martin....................................................guardian: Melchior BARE
John.......................................................guardian: Melchior BARE
Michael...................................................guardian: John WETZEL

Estate of Peter REESER, Lower Saucon Township—auditors' report (the heirs are all named as children in earlier reports:

widow
heirs: eldest son, not named
Anthony
Conrad
Peter
Paul
Phillip
Catherine

Estate of John MILLER, died about 18 years ago, Upper Saucon Township—request sale:

administrator: David REESER, administrator de bonis non:
administrator was John REESER, now deceased—had paid some of estate's debts
left widow and 5 children

**Court of 19 March 1765 (out of order)**
**Justices, the Esquires: Thomas ARMSTRONG, Lewis KLOTZ, John MOORE, Jacob ARNDT**

Estate of John MILLER, died about 18 years ago, Upper Saucon Township—request for audit:

auditors: John WAGLE, Henry ALSHOUSE, Henry KOCHIN

**Court on 19 September 1765**
**Justices, the Esquires: Lewis KLOTZ, John MOORE, Jacob ARNDT**

Guardians for minor children of Martin MYER (left 6 children, all minors):
administratrix: Mathalena MYER
6 children: Margaret, over age 14..............................guardian: Paul POLLIARD
Peter
Martin
John
Jacob
Catherine
guardians: for younger 5 children—Daniel SHNYDER and Michael NEWHART

Estate of Peter REESER: (note—Matthias BROSCH was appointed guardian on 16 May 1764)
widow
eldest son: Jacob—accepted the land
other children

**Court on 7 October 1767**
**Justices, the Esquires: Lewis GORDON, Christopher WAGNER, Henry KOOKIN**
**(note: Even though this date appears to belong to Volume D, these are additional notes written in Volume C, pertaining to the REESER estate.)**

Estate of Peter REESER—eldest son Jacob will accept the land:
securities: Anthony LARCH and Benedict LUTZ

**Court on 16 May 1768**
**Justices: not named**
**(note: Even though this date appears to belong to Volume D, these are additional notes written in Volume C, pertaining to the REESER estate. The notes refer the reader back to Volume B)**

Estate of Peter REESER—bond for shares for the minor children are given to Matthias OCH, guardian.

**End of Volume C**

**Volume D: 20 June 1765-20 December 1781:**

**Court on 20 June 1765**
**Justices, the Esquires: Lewis KLOTZ, John MOORE, Jacob ARNDT**

Estate of John CRACK, cordwainer of Whitehall Township—request sale:
administrator: Conrad CRACK, son
other children: not named
auditors: Myer HART, William LEDLIC, James TAYLOR

Guardians for minor children of Jacob FRANTZ (left 4 children):
administrator: Peter FRANTZ
4 children: Jacob, age 14..........................................guardian: Paul POLLIAT
Joseph, under age 14
John, under age 14
Peter, under age 14
guardians: for younger 3—Peter WASDRICH, David HAHN, and Paul POLLIAT

Guardians for minor children of John SHOVER, died about 1 ½ year ago (left 5 children, all minors):
widow: Anna Margaret, administratrix
guardians: for all five—Philip WERKMAN and Thomas EVERETT

Guardians for minor children of Henry TZINCK, killed by Indians in 1763 (left 5 children, all minors)—request a sale of 1/3 of the mill to pay debts:
land: saw mill over Blue Mountains in partnership with William CRAIG, Esq., & Neal GRAY
widow: Elizabeth, administratrix
children: Peter, age 14..........................................guardian: Abraham FREAT, Allen Township
the remaining 4 children, all under age 14:
Paul.......................................................guardian: Henry WEAVER
Catherine................................................guardian: Henry WEAVER
Henry.....................................................guardian: Peter FREED
Abram....................................................guardian: Peter FREED

Estate of John MILLER, Upper Saucon Township, yeoman,—return of sale by motion of Edward BIDDLE of the Council:
land: 71 acres adjacent to Hanes REESER, deceased, Christian SMITH, deceased, Peter MARSTELLER, vacant land, and John YODER
administrator: David REESER, administrator de bonis non, in place of his brother, John REESER, dec.
sold to: John ROTHROCK, Lower Saucon Township

Estate of Johannes MILLER, died 1750, Upper Saucon Township, 71 acres—complaint of Christian MILLER, eldest son, against the administrator, David REESER)
widow
children: Christian, eldest son
Peter
Daniel
Ann
Magdalen
Catherine

**Court on 20 June 1765, continued:**

Estate of Michael RISHEL, 535 acres in Macungie, Upper Milford, and Salisbury Townships—report of inquest by Sheriff Peter KACHLEIN, Esq.:

12 men:by oath—Christopher SMITH, Peter TREXLER (TRAXLER), Francis WESCO, Jacob SHNYDER, Jacob HANN, Christian STININGER, George HAMMER, Peter MILLER, Peter FOX, Peter HAAS, Martin GINCKER
by affirmation—Andrew GISENENHARD

(Note written in September 1765 before Lewis KLOTZ, John JENNINGS, Aaron DUPUI, and Daniel BRODHEAD—motion of James BIDDLE: "Some of the Jurors named in the foregoing Inquest were born aliens and not yet naturalized. The court Quash the said inquest and a new writ..." is issued.)

## Court on 8 July 1765
## Jacob ARNDT, Daniel BRODHEAD, Lewis GORDON

Guardians for minor children of Christian STAHL, Heidelberg Township, yeoman:

| | |
|---|---|
| next friend: | Everhard REICHMAN |
| children: | Elizabeth Margaret, over age 14 |
| | Katherine, over age 14 |
| | Paul, under age 14 |
| | Gertrude, under age 14 |
| guardian: | for all 4 children—Everhard REICHMAN & his wife Elizabeth |

## Court on 30 July 1765
## John MOORE, Christopher WAGGONER, Lewis GORDON

Guardians for 2 minor children of Abraham DELONG, died about 1756, Lynn Township, 200 acres:

| | |
|---|---|
| widow | |
| 9 children: | Matthias, the petitioner |
| | Lucas, over age 14 |
| | Edward, over age 14 |
| | others not named (all of age) |
| guardian: | for 2 minor children—Mark VANEMAKER |

## Court on 10 August 1765
## John MOOR, Lewis GORDON, Jacob ARNDT

Guardians of minor children of Christian MYER, Weisenberg Township:

| | |
|---|---|
| next friend: | Dewalt MYER |
| children: | Nicholas |
| | Peter |
| guardian: | for both children—Dewalt MYER |

## Court on 18 September 1765
## Justices not named

Estate of Simon FRIZE—request sale:

| | |
|---|---|
| land: | house and lot in Northampton Town and one moiety or ½ part of saw mill |
| administrator: | Phillip KOGLER |

**Court on 18 September 1765, continued:**

Guardians for grandchildren of Philip LEIBENGOOD, Whitehall Township (were other children):
petitioner: George LEIBENGOOD, older brother of Christina SWAP
grandchildren, children of Christina, late wife of Martin SWAP; she died about 5 years ago & left 2:
Adam SWAP
George SWAP
guardian: for both children—John SHAD (appointed)

Estate of John SHOVER, died about 2 years ago—request sale:
land: small improvement over the Blue Mountains
widow: Margaret, administratrix
5 small children

Estate of John CRACK—auditors' report:
administrator: Conrad CRACK
auditors: Will LEDLIE and James TAYLOR

**Court on 18 March 1765 (note: date was squeezed in here—out of order)**
**Hugh WILSON, Lewis KLOTZ, John MOOR**

Estate of John BEAR, died about 11 years ago, Heidelberg Township, 200 acres—request inquest:
widow
4 children: John BEAR, eldest son—petitioner
others not named

**Court on 18 March or 18 September 1765**
**(Uncertain which date for next three entries because of preceding entry)**

Estate of Michael KNAPPENBERGER, died about 14 years ago, Macungie Township—request inquest:
widow
5 children: Henry KNAPPENBERGER, eldest son—petitioner

Guardians for minor children of William BRAND, died about 11 years ago, Lower Saucon Township:
petitioner: George CREATER, Lower Saucon Township
3 children: Philip
Ragena
Matalena
guardian: for all 3 children—Anthony LARCH (appointed)

Request for new guardian for some of minor children of Andrew MYERS, Heidelberg Township:
guardian: former—Adam DESHLER, Whitehall Township—"...none of the children's money has been delivered to the Petitioner and that he Lives a good ways off and cannot well look after it...."
new—Michael OHL

**Court on 19 June 1766**
**George TAYLOR, Lewis KLOTZ, John MOOR**

Estate of Peter WALBERT , Macungie Township—request inquest:
widow: Elizabeth now wife of Matthias LUDWIG
8 children: George, eldest son
others not named

Estate of John HILLMAN, died about 2 years ago, 2 tracts in Hamilton Township—request inquest:
widow
12 children: James, eldest son, petitioner
others not named

(A note with next four entries says that the motions, though written on separate paper, do belong here.)

Guardian for minor child Jane BRINK, over age 14—motion by Nicholas WALN, Esq.:
guardian: John MOOR, Esq.

Estate of Rudolph ANDREAS—motion by Nicholas WALN, Esq. to have auditors appointed:
executors: Samuel UTRINGER and his wife Katherine Barbara
auditors: Bastian KNOWS, Adam KRAMMER, and Ludwig STELER

Estate of Michael RISHEL—auditors appointed:
administrators: Ludwig RISHEL, Adam GRAMMAR and Katherine his wife
auditors: Henry KOOKEN, Andreas KERING, and Adam SHULER

Estate of Stophel NARPLE—auditors appointed:
executors: John APPLE and Philip BUSHACRE
auditors: John OKELY, John RODROCK, and John NEWCOMER

Estate of Henry REES, Upper Milford Township, 250 acres—inquest report of Sheriff Peter KACHLEIN, Esq:
8 children: John REESE, eldest son—accepted the land
sureties: Jacob FLICKENGER, Peter MILLER
12 men: oaths of—George KNAUS, George GOOD, David DRESHLER, Michael HITTEL, Dewalt MECHLIN, John WETZEL, Peter MEYLIN, George Adam BLANK (Görg Adam BLANCK), Michael OTT
affirmation of—Bastian KNAUS, Isaac JERRET, George LEIBERT

Estate of Michael KNAPPENBERGER, Macungie Township, 275 acres—inquest report by Sheriff Peter KACHLEIN, Esq:
eldest son: Henry
securities: Melchior BARE, Deeter GOWER
12 men: all by oath—John KLINE, Deader GOWER, Jacob WAGGONER, Adam DESH, John REISS, Ludwig LARÜSH, Melcher BEAR, Godfred DEFENDORPHER, Christian ROOD, Peter KEISSER, Frantz WESKON, Lehard KOON

Guardians for Daniel, minor child of ____ BIDLEMAN, died several years ago, Lower Saucon Township (left two children):
children: Elizabeth, now married
Daniel, over age 14
guardians: John APPLE and Gratzer LERCH

**Court on 19 July 1766**
**George TAYLOR, John MOOR, Lewis GORDON**

Estate of Garret BRINK, died about 11 years ago, sundry tracts in Upper Smithfield Township—request inquest:
widow
5 children: Sarah, wife of the petitioner, Benjamin VAN de MARK, Upper Smithfield Township
Charity VAN GARDEN, widow of Peter VAN GARDEN, second daughter
Mary
Lydia
Jannicha

Estate of James MORDEN, died about 6 years ago, Mt. Bethel Township, 100 acres—request sale:
widow: Jane, now wife of Mr. VANETTA
9 children

**Court 18 September 1766**
**Hugh WILSON, Aaron DUPUI, Lewis KLOTZ**

Estate of Peter WALBERT, Macungie Township, 300 acres—report of inquest by Sheriff Peter KACHLEIN:
securities: George TOOT and Jacob BARE
12 men:all by oath—George SLEIGHER, Melcher BARE, John TREXLER, Simon HEIM, John BARE, Godfrey DEPENDORFER, Henry WETZEL, Ludwig MACKEL, John DUNKEL, John ROMICH, Andrew EISENHART, Jacob HERMAN

Estate of John HEILMAN, Hamilton Township, 40 acres—report of inquest by Sheriff Peter KACHLEIN, Esq.:
security: John DRAKE
12 men:all by oath—Dearck (Dirck) VAN FLEET, John DRAKE, Lawrence KUNKLE, Nicholas DUPUI, Evan MORGAN, Benjamin SHOEMAKER, Hugh PUGH, James LAWSON, Jacob STROUD, Abraham MILLER, Peter LABAR, Samuel DRAKE

Estate of John BEAR, Weisenberg Township, 260 acres—report of inquest by Sheriff Peter KACHLEIN, Esq.:
widow
children: John BEAR, eldest son—accepted the land
Jacob
Barbara, wife of Henry FETTER
Adam
securities: Abraham KNER and Henry FETTER
12 men:all by oath—John REINSMITH, Peter SELL, Simon QUIRE, John EBERT, Jacob BACHMAN, George BREINER, Frederick SHNYDER, Tobius EBERT, Henry KRICH, William MÖYER, George GEORGE, Andrew SINDEL

Estate of Garat BRINCK, Upper Smithfield Township, 350 acres—report of inquest by High Sheriff Peter KACHLEIN, Esq.:
second daughter, Charity, to accept the land and provide securities since first daughter refused land
securities: John BRINK and John VAN ETTEN
12 men:all by oath—Adam SHICK, Henry COURTRIGHT, David VANAKEN, Anthony BUNSCOTA, Alexander VANGARDEN, Gysbart VANGARDEN, James HYNDSHAW, Jacob SWARTHOOT, William SMITH, Manuel GENSALES, Barnard SWARTHOOT, Thomas SWARTWORTH

**Court 18 September 1766, continued:**

Estate of Enoch ARMITAGE, died about 11 years ago, of Philadelphia County—request sale:
land: on Colui's Creek, Mt. Bethel Township
administrators: Barbara and Benjamin ARMITAGE
6 children: Rachel wife of Mr. WHITE—the other 5 are minors:
Benjamin
James
Enoch
Elizabeth
Hannah

Guardians for 3 minor children of Jacob WETTERHOLD:
widow: Susannah, administratrix
3 children: Jacob
Susannah
Catherin
guardian: for all 3 children—John LICHTENWALDER the younger (appointed)

Estate of James MORDEN, Mt. Bethel Township—return of sale:
administrators: John VANETTA and his wife Jane
sold to: George BECK

**Court on 29 November 1766**
**George TAYLOR, Lewis GORDON, John MOOR**

Estate of Jacob HOWSER, died about 8 years ago, Plainfield Township, certain improvement already sold in Jacob's lifetime but for which he never made title; the widow wanted this title finalized for he, "...died so very poor that there was never any Inventory or appraisement taken...."—request final sale:
widow: Anna HOWSERIN, administratrix
left several small children

**Court on 16 December 1766**
**George TAYLOR, Lewis KLOTZ, John MOOR**

Estate of Jacob WETTERHOLT, Lynn Township, 150 acres—request sale (there were children):
widow: Susannah, administratrix, now wife of Michael KERN

Estate of Christopher HERPLE (had a will)—auditors' report:
executors: John APPLE and Philip BUCHACRE
left minor children
auditors: John OKELY, John NEWCOMER, Johannes ROTHROCK

Estate of Jacob HOWSER, Plainfield Township—return of sale:
administrator: Anna HOWSERIN
sold to: Jacob HUBLER, Sr. (for _15, "...to whom it was formerly sold.")

Estate of Michael RISHEL—auditors' report:
administrators: Ludwig RISHEL, Adam GRONER and his wife Katherine
left widow and 10 children
auditors: Henry KOOKEN, Adam SCHULER, Adam KERING

**Court on 16 December 1766, continued:**

Guardians for minor children of Peter VANGARDA, Upper Smithfield Township—motion of Nicholas WALN:
children: Charita
Jonathan
Peter
guardians: for all the children—Charity VANGARDA and John VENETTON (appointed)

Guardian for minor child, Jane BRINK, now over age 14—motion of Nicholas WALN:
guardian: John MOORE

**Court on 9 January 1767**
**John MOOR, Lewis GORDON, Jacob ARNDT, Christopher WAGNER**

Estate of Mr. BECK, Moore Township (left widow and 6 children)—request sale:
widow: now dead
eldest son: William, Moore Township

Guardian for Lovice, minor child of Michael ROUB (were other children)—motion of James TAYLOR:
guardian: John MOOR, Esq., of Forks Township

**Court on 15 January 1767**
**Lewis GORDON, Jacob ARNDT, John JENNINGS**

Estate of Jacob MAURER, died about 3 years ago, Bethlehem Township—request sale:
widow: Catherine, now wife of Mr. MIKLE
4 children

**Court on 21 January 1767**
**Lewis GORDON, John MOOR, Jacob ARNDT**

Estate of Peter WALBERT, Macungie Township—new security appointed:
eldest son: George
securities: former—Jacob BARE, about to remove from province into Carolina
other—George WALBERT, George TOST (not changed)
new—Leonard KOON, "a good freeholder"

**Court on 29 January 1767**
**Justices, the Esquires: Jacob ARNDT, John JENNINGS, Lewis GORDON**

Estate of Jacob MAURER—return of sale:
administratrix: Catherina MIKLE
sold to: Jonas HERTZEL

**Court on 17 March 1767**
**John MOOR, Thomas ARMSTRONG, Daniel BRODHEAD, Henry KOOCHEN**

Estate of Jacob WETTERHOLT—request audit, by motion of Edward BIDDLE:
administrators: Michael KERN and wife Susan (late WETTERHOLT)
auditors: John EVERET, Thomas EVERET, Jacob HORNER

**Court on 17 March 1767, continued:**

Guardians for minor children of Jacob KOON—motion of James TAYLOR:
- children: Magdalena
  - Jacob
- guardian: both chose France WESCO, Esq.

Estate of Balzer HAMON—request audit, by motion of Nicholas WALN:
- widow: Margaret, now wife of Paul THUSING
- auditors: Peter ROADS, George KNOWS, Daniel HURLOCHER

Estate of John MILLER, died about 11 years ago, Plainfield Township—request inquest:
- 11 children: John, eldest son
  - others not named

Estate of William SHOUP, died about 11 years ago, Upper Milford Township, 100 acres—request partition:
- 2 children: Bernard, eldest son
  - Margaret

Estate of Jacob KOON, died about 9 years ago—inquest requested:
- land: 2 small improvements in Salisbury and Macungie Townships
- 8 children: Leonard, eldest son
  - others not named

Estate of Frantz READ, died about 9 years ago—request inquest:
- land: Salisbury Township, 400 acres plus 50 acres of woodland
- widow
- 5 children, all minors:
  - Francis, eldest son
  - Henry
  - Maria
  - Elizabeth
  - Margaret

Estate of Adam FISHER, Salisbury Township—request sale:
- widow: Magdalena
- several small children

Estate of Rudolph ANDREAS—auditors' report:
- administrators: Samuel UTTRINGER and wife Katherine Barbara
- widow
- 3 children
- auditors: Sebastian KNAWS, Adam KRAMER, Ludwig STAHLER

Estate of Henry BECK, Moore Township—motion of Richard PETERS, Jr., stating administrator made fraudulent sale; the auditors appointed to inquire are ordered to produce evidence:
- administrator: William BECK, Moore Township
- sold to: George KINDT

**Court on 17 March 1767, continued:**

Guardians for minor HAMON children—motion of Nicholas WALN:

| | |
|---|---|
| children: | Jacob, over age 14 |
| | John George, under age 14 |
| guardian: | for both children—Leonard STEININGER, Whitehall Township |

Estate of Garet BRINK—motion of Nicholas WALN, that the land be adjudged to Garet's second daughter, Charity VANGARDA, widow, since eldest daughter refused to give security:

| | |
|---|---|
| securities: | John BRINK and John VANETTON |

**Court on 25 March 1767**
**Justices, the Esquires: George TAYLOR, Christopher WAGONER, Henry KOOCHEN**

Estate of Henry BECK, Moore Township—auditors' response to charges of fraud, "...no proof appearing that any fraud or deceit had been committed or intended." Sale approved.

| | |
|---|---|
| administrator: | William BECK |

Guardians for minor children of Jacob MAURER, died about 3 years ago (all under age 14):

| | |
|---|---|
| widow: | Catherine, petitioner, now wife of Mr. MIKLE, Bethlehem Township |
| 4 children: | Jacob |
| | Maria |
| | Margaret |
| | Catherine |
| guardians: | for all 4 children—Peter SHELP and Michael LAWALT |

Estate of John MILLER, Plainfield Township, 170 acres—report of inquest by Sheriff Peter KACHLEIN, Esq.:

| | |
|---|---|
| children: | John MILLER, eldest son—accepted the land |
| | others not named |
| securities: | Casper DOLL and Henry HAPPELL |
| 12 men:all by oath | —Casper DOLL, Nicholas DOLL, Diel BOWER, Peter HANN, Jacob DIETZ, Henry SPONOMER, John EBERT, William BEAR, Philip SHUCK, Andrew KLEIN, Simon HELLER, George CLAWELL |

**Court on 21 April 1767**
**Justices, the Esquires: John MOOR, Lewis GORDON, Jacob ARNDT**

Guardians for Susannah, under age 14, minor child of Michael WELTZ, Weisenberg Township (left several children):

| | |
|---|---|
| administrator: | Dewalt MÖYER |
| guardian: | Jacob HULBEY |

**Court on 16 June 1767**
**Justices, the Esquires: George TAYLOR, Lewis KLOTZ, Aaron DUPUI, Jacob ARNDT**

Guardians for minor children of Christopher DEMARK—motion of Nicholas WALN, Esq.:

| | | |
|---|---|---|
| children: | Barnabas, over age 14.................... | guardian: John CORTWRIGHT, L. Smithfield Tp. |
| | Christopher, under age 14.............. | guardian: John VAN CAMP |

Estate of Simon FREIS, left house and lot in Town of Northampton—request sale:

| | |
|---|---|
| petitioner: | Philip KOOGLER, Northampton Town |

**Court on 16 June 1767, continued:**

Estate of Peter MECHLIN, Salisbury Township, plantation and grist mill—request appraisal:
administrators: Barbara MECHLIN and Jacob MECHLIN
appraisers: Sebastian KNAWS, Peter ROTH, John WETZEL

Estate of Jacob WETTERHOLT—return of sale:
widow: Susannah, administratrix, now wife of Michael KERN
sold to: Peter BEISEL

Estate of Adam FISHER—return of sale:
administrator: Magdalena FISHER
sold to: Jacob MEYER

Estate of Frantz ROAD, Salisbury Township—report of inquest by Sheriff Peter KACHLEIN, Esq.:
children: Frantz, eldest son—accepted the land
others not named:
one brother, under age 21
rest are sisters, all under age 18
securities: Jacob GRIM and Peter HAAS
12 men:all by oath—John WETZELL, Dewalt MECHLIN, Jacob HERMAN, Peter TREXLER (TRECKLER), George Adam BLANCK, Henry FETTER (FEDER), Michael KITTLER (KÜTEL), Michael OTT, George KNAÜSS, Philip KÜNINO, Bastian KNAUSS, George LIEBERT

Estate of Jacob KOON, Macungie Township, 214 acres—report of inquest by Sheriff Peter KACHLEIN, Esq.:
children: Leonard, eldest son—accepted the land
others not named
securities: Jacob HERMAN and Jacob DANNER
12 men:all by oath—John WETZEL, Dewalt MECHLIN, Jacob HERMAN, Peter TREXLER, Jacob DANNER, Melchier BARE, Valentine KEISSER, Henry KNAPENBERGER, Godfried DEFFENDORPHER (DEBENDORFER), Jacob CRISTMAN, Andrew EISENHART, Isaac JARRET

Estate of William SHOUP, Upper Milford Township, 100 acres—report of inquest by Sheriff Peter KACHLEIN:
children: Bernard, eldest son—accepted the land
others not named
security: John JENNINGS
12 men:all by oath—Mathias OX, Peter EDELMAN, Jacob WETZELL, Christian FISHER, Peter WETZELL, Jacob SMITH, John MOYER, (Johannes MÖYER), Bencheman MEYER (MÖYER), Jacob (Jacobes) DUBS, Jacob STAHL, Andres (Andreas) ENGELMAN, George STALNECKER

Estate of Jacob WETTERHOLT—auditors' report:
widow: Susannah, now wife of Michael KERN
auditors: John EVERETT and Jacob HORNER

Estate of Jacob PRANG—motion of James BIDDLE, Esq. to sell part of land, the stone house and lot in Town of Northampton:
administrator: John WOOLSLAYER

**Court on 27 July 1767**
**Justices, the Esquires: Lewis GORDON, Jacob ARNDT, John MOOR**

Estate of Enoch ARMITAGE—return of sale:
administrator: Benjamin ARMITAGE
sold to: John MOODY

**Court of 22 September 1767**
**Justices, the Esquires: John MOOR, Aaron DUPUI, Christopher WAGNER, John JENNINGS, Henry KOOCHEN**

Estate of Jacob Frederich SHARDLY, died 2 years ago, Macungie Township, 60 acres—request sale:
widow: Christina
5 children

Estate of Nicholas HEIL, Plainfield Township, 170 acres—request inquest:
children: John, eldest son
others not named

Estate of Peter MECHLIN—auditors' report:
administrators: Barbara MECHLIN and Jacob MECHLIN
auditors: Sebastian KNAUSS, Peter RHOAD, John WETZELL
debts owed to: Conrad COLP
estate of Dewalt MECHLIN, deceased
Peter BOGARD
Elizabeth MECHLIN
William MECHLIN, for making the mill
Thomas MECHLIN
John DETER
George TIBERD and Peter SPANGLER
John SELER and Jarimia TUDX

**Court on 1 October 1767**
**Justices, the Esquires: John MOOR, Daniel BRODHEAD, Christopher WAGNER**

Estate of George HAMMER, died sometime ago, Upper Milford Township, 200 acres—request sale:
petitioners: Barbara HAMMER and Daniel TURNIE
widow
6 small children

**Court on 7 October 1767**
**Justices, the Esquires: Hugh WILSON, Lewis GORDON, Christopher WAGNER, Henry KOCKEN**

Guardians for minor children of Andreas SHOLL, Towamensing Township:
widow: Katherine, now wife of Godfriet MUSHLETS
4 children, all minors:
Henry, over age 14................................guardian: Frederich KLEIN
Daniel, over age 14................................guardian: Frederich KLEIN
Peter, under age 14................................guardian: Henry ALLSHOUSE
Nicholas, under age 14...........................guardian: Henry ALLSHOUSE

**Court on 22 December 1767**
**Justices, the Esquires: George TAYLOR, John MOOR, Joseph GASTON**

Estate of Peter MECHLIN, grist mill and plantation of 100 acres—return of sale:
administrators: Barbara MECHLIN and Jacob MECHLIN
sold to: George BADDER

Estate of Christopher BERGMAN, Lynn Township, 125 acres—request sale and audit:
administrator: Joseph EHRMAN
auditors: Peter TRAXLER, John WETZELL, Peter RHOAD

Estate of Andrew MYER—request partition:
widow: Ann Mary, now wife of John HANDWARCH
children: Christine
Peter
Catharine
Elisabeth
Jacob
Andrew
auditors: Michael OHL, Michael RUCH, William KEIM

Estate of Andrew SHOLL, died about 13 years ago, Towamensing Township, 80 acres—request sale:
widow: Catherine, now wife of Mr. MUSHLETS
4 young children

Estate of Nicholas HEIL, Plainfield Township, 170 acres—report of inquest by Sheriff Peter KACHLEIN, Esq., on motion of Richard PETERS:
6 children: John HEIL, eldest son—accepted the land
others not named
securities: Andreas DIEMER and Henry SCHUB
12 men:all by oath—Peter WALGERT, Andrew SHALE, John (Johannes) BARTHOLT, Philip STOLZ (Filib SOLTZ), Henry (Henrich) SHUB, Martin MAYER, Martin RERRIG, Nicholas SHNEIDER, John (Johannes) KLEBBINER, Andrew (Andreas) DIMER, Michael SHNEIDER, Nicholas ANDREWS

Estate of Michael WILHELM, died about 7 years ago, three tracts—request inquest:
land: two in Williams Township, 150 acres and 82 acres, other in Forks Township, 172 acres
widow
6 children: Jacob, eldest son
others not named

**Court on 21 January 1768**
**Justices, the Esquires: Lewis GORDON, Christopher WAGNER, Joseph GASTON**

Estate of Peter KREILING, died sometime ago—request audit:
administrators: Elizabeth KREILING and John ROTHROCK
widow and children
auditors: George SHIVE, Philip GEISSINGER, Cratyus LARCH

**Court on 21 January 1768, continued:**

Guardians for 4 minor children of Peter KREILING—(all under age 14) (were other children):

children: Salome<br>Sarah<br>Ann<br>Catharina<br>
guardians: for all 4 children—John ROTHROCK and John NEWCOMER

**Court on 22 March 1768**
**Justices, the Esquires: George TAYLOR, Aaron DUPUI, John MOOR, Daniel BRODHEAD, Christopher WAGNER**

Estate of Jacob STEPHEN, Macungie Township—request partition:

7 children: Jacob, eldest son<br>Susannah<br>Catharine<br>Elizabeth<br>Adam<br>Elizabeth Catherine<br>Mary

Estate of Frederich WRIGHTS, Whitehall Township—request partition:

7 children: Henry, eldest son<br>Margaret<br>Elizabeth<br>Ann<br>Eve<br>Jacob<br>Lawrence

Estate of Christopher BERGMAN, Lynn Township—request sale:

administrator: Joseph EHRMAN<br>
auditors: John WETZEL and Peter RHOADS

Guardians for minor children of Christopher MILLER, died about 3 years ago (left three children, all under 14):

administrator: Jacob MORREY, Upper Saucon Township<br>
3 children: Michael<br>William<br>Susannah<br>
guardians: for all 3 children—Philip GEISSINGER, Sr., and John NEWCOMER

Estate of Michael WILHELM, Forks Township—inquest report by Sheriff John JENNINGS:

widow<br>
6 children: Jacob, eldest son—accepted land<br>others not named<br>
securities: Valentine OPP and Frederick KOON<br>
12 men:all by oath—Jacob REICH, Charles BRIGGS (BIGGS), Philip OPP, Bernard KEPLER, John MOYER, Matthias BRUCH, Nicholas LANTZ, Francis HILLIARD (Frantz HILGERT), Christopher (Christophel) BITTENBENDER, George ROUP (RAUB), Michael ROUP (RAUB), Frederick KLINCHAUS

**Court on 22 March 1768, continued:**

Guardians for 4 minor children of Michael WILHELM, Williams Township:

widow: Margaret
4 children: Michael, over age 14
Elizabeth, over age 14
Mary, under age 14
Frederick, under age 14
guardian: for all 4 children—their mother

Guardians for minor children of the husbands of Elizabeth PORTZEN, a petitioner with Philip SCHUCH: "Jacob ROTH, late of Hamilton Township, was killed by the Indians in the year 1757, died intestate, leaving five Children..." who were cared for by, "... their Mother Elizabeth who Intermarried with George SHOLTZ, late of Plainfield Township, by whom she had one son named George Jacob now an Orphan....."

widow: Elizabeth, widow of Jacob ROTH and now widow of George SHOLTZ, deceased, Plainfield Twp.
5 children of Jacob ROTH:
Anna Maria, over age 14
Conrad, over age 14
Elizabeth, over age 14
Margaret, over age 14
George, under age 14
one son of George SHOLZ:
George Jacob, under age 14
guardians: for all the children: Joseph KELLER, Plainfield Township and George HARTLIEB, Hamilton Township
(possible error: Is Elizabeth's surname PORTZEN correct or should it be SHOLTZ? Perhaps she married a third time, to a Mr. PORTZ.)

Estate of Peter KREILING, Upper Milford Township—auditors' report:

administrator: John ROTHROCK
widow: Elizabeth
8 children: Jacob, eldest son
others not named
auditors: Philip GEISSINGER, George SHEIVE, Gratius LARCH

New guardian for minor children of Peter KREILING:

petitioner: Edward BIDDLE, Esq.
guardian: former—John NEWCOMER—refused, "...to accept the Trust reposed in him."
new—Mathias OX

**Court on 25 April 1768**
**Justices, the Esquires: Christopher WAGNER, Henry KOOKEN, Joseph GASTON**

Guardian for minor child, Peter, over age 14, son of Henry FRANTZ, Heidelberg Township:

guardian: Peter MISSMER, next friend

**Court on 22 June 1768**
**Justices, the Esquires: Aaron DUPUI, Lewis KLOTZ, Christopher WAGNER**

Estate of Christopher BERGMAN—return of sale:
administrator: Joseph EHRMAN
sold to: Jacob KOON

Estate of George HAMMER—return of sale:
administrators: Barbara HAMMER and Daniel TURNIE
sold to: Peter RAVENHOLT

Guardians for 3 minor children of Jacob SHYMER, died 4 years ago, Lower Saucon Township (all under 14):
administrators: Rosina SHYMER and Peter SEIP
widow
3 children: Peter
Samuel
John
guardians: for all 3 children—Rudolph OBERLY and Gratzius LARCH

Estate of Joseph KENNELL—request audit, on motion of Nicholas WALN, Esq.:
administrators: Sarah KENNEL and Casper PETER
auditors: Paul POLLIET, Adam DESHLER, Peter KOAHLER

Estate of William BRAND, Lower Saucon Township—request audit:
guardian: Anthony LERCH, petitioner
widow: now wife of George GREADER
3 small children
auditors: Rudolph OVERLY, George REIGLE, Philip GROSS

Estate of Jacob STEPHEN, 4 tracts of 400 acres in Macungie Township—report of inquest by Sheriff John JENNINGS, Esq.:
widow
7 children: Jacob, eldest son—accepted the land
others not named
securities: Melchior BARE and Jacob HARMAN
12 men:all by oath—Melchior BARE, Jacob HARMAN (HERMAN), Jacob DANNER, Dewalt MECHLIN, John ALBRIGHT, Henry (Heinrich) WETZELL, John ROMICH, Jacob BARE, Godfried DEFENDORFFTER, Valentine KASER, Leonard KOON (KUHN), Henry (Heinrich) MATTARN

Estate of Frederich WRIGHTS, Whitehall Township, 80 acres—report of inquest by Sheriff John JENNINGS:
7 children: Henry, eldest son—accepted the land
others not named
guardians: Adam GABLE and David BAHRRING (previously appointed)
securities: George KNAUSS and Peter HERR, both of Whitehall Township
12 men:by oath—Godfried KNOUSE (KNAUSS), John KRESEMORE, George GOOD, George KNOUSE, Bartholomus (Bartle) HUBER, Daniel GOOD, Jacob MORE (MOHR), George RUCH, Henry FETTER (Heinrich FEDER), George TOST, Christopher BLANK (Stophel BLANCK)
by affirmation—Daniel HORELOCKER (HORLACHER)

**Court on 22 June 1768, continued:**

Estate of Joseph KENNELL—auditors' report (auditors as before):

| | |
|---|---|
| administrators: | Sarah KENNELL and Casper PETER |
| widow | |
| 6 children: | Jacob |
| | Dewalt |
| | Peter |
| | others, 3 daughters, not named |
| | step-son |

**Court on 20 September 1768**
**Justices, the Esquires: George TAYLOR, Aaron DUPUI, Lewis KLOTZ**

Estate of Henry SCHÄNER, died about a year ago, Allen Township, 150 acres—request inquest:

| | |
|---|---|
| widow | |
| 11 children: | Matthais, eldest son |
| | Clara |
| | George |
| | Katharine |
| | Martin |
| | Peter |
| | Henry |
| | Susannah |
| | Adam |
| | Mary Elisabeth |
| | John |

Estate of John KLIPPEL—order to settle on motion of Edward BIDDLE, Esq.:

| | |
|---|---|
| executor: | Jacob REICH, surviving executor |
| child: | Mary Margaret, wife of Philip OPP |
| auditors: | Jacob ARNDT, William EDMONDS, James CRUICKSHANKS, gentleman |

Estate of Peter ALTIMUS—citation awarded against surviving administrator, Philip SERFAS on motion of Nicholas WALN, Esq.; why had the estate not been settled yet? The court ordered it to be done.

**Court on 1 October 1768**
**Justices, the Esquires: George TAYLOR, Lewis GORDON, Jacob ARNDT**

Estate of Alexander CAMPBELL, Mt. Bethel Township, two tracts of 400 acres—request sale:

| | |
|---|---|
| widow: | Jean CAMPBELL, administratrix |
| 7 children | |

**Court on 21 December 1768**
**Justices, the Esquires: George TAYLOR, Lewis KLOTZ, Christopher WAGNER, John MOOR**

Estate of Michael RAUB—motion of James TAYLER, Esq.:

| | |
|---|---|
| securities: | Martin LAHR and Lawrence RAMIE with Michael RAUB |
| minor children: | Christian |
| | Mary |
| | Loveis |

**Court on 21 December 1768, continued:**

Estate of John KLIPPELL—auditors' report:

| | |
|---|---|
| executor: | Jacob REICH, surviving executor |
| auditors: | Jacob ARNDT, William EDMOND, James CRUIKSHANK |

**Court on 22 March 1769**
**Justices, the Esquires: George TAYLOR, James ALLEN, Aaron DUPUI**

Guardians for 2 minor children of Henry WOLF, died 2 years ago, Bethlehem Township (both under age 14) (were other children):

| | |
|---|---|
| widow: | Ann Mary, administratrix |
| 2 children: | John |
| | Henry |
| guardian: | for both children—Peter SEIP |

Guardians for minor child, Margaret, over age 14, of Michael HELFRICH, died about 9 years ago, Macungie Township (were other children):

| | |
|---|---|
| administrator: | Christian STEININGER |
| guardian: | George Henry ONANGST |

Release of the guardian George REX for the following children (appointed in 1762). He was now infirm and incapacitated:

| | |
|---|---|
| children of Martin KOOCHER: | Martin |
| | Adam |
| children of Leonard STEIN: | Leonard |
| | Magdalena |
| | Albertina |
| children of Henry BOYER: | John |
| | Mary |
| new guardian: | for all 7 children—Adam DESHLER |

Guardians for minor SHADT children, both over age 14—motion of Nicholas WALN, Esq.:

| | |
|---|---|
| children: | Henry |
| | Rosina |
| guardian: | for both children—Jacob ARNDT |

Estate of Michael RAUB, Sr.—request audit on motion of James BIDDLE, Esq.:

| | |
|---|---|
| administrator: | Michael RAUB, Jr., son |
| auditors: | Peter KACHLEIN, Casper DOLL, Henry ALLSHOUSE |

Estate of William BEST, Lehigh Township—request partition:

| | |
|---|---|
| 6 children: | William, eldest son |
| | others not named |

**Court on 22 March 1769, continued:**

Estate of John ECKROTH, died about 13 years ago, Lynn Township—request partition:

widow

7 children: Henry, eldest son
George
Elizabeth
Christopher
Catharine
Margaret
Mary Elizabeth

Estate of Michael HELFRICH—request audit on motion of James TAYLOR, Esq.:

administrator: Christian STEININGER, surviving administrator

auditors: John WETZELL, Dewalt MECHLIN, Peter MILLER

**Court on 25 March 1769**
**Justices, the Esquires: Lewis GORDON, Aaron DUPUI, John MOOR**

Estate of Michael RAUB, Sr.—auditors' report:

widow

children: Michael, Jr., eldest son, administrator
Christian
Eve
Lovice

auditors: Peter KACHLEIN and Henry ALLSHOUSE

**Court on 11 April 1769**
**Justices, the Esquires: Lewis GORDON, Jacob ARNDT, Christopher WAGNER**

Estate of Michael RISHEL, died about 9 years ago—request partition:

land: 1) 300 acres in Macungie Township,
2) 2 tracts, 100 acres and 25 acres, in Upper Milford Township

widow: now wife of Adam GRAMMAR

10 children: Ludwick, eldest son
George
Jacob, died under age 21, unmarried and without issue
Martin, under age 21
John, under age 21
Michael, under age 21
Catharine, wife of Philip HAGER
Maria, wife of Henry KEMERER
Barbara, wife of George SWEYER
Rosina, under age 21

**Court on 28 April 1769**
**Justices, the Esquires: George TAYLOR, James ALLEN, Henry KOOKEN**

Guardians for minor children of Charles WILSON, died sometime ago (left 5 children, all under age 14):
widow: Margaret
5 children: Sarah
Christian
Hugh
John
Margaret
guardians: for all 5 children—Authur LATTEMORE and David CHAMBERS

**Court on 21 June 1769**
**Justices, the Esquires: George TAYLOR, James ALLEN, Lewis KLOTZ, Henry KOOKEN**

Guardians for minor children of Michael HELFRICH, Macungie Township (all under age 14)—motion of James TAYLOR, Esq.:
children: John
George
Michael
guardians: for all 3 children—George HELLFRICH and George PLANK

Estate of Philip SLOUGH, died about 14 years ago, Lower Saucon Township, 175 acres—request partition:
widow: now wife of Philip GROSS
7 children: George, eldest son—since died without issue
Jacob, now the eldest son
Margaret
Catharine
Clara
Rosina
Philip

Guardians for Philip, minor child, over age 14, of Philip SLOUGH (above estate):
guardian: Christopher WAGNER, Esq.

Estate of Michael RISHEL, Macungie Township, several tracts—300 acres, 100 acres, and 25 acres in Upper Milford Township—report of inquest by Sheriff John JENNINGS:
widow
8 children: Ludwig, eldest son—accepted the land
others not named
securities: Francis WESCOE, Macungie Township, and George THUT, Salisbury Township
12 men:by oath—Peter BOGARD (BOGERT), Nicholas MYER, Melchior SMITH, Jacob SLOUGH, John (Johannes) LICHTENWALTER, George TOST, Harman MOORE (Herman MOOR), Christopher STEDLER, George BADER, Daniel TURNEY, Adam EPLER
by affirmation—Henry FUNK

**Court on 20 September 1769**

**Justices, the Esquires: George TAYLOR, James ALLEN, Lewis KLOTZ, Daniel BRODHEAD, Jacob ARNDT, John MOOR**

Estate of Michael HELFRICH, Macungie Township—auditors' report:
administrator: Christian STEININGER, surviving administrator
settlements to: Jacob KEYSER
auditors: John WETZELL, Dewalt MECHLING, Peter MÜLLER

Guardian for Barbara BEST, minor child over age 14, of William BEST, Lehigh Township, yeoman—motion of Edward BIDDLE, Esq.:
guardian: Henry BEST, Barbara's brother

Guardians for minor children of William BEST, Lehigh Township (both under age 14)—motion of Edward BIDDLE:
children: Michael
Sibilla
guardian: for both children—Simon TRIESBACH, Lehigh Township

Estate of Philip HAMMEL, the elder, of Macungie Township—request inquest:
land: in Macungie and Heidelberg Townships
widow
2 sons, his only children:
Philip
Peter

Estate of William BEST, Lehigh Township, 157 acres—report of inquest by Sheriff John JENNINGS, Esq.:
widow
6 children: William, eldest son—accepted the land
others not named
securities: Michael RUCH and Jacob ROTH, both of Lehigh Township
12 men:by oath—Michael RUCH, John (Johannes) KERN, William (Wilhelm) KERN, Casper SNERR (SCHNERR), Leonard FORE (Leonart FÜHR), George WANAMAKER, John TURN (Johannes DORN), Paul EVERHARD, Jacob ROTH, John WASOM, Peter RECH (REEG)
by affirmation—John BEER

**Court on 19 December 1769**
**Justices, the Esquires: George TAYLOR, Aaron DUPUI, John MOOR, Daniel BRODHEAD**

Estate of Lawrence DERR, died sometime ago, Bethlehem Township, 100 acres—request sale:
widow: Mary Engle DERR, administratrix
9 children

**Court on 21 December 1769**
**Justices, the Esquires: not given**

Estate of John YEAGER (had will)—request audit:
executors: Michael OHL and Juliana YEAGER
widow and children
auditors: Peter KACHLEIN, Henry ALLSHOUSE, John WAGLE

**Court on 21 December 1769, continued:**

Estate of John YEAGER—auditors' report:
executors: Michael OHL and Juliana YEAGER
widow: Juliana
children: John
Adam

Report of debts owed to George ZINSINBAUGH from two estates, in his own right and in right of his wife—court found everything in order:
estates of: Felix BRUNNER, deceased—Adam WILHOWER, executor
Peter LYNN, deceased—Felix LYNN, executor

Estate of Garret BRINK—citation against Henry DECKER and his wife Charity, late Charity VANGARDA, to show why they have not paid shares to Benjamin VANDERMARH and wife Sarah.

**Court on 20 March 1770**
**Justices, the Esquires: George TAYLOR, Lewis KLOTZ, Jacob ARNDT**

Estate of Philip SLOUGH, Lower Saucon Township, 175 acres—report of inquest by Sheriff John JENNINGS:
widow
5 children: Jacob, eldest son—accepted the land
others not named
securities: Gratius LARCH and Jacob HARTZELL
12 men: by oath—George SHEIVE, Rudolph OVERLY, Adam KOOKER (KOCHERT), Adam EDELMAN, Nicholas SHULL, Tobias SHULL, Ulrich BRINKER (BRINCKER), Peter LABACH, John BLANK (Hannes BLANCK), Conrad RESALEY (REILI)
by affirmation—Kratzer (Gratius) LARCH, Reinhard LABACH

Estate of Lawrence DERR—return of sale:
administratrix: Mary Engle DERR
sold to: Vandle ESSICH

Guardians for minor children of Henry SHANER, Allen Township:
next friend: Garret SEISLOFF
children: Martin, over age 14................................guardian: Jacob MORREY
Peter, under age 14.................................guardian: Philips BEHM
Henry, under age 14...............................guardian: Philips BEHM

Guardian for Adam GOOD, over age 14, minor child of Lawrence GOOD, Whitehall Township:
guardian: Peter BURKHALTER

Estate of Philip HAMMEL, the elder, Macungie Township, two tracts—250 acres in Macungie Township and 193 acres in Heidelberg Township—report of inquest by Sheriff John JENNINGS:
children: Philip, Jr.—accepted the land
other is a brother, not named
securities: Adam THOMAS and Michael OHL
12 men: by oath—George KNOUSE (KNAUSS), Adam EPLER, Nicholas MYER, Harmon (Herman) MOOR, Adam HABERLY, Leonard STEININGER, George STEININGER, George HOFFMAN, Christopher STETLER, Dewalt KUNTZ, Jacob ACKER
by affirmation—Michael STREBY (STRIBY)

**Court on 20 March 1770, continued:**

Estate of Michael WALTZ—request audit and audit report on motion of Edward BIDDLE, Esq.:
administrator: Dewalt MYER
auditors: Harman SHNYDER, Henry ALLSHOUSE, Henry BARNET

Estate of Joseph STEIDLEY, died about 3 years ago, Lynn Township, 100 acres—request sale:
administrator: Marx WANNEMAKER
widow: Christina, administratrix
7 children

**Court on 21 March 1770**
**Justices, the Esquires: not named**

Another change in guardians for several children. Adam DESHLER, Whitehall Township, replaced George REX as guardian but now Adam was infirm and unable—requested that new guardians be appointed:

| | |
|---|---|
| children of Martin KOOCHER: | Martin |
| | Adam |
| children of Leonard STEIN: | Leonard |
| | Magdalena |
| children of Henry BOYER: | John |
| | Mary |
| new guardians: | for all 6 children—Peter BURKHALTER and John SHADE |

Guardian for Stophel NICHOLAS, minor child, over age 14, of John NICHOLAS, Whitehall Township—motion of James TAYLOR, Esq.:
guardian: Stophel BLANK, Whitehall Township

Citation from last court to Henry DECKER and wife—Henry said his wife was, "...indisposed and incapable of attending...." She was to appear later in June.

**Court on 26 March 1770**
**Justices, the Esquires: Lewis GORDON, Jacob ARNDT, Henry KOOKEN**

Estate of Christian KOLLUMBACH, died sometime ago, Moore Township, 65 acres—request sale:
widow: Elizabeth, administratrix, now wife of John DEEDER

Estate of Andreas SHOLL, Towamensing Township, 80 acres—request audit:
widow: Catharina, now wife of Godfrey MUSHLETS—stated that current husband brought in false charges and disbursements to the administration account
auditors: Abraham BERLIN, Peter KACHLEIN, David BAHRRINGER

**Court on 21 April 1770**
**Justices, the Esquires: Jacob ARNDT, Christopher WAGNER, Joseph GASTON**

Estate of Andreas STOLL, Towamensing Township, 80 acres—auditors' report:
widow: Catharina, now wife of Godfrey MUSHLETS
children: already had guardians, appointed at Easton
cash received: from Cap. REYNOLDS—soldiers money
from Nicholas OBLINGER
[also long list of men to whom cash was paid]

**Court on 26 May 1770**

**Justices, the Esquires: Lewis GORDON, Jacob ARNDT, Christopher WAGNER**

Guardian for Frederick, over age 14, minor child and one of the sons of Philips PIFER, yeoman:
guardian: Frederick KUHN

Estate of Bartholomew HOFFMAN, lot and house in Easton—request sale:
widow: Ann Mary, administratrix
6 children

**Court on 19 June 1770**
**Justices, the Esquires: George TAYLOR, James ALLEN, John MOOR, Jacob ARNDT**

Estate of Bartholomew HOFFMAN, lot in Easton—return of sale:
administratrix: Ann Mary HOFFMAN
sold to: Jacob TINKEY of Easton

Guardians for minor children of George STEININGER, Macungie Township:
administrator: John LITCHTEWALTER
widow: Elizabeth, administratrix
6 children: Ann Mary, over age 14............................guardian: Adam SMITH
the remaining children all under age 14:
Margaret
George
Christian
Elizabeth
John
guardians: for the 5 young children—Jacob SLOUGH and George STEININGER

**Court on 20 June 1770**
**Justices, the Esquires: not named**

Guardian for Rudolphus, Jr., over age 14, minor child and only son of Rudolphus SCHOONHOVEN, Sr., Delaware Township:
guardians: Amos OGDEN and James SCHOONOVEN

Guardians for minor children of Adam FISHER:
widow: Magdalena
5 children: George Michael, over age 14.............guardian: George STEININGER, Whitehall Twp.
Mary Elizabeth, over age 14.............guardian: Leonard STEININGER, Whitehall Twp.
remaining 3 children under age 14:
John George
Jacob
Ann Margaret
guardians: for younger 3 children—George and Leonard STEININGER

**Court on 21 June 1770**
**Justices, the Esquires: not named**

Guardians for 4 minor children of Henry COON:

| | |
|---|---|
| widow: | Margaret |
| 4 children: | Henry, over age 14 |
| | Mary, over age 14 |
| | Jacob, under age 14 |
| | Joseph, under age 14 |
| guardian: | for older two children— George KNOWS, Whitehall Township |
| | for younger two children—Peter BAGER |

Estate of Garret BRINK—citation held over against Henry DECKER & wife Charity; appraisal requested:

| | |
|---|---|
| appraisers: | William JEANS, Sr., Jacob STROUD, Benjamin SHOEMAKER |

**Court on 14 July 1770**
**Justices, the Esquires: Jacob ARNDT, Christopher WAGNER, Henry KOOKEN**

Guardians for minor children of Dietrick SCHMETZER (all under age 14):

| | |
|---|---|
| widow: | Magdalena, administratrix |
| 3 children: | Magdalena |
| | John Adam |
| | Jacob |
| guardian: | for all 3 children—Anthony LARCH |

**Court on 18 September 1770**
**Justices, the Esquires: James ALLEN, Lewis KLOTZ, Daniel BRODHEAD**

Guardians for minor children of Moses EVERETT, died about 2 years ago, Mt. Bethel Township, 87 acres—also request partition:

| | |
|---|---|
| widow | |
| 9 children: | Tenas, eldest son, administrator |
| | Ara |
| | Lucy |
| | Hannah |
| | Obed, over age 14 |
| | Abner, over age 14 |
| | Jerushah, over age 14 |
| | Moses, under age 14 |
| | Sarah, under age 14 |
| guardians: | for younger 5 children—Samuel RHEA and Thomas RUCHMAN |

Guardians for 3 minor children of Leonard FUHR, Heidelberg Township, yeoman (were other children):

| | |
|---|---|
| executor: | Catherina FUHR |
| 3 children: | Leonard, over age 14...............................guardian: Michael OHL |
| | Barbara, under age 14 |
| | Mary, under age 14 |
| guardians: | for younger two children—Christopher BEAR and Ulrich NEAF |

Report on citation of Henry DECHER and wife—they did owe money to Benjamin VANDERMARK and wife:

| | |
|---|---|
| auditors: | Jacob STROWD, Benjamin SHOEMAKER, William JAYNE |

**Court on 20 September 1770**
**Justices, the Esquires: not named**

Guardian for John, over age 14, minor child of Michael HELFRICH, yeoman, Williams Township:
guardian: George HELFRICH

**Court on 18 December 1770**
**Justices, the Esquires: George TAYLOR, Daniel BRODHEAD, Henry KOOKEN, Joseph GASTON**

Estate of Christian KOOLUMBOCH—return of sale:
widow: Elizabeth, administratrix, now wife of John DEEDER
sold to: Paul FLICK, Moore Township

**Court on 19 December 1770**
**Justices, the Esquires: not named**

Guardians for minor children of Henry PEAGLEY, Moore Township (both under age 14):
next friend: John PEAGLEY
children: Mary
Adam
guardian: for both children—Simon DRIESBACH

Guardians for 4 minor children of William MILLER, lately died (all under age 14):
uncle: Samuel MILLER, brother of deceased
4 children: not named
guardians: for all 4 children—Samuel REA and William McFARREN

Guardians for minor children of Andreas HAZLET (both over age 14)—motion of James TAYLOR:
children: William
Mary
guardian: for both children —Neal GRAY of Allen Township

**Court on 9 January 1771**
**Justices, the Esquires: John JENNINGS, Christopher WAGNER, Robert LEVERS, Henry KOOKEN**

Guardians for minor children of Adam MYER, died sometime ago:
administrator: Adam YOHE
children: Peter, over age 14....................................guardian: Peter SHELP
Adam, over age 14..................................guardian: Sebastian TRUCKMILLER
younger 5 all under age 14:
Barbara
Christian
Elizabeth
Conrad
Catharine
guardians: for younger 5 children—Lewis GORDON, Esq., and Peter SHELP

Guardians for minor grandchildren of Henry KOON, who left legacies to these children (all under age 14)
(Henry KOON was father-in-law of Peter KEAS and Henry ECKENROTH):
children of Peter KEAS...................................................guardian: Peter RHOADS
children of Henry ECKENROTH....................................guardian: Henry HAGENBUCH

**Court on 21 January 1771**
**Justices, the Esquires: Jacob ARNDT, John JENNINGS, Henry KOOKEN**

Estate of Jacob WIETMER, Whitehall Township, 100 acres—request sale:
administrator: Henry FUNCK
widow and 3 children

**Court on 16 February 1771**
**Justices, the Esquires: Lewis GORDON, Jacob ARNDT, Christopher WAGNER**

Estate of John RUSH, of Philadelphia County, yeoman, died several years ago, Williams Township, 375 acres—request inquest:
widow
4 children: John, eldest son, "having been about in remote parts for about ten years and upwards and has never been heard of since and is therefore in all likelihood dead...."
Peter, second son
other two not named

**Court on 19 March 1771**
**Justices, the Esquires: George TAYLOR, Aaron DUPUI, Lewis KLOTZ, Daniel BRODHEAD, Robert LEVERS, Henry KOOKEN**

Estate of John RUSH, the older, Williams Township, 375 acres—report of inquest by Sheriff Peter KACHLEIN:
widow
children: Peter, second son—accepted the land
eldest son—missing
two other children
securities: David BAHRRINGER and Melcher HAY
12 men:by oath—Conrad HESS, Frederick KUN, Christian PIPHER (PEIFER), Michael GRESS, Garret MOOR, Jacob PROTZMAN, John GATTART, Jacob BEST, Christopher BITTENBINDER, Jeremiah TREXLER, Dewalt DRUMHOLLER
by affirmation—Abraham BERLIN

**Court on 20 March 1771**
**Justices, the Esquires: not named**

New guardian for minor children of William MILLER—motion of Edward BIDDLE, Esq.:
guardians: former—Samuel REA and William McFARREN—they refuse to act
new—Joseph GASTON and Alexander MILLER, Sr.

Estate of Jacob WIETMER—return of sale:
administrator: Henry FUNCK
sold to: Nicholas MEYER, Whitehall Township

Guardians for minor children of Peter LINN (were other children):
children: John LINN, the petitioner, over age 14...guardian: John GREASAMORE
Elizabeth, under age 14...........................guardian: Peter WETZELL
Dewalt, under age 14..............................guardian: John HILLEGAS
grandfather: Felix BRUNNER, late of Upper Milford, left legacies to them

**Court on 21 March 1771**
**Justices, the Esquires: not named**

Estate of John DURHAM, Mt. Bethel Township, 438 acres—request partition:
widow
8 children: oldest son declined preference to accept land
James, second son
others not named

Estate of Andrew ISENHART, died March 1770, Macungie Township, 400 acres—request inquest:
widow
7 children: Andrew, eldest son
others not named

Estate of Jacob MEYER (had a will)—motion of Edward BIDDLE, Esq.; executors ordered to settle accounts:
widow: Elizabeth, executrix, now wife of Christopher BITTENBINDER

New guardian for Rudolphus, over age 14, minor child of Rudolphus SCHOONHAVEN—motion of Edward BIDDLE, Esq.:
guardian: former—Amos ODGEN
new—William SMITH

Estate of William MILLER (had a will)—motion of Edward BIDDLE, Esq.; request audit:
widow: Jean, executrix, now wife of William BAILEY
auditors: Peter MIDDAUGH, David ALLEN, Anthony MOOR

Guardians for minor children of Andrew ISENHART—motion of Daniel CLYMER, Esq.:
children: Margaret, over age 14..............................guardian: George LEIBERT
Simon, over age 14.................................guardian: Godfred DIFFENDOFFER
Hannah, under age 14..............................guardian: George LEIBERT

(Written here 28 December 1772: George LEIBERT received two bonds from Andrew ISENHART, Martin ROMICH, and Andrew GIERING for Margaret's and Hannah's shares; same to Godfred DIFFENDOFFER for Simon's share.)

**Court on 22 March 1771**
**Justices, the Esquires: George TAYLOR, Lewis KLOTZ, Daniel BRODHEAD**

Guardian for Henry, over age 14, minor child and one son of Henry FRIEDLEY, Lynn Township:
guardian: Jacob BILLMAN

**Court on 25 March 1771**
**Justices, the Esquires: Lewis GORDON, Jacob ARNDT, John JENNINGS**

Estate of Richard VAN ETTEN, Plainfield Township—request sale:
widow: Rosina, administratrix
children

**Court on 25 March 1771, continued:**

Guardians for minor children of Jacob SHANTZ, yeoman, Lehigh Township (all under 14) (were other children):

| | |
|---|---|
| widow: | Margaret |
| children: | Magdalena |
| | Christopher |
| | Jacob |
| | John |
| | Philip |
| | Catharina |
| guardians: | for all 6 children—Jost and Simon TRIESBACH |

**Court on 18 June 1771**
**Justices, the Esquires: George TAYLOR, Lewis KLOTZ, John MOOR, John JENNINGS, Robert LEVERS, Henry KOOKEN**

Guardian for Mary, over age 14, minor child of Peter LAHR, yeoman, Lower Saucon Township:

| | |
|---|---|
| guardian: | Matthias KERN |

**Court on 19 June 1771**
**Justices, the Esquires: not named**

Guardians for minor children of Richard VAN ETTEN, Plainfield Township (all under 14) (were other children):

| | |
|---|---|
| widow: | Rosina |
| children: | Joseph |
| | Peter |
| | Sarah |
| | Mary |
| | Derick |
| guardians: | Manuel GONSALES and Hans VAN ETTEN, both of Delaware Township |

Estate of Moses EVERETT, Mt. Bethel Township, 87 acres—report of inquest by Sheriff Peter KACHLEIN:

| | |
|---|---|
| children: | Tenas, eldest son—accepted the land |
| | others not named |
| securities: | Christopher BOWMAN and William CARNAGIE |
| 12 men: | all by oath—William CALDWELL, John MOORE, Alex'r CALBREATH, Fergus MANN, George (Jerg) REIMER, James HAMILTON, William MACK, John NIELSON, William CARNAGIE, Benjamin STACKHOUS, John DUNN, James OLIPHANT |

Estate of Andrew ISENHART, Macungie Township, 524 acres—report of inquest:

| | |
|---|---|
| 7 children: | Andrew (Andreas), eldest son—accepted the land |
| | others not named |
| securities: | Martin ROMICH and Andrew GIERING |
| 12 men: | all by oath—George KNAUS, Jacob DANNER, Jacob HERMAN, Dewalt MECHLING, Nicholas MYER, (Johan) Jacob STEPHEN, Harman MOHR, Hannes BÄHR (BÄR), Leonard KUHN, Leonard MYER (MEIER), Isaac JARRETT, Godfrey DEBENDORFFER |

## Court on 20 June 1771
## Justices, the Esquires: not named

Estate of Jacob YUNT, died about 11 years ago, Whitehall Township, yeoman, 278 acres—request inquest:
widow
6 children: Peter, eldest son
George
Mary
Daniel
Jacob
Abraham

Estate of Jacob MYER—motion of Edward BIDDLE, Esq.; request audit:
administrator: Christopher BITTENBENDER
widow: Elizabeth, administratrix, now wife of Christopher BITTENBINDER
auditors: John OKELY, Timothy HORSEFIELD, George KLEIN of Bethlehem

## Court on 18 September 1771
## Justices, the Esquires: Aaron DUPUI, Lewis KLOTZ, Christopher WAGNER, Robert LEVERS, Henry KOOKEN

Guardian for Abraham, under age 14, minor child of Jacob YUNT, Whitehall Township (were other children):
widow: Dorothy
guardian: John GREESEMORE

Estate of Jacob YUNT, Whitehall Township, 278 acres—report of inquest by Sheriff Peter KACHLEIN:
6 children: George, second son—accepted the land
Peter, eldest son—unable to give security
others not named
securities: John GREESAMORE and George KNOWS
12 men:all by oath—David DESHLER, Adam JOHE, Jacob KERN, Adam DESHLER, Martin DERR, Jacob MOOR (MOHR), Stoffel BLANCK, Jacob MECHLEY, John (Johannes) HOFFMAN, Peter BURCKHALTER, Peter RHOADS, Peter KOHLER

Estate of William MILLER—auditors' report:
executors: William BAILEY and wife, John MILLER, Alexander MILLER, Samuel MILLER
auditors: Peter MIDDAUGH, David ALLEN, Anthony MOORE

## Court on 1 October 1771
## Justices, the Esquires: Aaron DUPUI, Christopher WAGNER, Henry KOOKEN

New guardian for Abraham YUNT minor son of Jacob YUNT:
guardian: former—John GREESAMORE, Whitehall Township
new—Jacob SHRIEVER

**Court on 17 December 1771**
**Justices, the Esquires: Lewis KLOTZ, Henry KOOKEN, John JENNINGS, Christopher WAGNER**

Estate of Michael BROBST, miller, died about 5 months ago, Albany Township, Berks Co.—request inquest:
land: "Land situate in Lynn Township adjoining the Proprietary three hundred acres and Land of Jacob FRIER, Jacob BÄRR, and Valentine BROBST containing two hundred and fifty acres...."
widow: Margaret
10 children: Henry, eldest son
Martin
John
the remaining 7 are minors, under age 21:
Michael
Jacob
Valentine
Christian
George Michael
Catharine
Maria

**Court on 18 December 1771**
**Justices, the Esquires: not named**

Guardian for Jacob, over age 14, minor son of Jacob YUNT, Whitehall Township:
guardian: Philip Jacob SHREIBER

Guardians for minor children of Jacob KAMMERER, Upper Milford Township:
next friend: John FELLEMER
children: Regina, over age 14................................guardian: Adam REINHART
Elizabeth, over age 14............................guardian: Adam REINHART
Jacob, under age 14................................guardian: Andrew ENGLEMAN

Guardian for Rosina, over age 14, minor child of Lawrence SHADE:
guardian: George KLEIN of Bethlehem

Guardians for Jacob, under age 14, minor child of Henry TURNEY, Whitehall Township (were other children):
administrator: Daniel TURNEY
guardian: Jacob BEAR of Macungie Township

Estate of John DURHAM, Sr., Mt. Bethel Township, 438 acres—report of inquest by Sheriff Peter KACHLEIN:
children: James, second son—accepted the land
eldest son refused to accept land (on oath of Edward DURHAM and John DURHAM)
others not named
securities: William MACK and Jacob WOOD
12 men:John LONG, Sr, John LONG, Jr., Christian EÜLENBERGER, Charles (Karel) LABAR, William (Wilhelm) LABAR, Johannes DIETRICK, Henry DILDINE, Jacob WOOD, Elias DIETRICK, Henry (Hendrick) ATTEN, Jacob SHNEIDER, Valentine SENTEA (SENTEE)

**Court on 7 March 1772**
**Justices, the Esquires: John JENNINGS, Henry KOOKEN, Christopher WAGNER**

Estate of George WEAVER, Lower Saucon Township—order to settle the account:
executor: Valentine OPP
Until the executor settled the account, Anthony STOCK and his wife Barbara, late widow of George, "...shall possess the Plantation and Premises of the said deceased without Molestation they paying therefore a reasonable Rent, but to be allowed for bringing up and Educating the Children of the said deceased."

Guardians for minor children of George WEAVER, Lower Saucon Township (all under age 14):
widow: Barbara, now wife of Anthony STOCK
3 children: Catharine
Valentine
Mary
guardians: Gratius LARCH and John NEWCOMER, Sr.

**Court on 17 March 1772**
**Justices, the Esquires: George TAYLOR, Aaron DUPUI, Lewis KLOTZ, John JENNINGS, Henry KOOKEN**

Estate of Henry BRUNNER, Upper Saucon Township (had a will)—request audit:
executors: Jacob MORRY and George PLANCK
widow and children
auditors: Peter ROADS, Peter KNAPLEY, George STALLNECKER

**Court on 18 March 1772**
**Justices, the Esquires: not named**

Guardian for David, over age 14, minor child of Nicholas SMITH, Lowhill Township:
guardian: Jacob EKER

Estate of Michael BROBST, Lynn Township, 250 acres—report of inquest by Sheriff Peter KACHLEIN, Esq.:
9 children: Henry, eldest son—accepted the land
others not named
securities: Peter KACHLEIN and Henry ALLSHOUSE
12 men:by oath—Philip MOSER, Melcher DERR, George HERMANI, Jacob WETZEL, Peter SHOLL
by affirmation—Peter LUTZ, George KISTLER, Michael BUCK, Daniel OSWALT, Zachariah HALLER, Philip ENIS, Frederick SECHLER

Estate of William RITCHART, died about 1 year ago, Mt. Bethel Township, 3 tracts totaling 250 acres—request inquest:
widow
7 children: Robert, eldest son
others not named

Estate of John BUSSINGER, died about 17 years ago, Weisenberg Township, 100 acres—request inquest:
widow
4 children: Conrad, eldest son
others not named

## Court on 17 June 1772
## Justices, the Esquires: George TAYLOR, Lewis KLOTZ, Christopher WAGNER, Henry KOOKEN, Joseph GASTON

Guardians for minor children of Henry SMITH, died about 2 months ago, Heidelberg Township (all under 14):
widow: Juliana
6 children: Christian
Henry
John
Michael
Elizabeth
Catharine
guardians: John SMITH and Philip MOSER

Estate of Christian STAHL, died about 16 years ago, Heidelberg Township—request audit:
petitioner: John DELONG, Lynn Township—found mistake in account
administrators: Peter MESSIMER and Jacob PETER
widow and 4 children
auditors: Mathias PROBST, Henry GEIGER, Peter KOHLER

Guardians for minor children of Jacob WEIS, died about 1 year ago, Lower Saucon Township:
widow: Ann Margaret, now wife of Jacob LUDWIG
6 children: Magdalena, over age 14..........................guardian: John RODROCK
Elizabeth, over age 14............................guardian: Benjamin RIEGEL
remaining children all under age 14:
John
Matthias
Jacob
Catharine
guardians: for younger 4 children—Baltzar BOYL and Jacob GEESEY

Estate of John BUSSINGER, Weisenberg Township, 100 acres—report of inquest by Sheriff Peter KACHLEIN:
widow
4 children: Conrad, eldest son—accepted land
others not named
securities: Peter HAAS and Michael POBST
12 men:all by oath—Jacob HOLBEN, Adam GIFFS, Nicholas GIFFS, Peter BIEBER, Stoffel TRESHER, Philip BOGER, Adam WILD, John GABEL, Christian MARBURGER, Michael POBST, Daniel ZERICH, Valentine GRAMLICH

## Court on 24 June 1772
## Justices, the Esquires: George TAYLOR, Lewis KLOTZ, Christopher WAGNER

Estate of Moses MATHEWS, Lower Smithfield Township—request sale:
land: 237 acres and 1/3 part of saw mill erected on that land
administrator: John SEELY
widow and one son

## Court on 22 September 1772
## Justices, the Esquires: George TAYLOR, Aaron DUPUI, Lewis KLOTZ, Christopher WAGNER, Henry KOOKEN

Guardian for William, over age 14, minor son of James YOUNG, Allen Twp.:
guardian: William CRAIG, Allen Twp.

## Court on 23 September 1772
## Justices, the Esquires: not named

Guardian for minor children of Henry BUCHACKER, Upper Saucon Township (both under age 14):
administrator: Philip SHEARER
widow
2 children: Magdalena
Elizabeth
guardian: for both children—George SWANKER

Guardians for minor children of Claudy KEINHART, Macungie Township ( both over age 14):
children: Michael
Catharina (deaf and dumb)
guardian: for both children—Sebastian TRUCKENMILLER

Guardians for minor children of Joseph STEIDLEY, Lynn Township (were other children):
widow: Christina
3 children: Christina, over age 14..............................guardian: Matthias DELONG
Christiana, over age 14............................guardian: John SMITH
Philip, under age 14................................guardian: John SMITH

Estate of Andrew LYE, Williams Township, 50 acres—request sale:
administrator: Benedict LUTZ

Estate of Frederick BERKENSTOCK, Upper Milford Township—request sale:
land: 99 acres 6 perches, being part of the estate, adjoining Michael SMITH, Philip HALL, Samuel GEISINGER, and others
widow: Magdalena, administratrix
two children

Estate of Jacob DOREMYER, Whitehall Township, 130 acres—request sale:
widow: Elizabeth, administratrix, now wife of Mr. SNERR
4 children

## Court on 24 September 1772
## Justices, the Esquires: not named

Estate of Michael ROUP, Lower Smithfield Township—motion to accept securities by James TAYLOR, Esq.:
eldest son: Michael ROUP
securities: George HARTLIEB and Frederick GEWINNER

Estate of Christian STAHL—auditors' report on motion of Edward BIDDLE, Esq.:
administrators: Peter MESSIMER and Jacob PETER
auditors: George KNOUSE, Philip MOSER, and Peter RHOADS

**Court on 2 October 1772**
**Justices, the Esquires: Lewis GORDON, Henry KOOKEN, Joseph GASTON**

Estate of Valentine TICKENSHIT, Upper Milford Township—request sale:
land: 150 acres adjoining John SHOUT, Peter SLOSER, and others
administrator: Abraham ARNDT
widow: Eve, administratrix, now wife of Mr. KOOKEN
4 children

Guardian for minor children of James MARTIN, Mt. Bethel Township (were other children):
children: Joseph, the petitioner
Thomas, under age 14
James, under age 14
guardian: for both sons—John RALSTON of Allen Township

**Court on 22 December 1772**
**Justices, the Esquires: George TAYLOR, Aaron DUPUI, Lewis KLOTZ, Christopher WAGNER, Henry KOOKEN**

Estate of Henry PEAGLEY, Moore Township—request audit:
administrator: David MARSH
guardian: Simon DREISBACH (already appointed)
auditors: James HUTCHISON, Robert LATTEMORE, Conrad CREIDER

**Court on 23 December 1772**
**Justices, the Esquires: not named**

Allowance for maintenance of 3 minor children of Henry BRUNNER, Upper Saucon Township (were other children):
petitioner: Peter LAUBENSTEIN, Upper Saucon Township
widow: now wife of the petitioner, Peter LAUBENSTEIN
children: 3 minor ones had been under care of petitioner for a year past who had applied for an allowance from the executors

Guardians for minor children of Jacob BRANG, Town of Northampton, mason (were other children):
children: George, the petitioner
Christopher, over age 14
Jacob, under age 14
Peter, under age 14
guardian: for younger 3 children—George KNAUSE

Estate of Christian STAHL—auditors' report:
administrators: Peter MESSEMIRE and Jacob PETER
widow and 4 children
auditors: George KNOUSS, Philip MOSSER, Peter RHOADS

Estate of Richard VAN ETTEN—return of sale:
widow: Rosina, administratrix
sold to: Peter BENDER, Plainfield Township

**Court on 23 December 1772, continued:**

Estate of Valen TICKENSHIT—return of sale:
administrators: Eve KOOKEN and Abraham ARNDT
sold to: Conrad WORMAN, Solford Township, Philadelphia County

Estate of Frederick BERKENSTOCK—return of sale:
administrator: Magdalena BERKENSTOCK
sold to: Peter WETZELL, Upper Milford Township

**Court on 24 December 1772**
**Justices, the Esquires: not named**

New guardians for minor children of William MILLER:
guardians: former—Joseph GASTON and Alexander MILLER, Sr., appointed in 1771
new—Anthony MOOR and Robert McCRACKEN, Sr.

**Court on 16 March 1773**
**Justices, the Esquires: George TAYLOR, Lewis KLOTZ, John JENNINGS, Henry KOOKEN, Christopher WAGNER, Robert LEVERS**

Guardians for minor children of John STANTON, Allen Township (left two children):
petitioner: William CONGLESTON, Allen Township
children: Elizabeth, over age 14............................guardian: John LATTEMORE
John, under age 14..................................guardian: Niegal GRAY

Estate of George WEAVER, Lower Saucon Township, yeoman (had a will)—request audit:
petitioners: the children's guardians—John NEWCOMER and Gratius LARCH
executor: Valentine OPP
auditors: John OKELY, Simon DREISBACH, John BUNN

Estate of Henry PEAGLEY—auditors' report:
administrator: David MARSH
cash received: George DREISBACH
John LEYDIE
John PEAGLEY
Valentine MARSH
Simon DREISBACH, guardian
auditors: James HUTCHISON, Robert LATTEMORE, Conrad KREILER

**Court on 17 March 1773**
**Justices, the Esquires: not named**

Estate of Diedrick BALDAUFF, yeoman, Lynn Township, 200 acres—request inquest:
petitioner: Casper BALDAUFF, eldest son
widow and 4 children

Guardian for George, over age 14, minor son of Philip KIBLER, Macungie Township:
guardian: Jacob HARMAN

**Court on 17 March 1773, continued:**

Estate of George REX, Sr., yeoman, Heidelberg Township—partition request:
land: 250 acres with proprietary patent and two tracts of 150 acres and 119 acres
widow
8 children: William REX, Jr., eldest son
others not named

Guardian for minor children of George REX, Sr. (both under age 14):
children: Catharine
Salome
guardians: for both children—George KNOUSE and Daniel KNOUSE

Estate of Andrew LYE—return of sale:
administrator: Benedick LUTZ
sold to: Adam MAUNY

Estate of Moses MATTHEWS—return of sale of 1/3 land and 1/3 saw mill:
administrator: John SEELY
sold to: Samuel SEELY

**Court on 18 March 1773**
**Justices, the Esquires: not named**

Estate of John APPLE—distribution of estate on motion of James ALLEN, Esq.:
children: John, eldest son—to get 2/3 of estate
Catherine—has 4 children who share 1/3 of estate

Guardians for minor APPLE children, nieces and nephews of Martin APPLE who left his estate to them—motion of James ALLEN, Esq.:
children, the nieces and nephews:
Paul APPLE
Jacob APPLE
Andrew APPLE
Elizabeth APPLE
Mary APPLE
guardian: John APPLE, their father

**Court on 25 March 1773**
**Justices, the Esquires: George TAYLOR, Robert LEVERS, John JENNINGS**

Estate of Leonard FUHR, yeoman, Heidelberg Township, 300 acres—request valuation:
widow: survived her husband but now deceased
6 children: John, eldest son—accepted the land
others not named

Estate of Thomas SILLYMAN, two tracts in Mt. Bethel Township—request sale:
land: 1) 50 acres adjoining to John MILLER and vacant land
2) 100 acres adjoining James HUTCHISON and Parises tract
administrator: Thomas SILLYMAN

**Court on 25 March 1773, continued:**

Guardian for Daniel, over age 14, minor son of George REX, yeoman, Heidelberg Township:
guardian: Daniel KNOUSE

**Court on 23 June 1773**
**Justices, the Esquires: George TAYLOR, Lewis KLOTZ, Robert LEVERS, Henry KOOKEN, John JENNINGS**

Guardians for minor children of Michael FLORES, yeoman, Upper Milford Township (were other children):
children: Michael, the petitioner, over age 14
Margaret, under age 14
guardian: for both children—Jacob DILLINGER

Estate of Thomas SILLYMAN—return of sale:
administrator: Thomas SILLYMAN
sold to: David ALLEN, Mt. Bethel Township, yeoman

**Court on 24 June 1773**
**Justices, the Esquires: not named**

Estate of Philip WAGGONMAN, yeoman, Weisenberg Township (8 children)—request sale:
land: 100 acres adjoining Philip BOGER, Nicholas GERRINGER, Bastian GERRINGER, Nicholas GIFT, and John MOURER
widow: Susannah, administratrix

Estate of George REX, Sr.—report of inquest by Sheriff Peter KACHLEIN, Esq.:
widow
8 children: William, eldest son—accepted the land
others not named
securities: William KERN and Peter MISSIMER
12 men:all by oath—Henry GEIGER, William (Wilhelm) KERN, John (Johannes) KERN, Jacob REX, William REX, Frederick SHICKER, Frederick KERN, Rudolf PETER, John WASSOM, Casper SHNERR, George HAFF, Ulrich BENNINGER

Estate of Diedrick BALDAUFF, Lynn Township, 200 acres—report of inquest by Sheriff Peter KACHLEIN:
widow
4 children: Casper, eldest son—accepted the land
others not named
securities: Philip ANTHONY, Lynn Township, and Jacob PETER, Heidelberg Township
12 men:all by oath—Michael OHL, Philip MOSER, Burghart MOSER, Melcher DERR, Frederick SHNYDER, John SMITH (Johannes SHMIT), Peter SHOLL, John (Johannes) RUMFIELD, Conrad ____, Jacob PETER, Jacob RINDY, Simon CREÜTZ

Estate of Leonard FUHR—report of inquest by Sheriff Peter KACHLEIN:
6 children: John, eldest son—accepted the land
others not named
securities: John SHAD, Whitehall Township, and William KERN, Heidelberg Township
12 men:all by oath—Henry GEIGER, William (Wilhelm) KERN, John (Johannes) KERN, Jacob REX, William REX, Fred'k SHLEIGER, Frederick KERN, Rudolph PETER, John WASSOM, Casper SNERR, Ulrick BENNINGER (BENNICK), George HAFF

**Court on 3 September 1773**
**Justices, the Esquires: George TAYLOR, Lewis KLOTZ, Robert LEVERS, Henry KOOKEN, John JENNINGS**

Estate of John George NUNGESSER, Lynn Township (had a will)—request audit:
petitioner: George HUBNER
executors: Eve NUNGESSER and Frederick ROMICH
auditors: Peter RHOADS, Valentine OPP, Daniel KNOWS

**Court on 21 September 1773**
**Justices, the Esquires: George TAYLOR, Lewis KLOTZ, Robert LEVERS, Henry KOOKEN, John JENNINGS, Joseph GASTON**

Estate of Jacob BRANG, died some years ago, of Town of Northampton, house and lot in town—request inquest:
widow
several children: George, eldest son
others not named

**Court on 22 September 1773**
**Justices, the Esquires: not named**

Estate of William BRANDT, died several years ago, Lower Saucon Township, 56 acres—request inquest:
widow: now wife of George CREADER
3 children: Philip—"has been absent in remote parts for about eighteen years and upwards and has never been heard of since and is therefore in all likelihood dead,..."
Regina, elder daughter, wife of Melcher EDDINGER, Lower Saucon Township
Magdalena

Guardians for minor children of Jacob CHRISTMAN, yeoman, Upper Milford Township (both over age 14) (were other children):
children: Philip.....................................................guardian: Michael SHAFFER
Henry.....................................................guardian: Anthony STAHLER

Estate of George WEAVER—motion by Edward BIDDLE on behalf of guardians of children:
guardians: John NEWCOMER and Gratius LARCH
executor: Valentine OPP—to deliver up bonds and money

New guardians for minor children of Jacob SHANTZ, Lehigh Township:
guardians: former—Jost DREISBACH and Simon DREISBACH, both of Lehigh Township, appointed guardians in 1771 but did not receive the order until two months ago
new—Barnet KUNTZ and Peter ANTHONY

**Court on 23 September 1773**
**Justices, the Esquires: not named**

Estate of Philip WAGGONMAN—report of sale:
administratrix: Susannah WAGGONMAN
sold to: Abraham STEANBROOK, yeoman, Weisenberg Township

Estate of James DUNBAR, yeoman, Mt. Bethel Township, 40 acres—request sale:
widow: Ann, administratrix

**Court on 23 September 1773, continued:**

Estate of George WEAVER—auditors' report:
executor: Valentine OPP
widow and children
auditors: J. OKELY, Simon DREISBACH, John BONN

**Court on 2 October 1773**
**Justices, the Esquires: George TAYLOR, Henry KOOKEN, Robert LEVERS**

Estate of George WEAVER—admitting securities for the executors:
executor: Valentine OPP
securities: John RODROCK and Jacob OPP

**Court on 22 December 1773**
**Justices, the Esquires: Lewis KLOTZ, Robert LEVERS, John JENNINGS, Henry KOOKEN, Christopher WAGNER**

Guardians for 4 minor children of Henry DEAL, yeoman, Moore Township:
widow: Mary
4 children: Susannah, over age 14............................guardian: William BECK
Margaret, over age 14............................guardian: William BECK
George, over age 14...............................guardian: Philip DROOM, Sr.
Frederick, under age 14..........................guardian: Philip DROOM, Sr.

**Court on 23 December 1773**
**Justices, the Esquires: not named**

Guardian for Jacob, over age 14, minor child of Frederick REITZ, yeoman, Whitehall Township:
guardian: John GRESSAMER

Estate of William RICHART, Mt. Bethel Township 3 tracts of 250 acres—report of inquest by late Sheriff Peter KACHLEIN:
children: Robert, eldest son—accepted the land
other brothers and sisters not named
securities: Henry SMITH and William BARE
12 men:all by oath—Alex'r CALBREATH, Thomas McCRAKEN, John BORLEN, George DAVID, Thomas ROSS, Elisha BARTON, Robert McCRAKEN, Samuel MILLER, John BROWN, John MOOR, Patrick DUNN, George BARD

Estate of Frederich WEAVER, yeoman, Lower Saucon Township, 120 acres—request inquest:
5 children: Jacob, eldest son
others not named

**Court on 20 January 1774**
**Justices, the Esquires: Lewis KLOTZ, John JENNINGS, Henry KOOKEN**

Estate of Peter SHNYDER, yeoman, Easton—request sale:
land: house and lot on north side of Northampton Street, #166
administrators: Casper DOLL and Henry ALLSHOUSE

**Court on 22 March 1774**
**Justices, the Esquires: George TAYLOR, Lewis KLOTZ, Robert LEVERS, Henry KOOKEN, John JENNINGS, Christopher WAGNER**

Estate of Baltzer HAMMON, died about 19 years ago, Whitehall Township, 200 acres—request inquest:
widow
4 children: Jacob, eldest son
others not named

Estate of George HENRY, Whitehall Township, yeoman—request sale:
land: 100 acres adjacent to Casper WISTER, George REECK, and Jacob DORMYER
widow: Elizabeth, administratrix, now wife of Mr. WOLF
6 children

**Court on 23 March 1774**
**Justices, the Esquires: not named**

Guardian for minor child named Philip HITTELL, over age 14:
guardian: Christian STEININGER

Guardians for minor child of Michael FEGER, Lower Saucon Township, yeoman:
petitioner: Melchior KNAPLEY, executor
2 children: Catherine, over age 14............................guardian: George RINEHART
Valentine, since deceased

Guardian for minor child, Elizabeth, over age 14, daughter of George NUNGESSER, Lynn Township, yeoman:
guardian: Abraham LEVAN

Guardian for minor child, Ann Eve (no comment on age), daughter of George NUNGESSER:
petitioner: Christian HUCK, Esq.
guardian: Abraham LEVAN (she chose him)

Estate of Jacob BRANG, Town of Northampton—report of inquest by Sheriff Henry FULLERT, Esq.:
land: house and lot on west side of Allen Street
widow
6 children: George, eldest son—accepted the land
security: George MYER, Allen Township
12 men:by oath—David DESHLER, George SHREIBER, Peter MILLER, Martin FRALEY, Jacob MOOR, Martin DERR, Frederick SHECKLER, Leonard ABLE (ABELL)
by affirmation—Peter RHOADS, Christopher (Stoffel) GANGWARE, Philip BEAM, Henry HAGENBUCH

Estate of Frederick WEAVER, Lower Saucon Township—report of inquest by Sheriff Henry FULLERT, Esq.:
widow
5 children: Jacob, eldest son—accepted the land
others not named
securities: Christopher GANGWARE, Salisbury Township and William BECK, Moore Township
12 men:by oath—David DESHLER, Stoffel HELLER, Michael HELLER, John (Johannes) HAAS, Ludwig HELLER, Jacob ROTH, Daniel HELLER
by affirmation—John (Johannes) ROTHROCK, Jacob GIESEY, Jacob ESHELMAN, Henry GEISSINGER, John (Hannes) BACHMAN

**Court on 23 March 1774, continued:**

Estate of William MORREY, died about 11 years ago, Upper Saucon Township, yeoman—request inquest:
- land: two tracts, 300 acre plantation and 95 acres woodland
- widow
- 4 children
- eldest son: Godhart, petitioner

## Court on 25 March 1774
### Justices, the Esquires: Lewis GORDON, Lewis KLOTZ, Robert LEVERS, Peter KACHLEIN

Estate of Thomas OSTERSTOCK, Forks Township—request sale:
- land: 118 acres adjacent to Michael KOCHER and George SIGMAN
- widow: Mary Elizabeth, administratrix, now wife of Mr. WOLF
- 6 children

Guardians for minor children of Thomas OSTERSTOCK:
- widow: Mary Elizabeth, now wife of Mr. WOLF
- children: Leonard, over age 14..............................guardian Henry ALLSHOUSE
  - remaining 5 children under age 14:
  - Henry
  - Mary
  - Thomas
  - John
  - Elizabeth
- guardians: for 5 younger children—Abraham LABAR

Estate of Jacob SHANTZ, Lehigh Township, yeoman—request audit:
- administratrix: Mary KRAFT, late Mary SHANTZ
- children: Henry—thought there were errors in administration account
- auditors: Simon TREISBACH, Arthur LATTIMORE, Conrad KREIDER

Estate of Peter SHNYDER, house and lot—return of sale:
- administrators: Casper DOLL and Henry ALLSHOUSE
- sold to: Peter KACHLEIN, Jr., of Easton, yeoman

## Court on 23 April 1774
### Justices, the Esquires: Lewis GORDON, Peter KACHLEIN, John OKELY, Jacob LERCH

Estate of Thomas OSTERSTOCK, Forks Township, yeoman—return of sale:
- widow: Mary Elizabeth, administratrix, now wife of Mr. WOLF
- sold to: Leonard KERN of Plainfield Township

Guardians for minor children of John DIEDER, Sr., died about 1 year ago, Moore Township, yeoman (all under age 14) (were other children):
- widow: Elizabeth, now wife of Mr. EVERET
- children: Elizabeth
  - Margaret
  - Susannah
  - Henry
- guardians: for all the minor children—Simon TREISBACH

**Court on 22 June 1774**
**Justices, the Esquires: George TAYLOR, Lewis KLOTZ, Robert LEVERS, Henry KOOKEN, Peter KACHLEIN, Lewis NICOLA**

Estate of Baltzer HAMMAN, Whitehall Township, 200 acres—report of inquest by Sheriff Henry FULLERT:
widow
4 children: Jacob, eldest son—accepted the land
others not named
securities: George KNOUSE and George STEININGER
12 men:all by oath—Adam HABERLEY, George KNOWS, Sr. (Görg KNAUSS), John GREESAMORE (Johannes GREASEMER), Adam EPLER, George HOFMAN, Andrew WINNER (Andreas WENNER), George Frederick KNOUSE, Daniel TORNEY (DORNI), Adam TORNEY (DORNY), George LITZENBERGER, George STEININGER, Jacob BÄRR

Estate of William MORREY, Upper Saucon Township—report of inquest by Sheriff Henry FULLERT, Esq.:
widow
4 children: Godhart, eldest son—accepted the land
others not named
securities: Jacob MORREY and Philip BUCKACKER, both of Upper Saucon Township
12 men:by oath—David DESHLER, Henry KECK, Baltzer BEIL, Ehrhart WEAVER (WEBER)
by affirmation—Jacob MORRY, Henry WEAVER (WEBER), David OWEN, Aquilla TOOLL, Peter KNAPLEY (KNAPPLY), Andrew WIND, John (Johannes) NEWCOMER, Jr., Henry WIND

Guardians for minor children of Frederick NUNGESSER, Easton, yeoman (were other children):
widow: Christina
children: Elizabeth, over age 14............................guardian: her husband, Isaac LIDMAN
remaining 3 are under age 14:
Frederick
George
John
guardians: for younger 3 children—Peter KACHLEIN, Esq., and Henry ALLSHOUSE

Guardian for Catherine, over age 14, daughter of George SMITH, Lehigh Township:
guardian: William BECK

**Court on 11 August 1774**
**Justices, the Esquires: Lewis GORDON, Peter KACHLEIN, Jacob NICOLA**

Estate of Conrad BITTENBINDER, died about 17 years ago, Hamilton Township, yeoman, 300 acres adjacent to George HARTLIEB, Philip BUSSERT, Nicholas YOUNG, and Jacob STERNER—request inquest:
land:
widow: since deceased
4 children: George, eldest son
Christopher
Jacob
Conrad

Estate of Conrad BITTENBENDER—report of inquest by Sheriff Henry FULLERT, Esq.:

children: George, eldest son—refused to accept land
Christopher, Jr., second son—accepted the land

securities: Christopher BITTENBENDER, Sr., of Easton, blacksmith, and John BITTENBENDER, Hamilton Township

12 men:all by oath—Melcher STACHER, Jacob BRINKER, Jacob STERNER, Henry BUSERT, Melchior BUSERT (BOSSERT), William SERFASS, Michael RAUB, Lawrence RAMEY, Adam STECHER, Nicholas YOUNG, Bartholomew (Bartel) SHEIBLE, Philip BUSERT (BOSSERT)

**Court on 22 September 1774**
**Justices, the Esquires: not named**

Guardians for minor children of Henry ATTEN, died about one year ago, Mt. Bethel Township:

children: Henry, eldest son, over age 14.................guardian: Derrick ATTEN
Thomas, over age 14...............................guardian: Adrijan ATTEN
remaining 4 children are under age 14:
Mary
John
Sarah
George

guardians: for younger 4 children—Derrick and Adrijan ATTEN

Estate of Peter VANDERMARK, Lower Smithfield Township—request audit:

land: 93 acres adjoining Samuel DRAKE and Jacob MINOR
administrator: Benjamin SCHOONOVEN
auditors: John VAN CAMPEN, Nicholas DEPUI, and Jacob STROWD

**Court on 21 December 1774**
**Justices, the Esquires: George TAYLOR, Henry KOOKEN, Christopher WAGNER, Robert LEVERS, Peter KACHLEIN, John OKELY, Lewis NICOLA**

Guardians for minor children of John FREEZE, Lynn Township, yeoman (all under age 14):

administrator: Thomas EVERET
4 children: Peter
Elizabeth
John
Daniel

guardians: for all 4 children—Jacob FREEZE and Daniel OSWALD

Guardian for minor child, Nicholas, over age 14, Lower Saucon Township, yeoman, child of Charles BEETCH—Nicholas requested a guardian for his estate left him by his father, "who died in Germany some years ago...":

guardian: John APPLE of Upper Saucon Township

Estate of George HENRY, Whitehall Township, yeoman—return of sale:

administratrix: Elizabeth WOLF
sold to: Michael TEIBERT of Lowhill Township

**Court on 22 December 1774**

**Justices, the Esquires: not named**

Estate of Adam SHRADER, Weisenberg Township, yeoman—request audit:

| | |
|---|---|
| widow: | Magdalena, administratrix |
| children: | George—said he found errors in administration account |
| | others not named |
| auditors: | Nicholas MYER, Daniel KNOWS, John LICHTEWALTER |

Estate of George WEAVER—complaint by minor children's guardians, John NEWCOMER & Gratius LARCH:

| | |
|---|---|
| children: | Catherine |
| | Valentine |
| | Mary |

"...their father George WEAVER died in the lifetime of his Father Frederick WEAVER which said Frederick is since dead leaving a considerable Personal and Real Estate." Jacob WEAVER, eldest son of Frederick, accepted the land and was to pay the other heirs a share. A rehearing was requested.

**Court on 22 March 1775**
**Justices, the Esquires: George TAYLOR, Lewis KLOTZ, Henry KOOKEN, Robert LEVERS, Jacob LERCH, Lewis NICOLA, John OKELY, Jacob MORRY**

Estate of Martin KARG, died sometime ago, Weisenberg Township, yeoman—request sale:

| | |
|---|---|
| land: | 51 acres adjoining to David KNOWS, Melchior SEIP, and John LICHTEWALTER |
| administrator: | Bartholomew MILLER |
| left widow but no children | |

Guardian for minor children of Frederich BERKENSTOCK, Upper Milford Township, yeoman (both under 14):

| | |
|---|---|
| next friend: | Peter FOX |
| children: | John |
| | Abraham |
| guardian: | for both sons—Peter FOX |

Estate of John DRAKE, Sr., died sometime ago, Lower Smithfield Township—request sale:

| | |
|---|---|
| land: | 128 acres adjoining to Derrick VAN VLIET, Benjamin SHOONHAVEN, and John DRAKE, Jr. |
| administrator: | Jacob STROWD |

**Court on 23 March 1775**
**Justices, the Esquires: not named**

Estate of William McILLHENNY, died sometime ago, Mt. Bethel Township—request inquest:

| | |
|---|---|
| land: | 373 acres in two tracts adjoining each other & Alexander McILLROY and the late Alexander CAMPBELL |
| widow | |
| 4 children: | James, only son |

**Court on 24 March 1775**

**Justices, the Esquires: not named**

Estate of Henry BYER, died about 19 years ago, Towamensing Township, yeoman—request inquest:

land: 1) 150 acres in Towamensing Township adjoining to Andrew OLLEWINE and Nicholas HORNER
2) 150 acres in Lynn Township adjacent to Melchier DERR and others

widow

7 children: Frederich, eldest son
others not named

Response to complaint of WEAVER children on 22 December 1774 concerning estate of Frederich WEAVER, their grandfather, against their uncle Jacob WEAVER:

Their father, George WEAVER, had received no advancement from his father during his lifetime. The children came to court and received their shares of their grandfather's estate.

**Court on 25 March 1775**
**Justices, the Esquires: Lewis GORDON, Jacob LERCH, Jacob MORRY**

Estate of Peter VANDERMARK—auditors' report:

administrator: Benjamin SCHOONHAVEN—the administration account was declared just
auditors: Jacob STROWD, Nicholas DUPUI, John VAN CAMPEN

Estate of Peter VANDERMARK, Lower Smithfield Township, 150 acres adjacent to Samuel DRAKE and Jacob MINER—request sale:

administrator: Benjamin SCHOONHOVEN

**Court on 8 April 1775**
**Justices, the Esquires: John OKELY, Peter KACHLEIN, Jacob LERCH, Jacob MORRY**

Estate of Christopher SHNYDER, Whitehall Township, yeoman—request sale:

widow: Elizabeth, administratrix

no children

Christopher had bought two tracts from Christopher KERN in partnership with George KOHLER, also of Whitehall Township—one of 81 acres, adjacent to Jacob SHOWALTER, George KERN, Jacob SHOWALTER, and west branch of Delaware River; other of 19 acres, adjacent to Jacob SHIVER, Adam DECHLER, Peter BASLER, and west branch of Delaware River. The partners had partitioned the land, George KOHLER got 27 acres 142 perches of first tract and the deceased got 53 acres 18 perches of first tract and second tract, totaling together 72 acres 18 perches.

**Court on 15 May 1775**
**Justices, the Esquires: Lewis GORDON, Peter KACHLEIN, Jacob LERCH**

Guardians for minor children of Moses BEAR, died sometime ago, Lehigh Township, yeoman (all under age 14):

widow: Catherine

4 children: Samuel
David
Jacob
Rachel

guardians: for all 4 children—Simon TREISBACH and Conrad KREIDER

**Court on 21 June 1775**

**Justices, the Esquires: George TAYLOR, Lewis KLOTZ, Henry KOOKEN, John OKELY, Peter KACHLEIN, John WETZELL, Jacob LERCH**

Guardians for minor children of Derrick VAN VLIET, Sr., Lower Smithfield Township:
next friend: Derrick VAN VLIET, Jr., of Lower Smithfield Township
children: Lydie, over age 14
Joseph, over age 14
Cornelia, under age 14
guardian: for all 3 children—Jacob STROWD

Guardians for minor children of Samuel GEISSENGER, Milford Township, yeoman (all under age 14):
next friend: Philip GEISSENGER, the younger—children's uncle
children: Philip
John
Mary
Elizabeth
guardians: for all 4 children—John NEWCOMER, Sr., and John GEISSENGER

Guardian for minor child, Christina, over age 14, daughter of Lawrence HARTMAN, Chestnuthill Township:
guardian: John JENNINGS, Esq.

Estate of Moses MARSHALL, Bucks County, yeoman—request audit:
administrator: Jacob WOOD of Mt. Bethel Township
widow: Sarah
auditors: Henry BARNET, Abraham BERLIN, Henry ALLSHOUSE

Estate of Martin KARG, Weisenberg Township, yeoman—return of sale:
administrator: Bartholomew MILLER
sold to: John YAMPERT of Weisenberg Township

**Court on 22 June 1775**
**Justices, the Esquires: not named**

Estate of Christopher SHNYDER, Whitehall Township—return of sale:
widow: Elizabeth SHNYDER, administratrix
sold to: Christopher KERN of Whitehall Township

**Court on 20 September 1775**
**Justices, the Esquires: George TAYLOR, Robert LEVERS, Henry KOOKEN, John OKELY, Peter KACHLEIN, Jacob LERCH**

Estate of William McILLHENNY, Mt. Bethel Township—report of inquest by Sheriff Henry FULLERT, Esq.:
widow
children: James, only son—accepted the land
3 daughters
securities: Samuel REA and James BEARD, both of Mt. Bethel Township
12 men:all by oath—Samuel REA, William MOORE, Thomas ROCKMAN, William McFARREN, Thomas ROSS, James BEARD, John DEPUE, Benjamin DEPUE, John MOORE, Elisha BARTON, John CRAWFORD, Anthony MOORE

**Court on 20 September 1775, continued:**

Estate of John DRAKE, Sr.—return of sale:
administrator: Jacob STROWD
sold to: John BUSH

**Court on 19 December 1775**
**Justices, the Esquires: George TAYLOR, Robert LEVERS, Henry KOOKEN, Christopher WAGNER, Peter KACHLEIN**

Guardians for minor children of William GABLE, died sometime ago, Penn Township, yeoman (all under 14):
administrator: Thomas FARMER
widow
6 children: Thomas
William
Israel
Barnet
Catherine
Elizabeth
guardians: for all 6 children—Burghart MOSER and Michael OHL

Guardians for minor daughters of George Jacob RIFFLE died sometime ago, Whitehall Township, yeoman (both under age 14):
grandfather: Christian HENRY, petitioner, father-in-law of the deceased
widow
daughters: Magdalena
Elizabeth
guardians: for both daughters—Michael POBST and John LICHTEWALTER

Estate of Jacob YEANTZER, died sometime ago, Weisenberg Township, yeoman, two tracts—request inquest:
land: 1) 230 acres in Weisenberg Township adjacent to Philip BOGER, Dewalt MYER, and Christian MARBURGHER
2) 130 acres, adjacent to Christopher SUNDAGH and George KRIM
widow
4 children: Jacob, eldest son
others not named

**Court on 20 December 1775**
**Justices, the Esquires: not named**

Estate of Jacob MORITZ, Town of Northampton, yeoman—request sale:
land: house & lot on west side of James Street, lot #490 measuring 60' front, X 230' depth
administrator: Jacob MILLER

**Court on 15 January 1776**
**Justices, the Esquires: Lewis GORDON, Christopher WAGNER, Jacob MORRY, Jacob LERCH**

Estate of Jacob MORITZ—return of sale:
administrator: Jacob MILLER
sold to: George OTT, Salisbury Township

**Court on 19 March 1776**

**Justices, the Esquires: George TAYLOR, Robert LEVERS, Henry KOOKEN, Christopher WAGNER, Peter KACHLEIN, Jacob MORRY**

Guardian for minor child, Ann Mary, under age 14, daughter of Jacob BACHER, Lynn Township:
next friend: Nicholas BACHER
guardian: Matthias PROBST

**Court on 20 March 1776**
**Justices, the Esquires: not named**

Estate of Frederick SHAFFER, died sometime ago, Hamilton Township, yeoman—request sale:
land: 100 acres bounded by George HARTLIEB, Simon HELLER, and George DOLL
administrator: Christian WILLOUR
widow and 9 children

Estate of Alexander CAMPBELL, Mt. Bethel Township, 100 acres—return of sale:
administratrix: Jane CAMPBELL
sold to: John BROWN of Mt. Bethel Township

Guardians for minor children of Jacob YENTZER, Sr., died sometime ago, Weisenberg Township (both under age 14) (were other children):
widow: Catherine
children: Otilla
Barbara
guardian: for both daughters—Daniel KNOWS

Estate of Jacob YENTZER, Weisenberg Township, two tracts—report of inquest by Sheriff Henry FULLERT:
land: 1) 230 acres in Weisenberg Township adjacent to Philip BOGER, Dewalt MYER, and Christian MASBURGER
2) 130 acres in Lynn Township adjacent to Christopher SUNDAGH and George KRIM
children: Jacob, eldest son—accepted the land
others not named
securities: Jacob GRENEWALT and George GRIM, both of Weisenberg Township
12 men:all by oath—Nicholas MYER, Daniel KNOWS, John LICHTEWALTER, Michael POBST, Jacob GRENEWALT, George GRIM, Adam GROH, Nicholas BEESACKER, Matthias PROBST, Jacob HANS, Bernhart SMITH, Michael FINSTERMACHER

**Court on 25 March 1776**
**Justices, the Esquires: Lewis GORDON, John WETZEL, Jacob MORRY**

Request sale and guardians for minor children of John WERTZ, died sometime ago (all under age 14):
land: Lehigh Township, 160 acres bounded by Frederick SHECKLER, John DREISBACH, Martin SWAB, and Michael HOLSTEIN
widow: Barbara now wife of Jacob KERSTER
5 children: John
Margaret
Catherine
Barbara
Peter
guardians: for all 5 children—Peter ANTHONY and Nicholas SHNYDER

**Court on 25 March 1776, continued:**

Estate of Alexander CAMPBELL, died some years ago, Mt. Bethel Township—request sale:
land: 220 acres bounded by Henry SMITH, James TAYLOR, James OLIPHANT, and others
widow: Jane

Estate of Martin HERBSTER, died sometime ago, Moore Township—request sale:
land: 150 acres bounded by Nicholas NELICH, Michael ESH, and others
administrator: Paul FLICK, acting admininistrator

New guardian for minor children of Charles WILSON:
guardians: former—Arthur LATTEMORE of Allen Township and David CHAMBERS, appointed 28 April 1769—CHAMBERS "has since removed" out of the province
new—John McNAIR, in place of David CHAMBERS

**Court on 15 April 1776**
**Justices, the Esquires: Lewis GORDON, Christopher WAGNER, Jacob MORRY**

New guardians for minor children, of Frederich NUNGESSER, died sometime ago, Easton (were other children):
widow: Christina
children: Frederick
George
John
guardians: former—for all 3 children when they were all under age 14—Peter KACHLEIN and Henry ALLSHOUSE
new—for Frederick, now over age 14......Rudolph OBERLEY
new—for George, under age 14,
and John, under age 14..................their mother

**Court on 18 June 1776**
**Justices, the Esquires: Lewis KLOTZ, Christopher WAGNER, Peter KACHLEIN, Jacob LERCH, Jacob MORRY**

Estate of Alexander CAMPBELL—return of sale:
administratrix: Jane CAMPBELL
sold to: Samuel TAYLOR, Mt. Bethel Township—200 acres
Henry SMITH, Mt. Bethel Township—20 acres

Estate of Martin HERBSTER—return of sale:
administrator: Paul FLICK
sold to: Daniel SWARTZ, Allen Township

Estate of John WERTZ—return of sale:
widow: Barbara, now wife of Jacob KERSTER
sold to: Leonard HOESLEY, Lehigh Township

**Court on 14 August 1777**

**Justices, the Esquires: John ARNDT, Samuel REA, Thomas SYLLYMAN, Robert LEVERS, Benjamin DUPUI**

**"At an Orphans Court held at Easton in and for the County of Northampton in the Commonwealth of Pennsylvania...."**

Estate of Charles BRIGGS, died sometime ago, Williams Township—inventory ordered:
children: Joseph BRIGGS, administrator
Sarah, wife of John DYER—said that Joseph left things out of the administration account

Guardian for Jonathan, under age 14, minor son of James NELSON, died sometime ago, Mt. Bethel Township (left widow and one son):
petitioner: Jonathan NELSON, grandfather, Mt. Bethel Township—said he would maintain his grandson without charge but the child would continue to live with his mother.
guardian: Robert FORDSMAN, Sr.

Estate of Peter BOYER, died sometime ago, Plainfield Township—request sale and guardians:
land: 150 acres bounded by Deeter BAUER, Adam BUTZ, and Henry HAUSER
widow: Elizabeth, administratrix
2 children: Leonard, under age 14............................guardian: Casper SHOLL
Abraham, under age 14...........................guardian: Conrad GERMANTOWN

**Court on 17 September 1777**

**Justices, the Esquires: Thomas SILLYMAN, Jacob MOREE, Thomas HARTMAN, Benjamin DUPUI, Samuel REA, William McNAIR, Lewis STACKER, James VANAKEN, Frederick LEIMBACH, Peter MOYER**

Estate of Charles BRIGGS, died sometime ago, Williams Township—request inquest:
land: 200 acres adjacent to Isaac STOUT, Conrad MILLER, Abraham BEIDLEMAN, and Abraham ARNDT
widow
one son and one daughter—the only surviving children:
Joseph, only son
only daughter, not named

Guardian for John, under age 14, minor son of John KNIGHT, died sometime ago, Bethlehem Township:
widow: Mary Magdalena
guardian: the mother and Peter SEIP

Estate of Jacob SWARTWOOD—return of sale:
administrator: Peter SWARTWOOD
sold to: Harman COAL, Walpack Township, Sussex County, New Jersey, signed on 6 July 1776

**Court on 18 September 1777**

**Justices, the Esquires: not named**

Estate of Peter BOYER—return of sale:
widow: Elizabeth, administratrix
sold to: Henry HOUSER, Plainfield Township

**Court on 18 September 1777, continued:**

Estate of Henry NELICH, Whitehall Township (had will)—request appraisal on motion of Robert TRAILL, Esq.:

executor: John KUNTZACHER
appraisers: Peter KOHLER, Christopher BARE, Daniel SHNYDER

Guardian for minor children of Henry NELICH—motion of Robert TRAILL, Esq:

children: Paul, over age 14....................................guardian: Nicholas NELICH, Moore Twp.
Henry, under age 14...............................guardian: Peter KOHLER, Whitehall Twp.

Guardians for 2 sons of Rudolph PETER, Heidelberg Township (both under age 14)—motion of Robert TRAILL, Esq.:

sons: Henry...................................................guardian: George BLOSS, Heidelberg Twp.
Adam....................................................guardian: Casper PETER, Heidelberg Twp.

Guardian for Robert, under age 14, minor son of Robert HANNA, Lower Smithfield Township—motion of John CURRIE, Esq.:

guardian: Benjamin BONNELL, Lower Smithfield Township

Guardian for minor children of Peter SHOP, Weisenberg Township (both under age 14)—motion of Robert TRAILL, Esq.:

children: Peter
Eve Barbara
guardian: for both children—John BARE, Weisenberg Township

Estate of George HIND, Lowhill Township, 98 acres—request to confirm sale on motion of Robert TRAILL and John CURRIE, Esq.:

executrix: Christina, now wife of Martin EILERT
sold to: Martin BUCHANAN

**Court on 1 October 1777**
**Justices, the Esquires: Thomas HARTMAN, Benjamin DUPUI, Robert LEVERS**

Guardian for John, over age 14, minor child & one son of Paul BALLIET, died sometime ago, Whitehall Twp.:

guardian: David HAHN, Whitehall Township

Guardians for minor children of Joseph MIM, Easton, tailor (both under 14, left only two children):

administrator: Peter EALER
widow: Mary, administratrix
2 children: John......................................................guardian: Henry BARNET, Easton, tanner
Elisabeth...............................................guardian: Lodowick KNAUS, Easton, saddler

**Court on 16 December 1777**
**Justices, the Esquires: Thomas SILLYMAN, Samuel REA, Jacob MOREE, Benjamin DUPUI**

Guardian for Ulrich, over age 14, minor son of Rudolph PETER, Heidelberg Township—motion of Robert TRAILL, Esq.:

guardian: Jacob PETER, Heidelberg Township

**Court on 16 December 1777, continued:**

Estate of Rudolph PETER, Heidelberg Township—request audit on motion of Robert TRAILL, Esq.:
- executor: John HUNSACKER
- auditors: Peter KOHLER, Daniel SHNYDER, Christopher BARE

Guardians for minor children of Paul BALLIET, Whitehall Township (all under age 14):
- widow: Magdalena
- 3 children: Paul.......guardian: Peter BURKHOLDER, Whitehall Twp.
  - Nicholas.......guardian: Peter KOHLER, Whitehall Twp.
  - Magdalena.......guardians: Nicholas and Peter RHODES, Town of Northampton

**Court on 29 January 1778**
**Justices, the Esquires: Robert LEVERS, Peter TREXLER, John ARNDT**

Estate of George KNAUS, Whitehall Township, 240 acres—request inquest:
- land: tenement grist mill and tract bounded by Conrad KRUMBACH, Daniel TURNER, and land of the late Lynford LARDNER
- widow
- 7 children: George Frederick—petitioner
  - others not named

Guardian for minor children of George KNAUS:
- children: Margaret, under age 21.......guardian not named
  - Elisabeth, under age 14.......guardian: Adam TONEY

**Court on 17 March 1778**
**Justices, the Esquires: Thomas SILLYMAN, Jacob MORRY, John ARNDT, Samuel REA, William McNAIR, Benjamin DUPUI, Jacob HORNER**

Guardians for minor children of Benjamin REEGLE, Lower Saucon Township (were other children):
- next friend: John RODROCK
- children: Matthais, over age 14.......guardian: John RODROCK
  - the remaining 4 are under age 14:
  - Margaret.......guardian: John BOYL
  - John.......guardian: John BOYL
  - Catherine.......guardian: Daniel DIEL
  - Jacob .......guardian: Daniel DIEL

Guardian for Susanna, under age 14, minor and only child of Adam GOODAKUNTZ, Macungie Township:
- brother-in-law: Melchior SEIP, Macungie Township, petitioner
- guardian: John LICKSERWALTER

**Court on 18 March 1778**
**Justices, the Esquires: not named**

Guardians for 5 minor children of Jacob ENGLER, Plainfield Township (were other children):

| | | |
|---|---|---|
| widow: | Ann Mary | |
| children: | Jacob, over age 14 | guardian: Adam ENGLER, Plainfield |
| | Simon, under age 14 | guardian: Casper SHOLL, Plainfield |
| | Susanna, under age 14 | guardian: Casper SHOLL, Plainfield |
| | Adam, under age 14 | guardian: Teetrich BAUER, Plainfield |
| | Ann Mary, under age 14 | guardian: Teetrich BAUER, Plainfield |

Guardians for 5 minor children of Felix ARNER, Whitehall Township (were other children):

| | | |
|---|---|---|
| widow: | Elizabeth, now wife of Peter ANTHONY | |
| children: | Salome, over age 14 | guardian: Peter SCHLOSSER |
| | John, over age 14 | guardian: Nicholas MOREPS, Whitehall Twp. |
| | Felix, under age 14 | |
| | William, under age 14 | |
| | Dorothea, under age 14 | |
| guardian: | for younger 3 children—Daniel SNIDER, Whitehall Township | |

**Court on 19 March 1778**
**Justices, the Esquires: not named**

Guardians for minor children of John RIDDLE, Allen Township (were other children):

| | | |
|---|---|---|
| children: | David, over age 14 | guardian: James CARR, Allen Twp. |
| | Sarah, over age 14 | guardian: William McNAIR, Allen Twp. |
| | Susanna, under age 14 | guardian: William McNAIR, Allen Twp. |

**Court on 25 March 1778**
**Justices, the Esquires: Thomas SILLYMAN, Samuel REA, Benjamin DUPUI, Lewis STACKER**

Guardians for 2 minor children of Benjamin REEGLE, Lower Saucon Township (both under age 14) (were other children):

| | |
|---|---|
| grandfather: | John HAAS, petitioner |
| children: | Elisabeth |
| | Benjamin |
| guardians: | for both children—Peter SEHN and Daniel BEIDLEMAN |

Guardians for 2 minor children of George BENDER, Plainfield Township (both under age 14):

| | |
|---|---|
| widow: | Catherine |
| 2 children: | Christian |
| | Elisabeth |
| guardians: | for both children—Casper SHOLL and Philip YANT |

New guardian for Henry, now over age 14, one son of Thomas OSTERSTOCK, Forks Township:

| | |
|---|---|
| guardian: | former—Abraham LABAR, Easton, to whom Henry was willing to be an apprentice; "Indentures cannot be properly drawn without his having another Guardian...." |
| | new—Lodowich KNAUS, Easton |

**Court on 25 March 1778, continued:**

William COUNGELSON—soldier requesting half-pay:

William produced a certificate signed by Colonel Stephen BALLIET that he, by an accident in militia service, was incapable of doing further duty or procuring livelihood for self or family. He wanted the court to approve an order on Lieutenant of County, Lt. John WETZELL, Esq., for ½ pay—approved by the court.

**Court on 16 June 1778**
**Justices, the Esquires: Thomas SILLYMAN, Jacob MORREE, Samuel REA, John ARNDT, Nicholas DUPUI, Benjamin DUPUI, William McNAIR**

Guardians for 3 children, of Samuel BEER, Towamensing Township (all minors under age 14):

| | |
|---|---|
| widow: | Susanna |
| 3 children: | Ann |
| | Lawrence |
| | Elisabeth |
| guardian: | for all 3 children—Henry SHAP |

Estate of Matthais RIEGLE (made will and left legacies to diverse persons)—request audit:

| | |
|---|---|
| petitioners: | John REIGLE, Conrad JACOBE, Jacob LUDWIG, all yeomen |
| executor: | Benjamin RIEGLE, eldest son (sole executor)—died soon after his father |
| administrator: | John RODRICK, plus the petitioners |
| auditors: | Anthony LERGH, Gratzuis LERGH, Adam KOCHERT |

**Court on 17 June 1778**
**Justices, the Esquires: not named**

Estate of John MELCHIOR (had a will) & guardian for grandchildren—motion of Daniel CLYMER, Esq.:

| | |
|---|---|
| executor: | Christopher WAGGONER |
| children: | Michael, died intestate and left two children, both under age 14: |
| | Michael......guardian: William BECKER |
| | Elizabeth......guardian: Peter RHOADS |
| | Catherine, wife of Leonard KESLER |

Guardians for minor children of Jacob GRASSEL, Heidelberg Township—motion by Robert TRAILL, Esq.:

| | |
|---|---|
| children: | Jacob, over age 14......guardian: John HANDWERK |
| | remaining children are all under age 14: |
| | Magdalena |
| | John |
| | Adam |
| | Bernhardt |
| | Catherine |
| guardians: | for younger 5 children—Peter HANDWERK and Henry HARTMAN |

Guardians for minor children of Abraham KNERR, Jr., Weisenberg Township (all under age 14)—motion by Robert TRAILL, Esq.:

| | |
|---|---|
| children: | Ann Elisabeth......guardian: Jacob HORNER |
| | Andrew......guardian: Jacob HORNER |
| | Abraham......guardian: Henry KOCH |
| | Susan......guardian: Henry KOCH |

**Court on 17 June 1778, continued:**

Guardians for minor children of Bernard SELL, Lowhill Township (all under 14)—motion by Robert TRAILL:

children: Peter
John George
John

guardian: for all 3 children—Henry KROCOLO

Guardians for minor children of Rudolph ZECHLER, Macungie Twp. (all under age14)—motion by Robert TRAILL, Esq.:

children: Jacob
John
Christina

guardians: for all 3 children—Jacob and Frederick ZECHLER

Guardians for minor children of Samuel WEST, Weisenberg Township (all under age 14)—motion by Robert TRAILL, Esq.:

children: Peter
Ann Mary
Catherine
Susanna

guardians: for all 4 children—Michael POBST and John EBERT

**Court on 18 June 1778**
**Justices, the Esquires: not named**

Estate of Gottfridt KNAUS, Whitehall Township, 140 acres (had a will)—motion on John CURRIE, Esq.:

administrators de bonis non: George Frederich KNAUS, Philip KNAUS, Gottfridt KNAUS, and Paul KNAUS

The administrators asked the court to be empowered to make a deed to Peter RHOADS of the Town of Northampton who purchased the property from George KNAUS, executor of the will, but who died before he made the deed.

Guardian for Solomon BONNEL, the younger, who was in a state of lunacy—motion of John CURRIE, Esq.:

guardians: as long as he remained in a state of lunacy—Solomon BONNEL, the elder, William JEANE, and Benjamin VANCAMPEN

Guardian for Robert, under 14, minor son of Robert HANNA, Delaware Township—motion of John CURRIE:

guardian: Solomon BONNEL, the elder

**Court on 23 September 1778**
**Justices, the Esquires: Thomas SILLYMAN, Samuel REA, Jacob MORRY, John ARNDT, Benjamin DUPUI, Jacob HORNER, Peter MOYER, William McNAIR, Matthias PROPST, Frederick LEIMBACH**

Estate of Matthais RIEGLE—auditors' report:

administrators: John RODRICK and others—said that Benjamin RIEGLE son of Matthais did not, in his lifetime, account unto the other heirs for a sum of money left in his hands

auditors: Anthony LERCH, Gratzuis LERCH, Adam KOCHERT

**Court on 23 September 1778, continued:**

Guardians for minor children of Henry ALLISE, Upper Saucon Township (all under age 14):
grandfather: Christian BUSE, Bucks County
widow
4 children—one son and three daughters:
Elisabeth.......................................guardian: Jacob MORRY, Esq.
Mary.............................................guardian: Jacob MORRY, Esq.
two younger....................................guardian: Philip BAHL

Guardian for minor children of Nicholas GABLE, Salisbury Township (both under age 14):
next friend: Hubertus LARE, Salisbury Township
widow
2 children: Christina
Elizabeth
guardian: for both children—Jacob SPINNER

Guardians for 4 minor children of Christopher GANGWARE, Salisbury Township (were other children):
administrators: Michael GANGWARE and Catherine GANGWARE
children: Elisabeth, over age 14............................guardian: Michael HELLER
remaining 3 are under age 14:
Sivilla
Daniel
David
guardian: for younger 3 children—Philip BAHL

Guardians for 2 minor children of Peter LONG, Upper Milford Township (both under age 14):
widow: Elisabeth
8 children: older six not named
Mary.............................................guardian: John SNIDER
Francis..........................................guardian: Peter SCHLOSSER

Estate of Andrew LINE, Salisbury Township—request inquest:
land: 100 acres bounded by Bernard STRAUP, Jacob GISSEY, and Christian GEESE
widow
only child: William

Estate of Henry ATEN, died some years ago, Mt. Bethel Township, two tracts—request inquest:
land: 1) 150 acres, for which there is a deed, bounded by Derrich ATEN and others
2) 200 acres bounded by Derrich ATEN and others
widow: since remarried
6 children: Henry, eldest son
others not named

**Court on 24 September 1778**
**Justices, the Esquires: not named**

Estate of John ECKENROTH, died about 21 years ago, Lynn Township—request inquest:
land: 250 acres adjacent to Christian HENRY, Frederich LYSER, and John NYER
widow
8 children: Henry, eldest son, others not named

**Court on 24 September 1778, continued:**

Guardians for 3 minor children of Henry MILLER, younger, Lower Saucon Township (all under age 14):
next friend: John MILLER
children: Henry
Peter
Catherine
guardian: for all 3 children—Anthony LERCH

Guardians for minor children of Henry MILLER, the elder, Williams Township (were other children):
children: John, eldest son, the petitioner
Jacob, over age 14..................................guardian: Edward SHYMAN
Andrew, over age 14..............................guardian: Edward SHYMAN
Philip, under age 14
Peter, under age 14
Elisabeth, under age 14
guardian: for younger 3 children—Nicholas BAST

Guardians for minor children of Henry SHNYDER, Easton:
next friend: Nicholas TRAXEL, Easton
widow: since remarried
6 children: Margaret, over age 14.............................guardian: Peter KACHLEIN, Esq.
the remaining children are all under age 14:
Peter
Henry
Elisabeth
Catherine
Juliana
guardians: for younger 5 children—Lewis KNAUS and Jacob OPP

**Court on 28 September 1778**
**Justices, the Esquires: Thomas SILLYMAN, John ARNDT, Robert LEVERS**

Estate of John JENNINGS, Town of Northampton, land and tenement and two lots in town—request sale:
widow: Anna, administratrix
no children mentioned—"...leaving the Petitioner, his widow...."

**Inquest on 16 December 1778**
**Before: High Sheriff Jonas HERTZEL, Esq.**

Estate of John ECKENROTH, taken at Lynn Township—report of inquest:
land: 250 acres adjoining Christian HENRY, Fridrick LYSER, and John NYER
12 men:by oath and affirmation—Thomas EVERETT, Martain (Johann Martin) MOTZER, George BRICK, Jacob MILLER, Zacherius HALLER, Jacob WITZEL, Jacob GREINENMAYER (GREINNMŸER), John LEESER (LISAR), Daniel OSEWALD, Michael BOCK, Daniel HAM, Henry KING (Heinrich KÖNIG)
{Note: this entry is on a loose sheet of paper and appears to be the actual paper signed by the 12 men after they had toured the property. There is no mention of an heir accepting the estate nor of securities being appointed)

**Court on 22 December 1778**
**Justices, the Esquires: Thomas SILLYMAN, Nicholas DUPUI, John ARNDT, Jacob MORREY, Samuel REA, Peter MOYER, Jacob HORNER**

Guardians for minor children of Lewis GORDON, Esq., Easton (both over age 14)—motion of Robert TRAILL:
children: William
Alexander
guardians: for both children—Henry FULLERT and Henry ALLSHOUSE of Easton

**Court on 23 December 1778**
**Justices, the Esquires: not named**

Guardian for John George, over age 14, minor son of John DINGLER, Easton—motion of Robert TRAILL:
guardian: Nicholas TRAXEL

Guardian for Mary Barbara, under age 14, minor child of George HAFT, Heidelberg Township—motion of Robert TRAILL, Esq.:
guardian: Casper SNERR

Guardian for minor children of Jacob MILLER, Forks Township (both over age 14)—motion of Robert TRAILL:
children: Hannah
Margaret
guardian: for both children—John ERICH, Forks Township

William COUNGELSON, soldier requesting half-pay:
Lieutenant of County, Lt. John WETZELL was ordered to so pay

Guardian for Elisabeth, under age 14, child of George RIFFLE, Whitehall Township:
next friend: Andrew TAPPER
guardian: Christian TAPPER

Guardian for minor children of Joseph STOUT, Plainfield Township (both under age 14):
next friend: Deal BOWER
children: John
Christian
guardian: for both children—Christian STOUT

Guardians for minor children of Casper RUMMAGE, Lower Smithfield Township—motion of Robert TRAILL:
children: Ludwig, over age 14................................guardian: Peter KACHLEIN, Esq.
Elisabeth, over age 14.............................guardian: Peter KACHLEIN, Esq.
remaining 4, all under age 14:
Jacob
Christina
Mary
Magdalena
guardian: for younger 4 children—Jacob STROWD

Guardians for minor children of Henry KRATZER (both over age 14)—motion of John CURRIE, Esq.:
children: Hannah..................................................guardian: Simon DREISBACH
Philip....................................................guardian: John OVERLEY

**Court on 23 December 1778, continued:**

Guardians for minor children of Philip FOX, Bethlehem Township (all under age 14)—motion of Robert TRAILL:

| | | |
|---|---|---|
| children: | Conrad | guardian: Simon DREISBACH, Esq. |
| | Peter | guardian: Simon DREISBACH, Esq. |
| | Anna Maria | guardian: Peter FOX |
| | Maria Margaret | guardian: Peter FOX |

Estate of John JENNINGS, Town of Northampton—return of sale:

widow: Anna
sold to: William GRINDING of City of Philadelphia, gentleman

**Court on 24 December 1778**
**Justices, the Esquires: not named**

Guardian for minor children of Andrew SLEPPY, Bethlehem Township (both under age 14):

next friend: Jacob RHOADS
children: Katherine
Susanna
guardian: for both children—William HENRY

Estate of Rudolph PETER, Heidelberg Township—auditors' report and distribution:

executor: John HUNSACHER
widow: Susanna
4 children

Estate of Henry ATEN—motion of John CURRIE, Esq. for new writ to be issued—only 11 jurors had signed the partition inquest:

eldest son: Henry, petitioner

Estate of Andrew LINE—motion of John CURRIE, Esq. for new writ to be issued:

widow: was not satisfied with earlier valuation
only son: William

Guardian for Leonard, over age 14, son of William BECK, Moore Township—motion of Collison READ, Esq.:

guardian: Casper ERB

**Court on 8 February 1779**
**Justices, the Esquires: Thomas SILLYMAN, John ARNDT, Robert LEVERS**

Estate of William BECK, Moore Township, two tracts—request inquest:

land: 1) 100 acres bounded by Paul FLICK and Philip DRUM
2) 60 acres adjoining the other tract
widow: deceased since husband's death
6 children: Frederick, eldest son
others not named

**Court on 8 February 1779, continued:**

New guardians for minor children of Henry DEAL, Moore Township:
petitioner: Adam LECHNER, Moore Township
widow: Mary
children: Margaret, over age 14..............................new guardian: Paul FLICK
Frederich, under age 14...........................new guardian: Jost DREISBACH
guardians: former—appointed on 22 December 1773—William BECK, now deceased, and Philip DRUM—"Through age and infirmities," declines

**Court on 17 March 1779**
**Justices, the Esquires: Thomas SILLYMAN, Jacob MORRY, Samuel REA, John ARNDT, William McNAIR, Peter MYER, Jacob HORNER**

Guardians for minor children of Daniel WERNER, Jr., Penn Township (all under age 14)—motion of Robert TRAILL, Esq.:
children: Elisabeth
Sarah
Bathia
Edward
guardian: for all 4 children—Daniel WERNER, their grandfather

New guardian for 3 minor children of Henry MILLER, the younger, Lower Saucon Township—motion of Robert TRAILL, Esq.:
children: Henry
Peter
Catherine
guardian: former—appointed 24 September last, Anthony LERGH who declined
new—Abraham ARNDT

New guardian for 3 minor children of Henry MILLER, the elder, Williams Twp.—motion of Robert TRAILL:
children: Philip
Peter
Elisabeth
guardian: former—Nicholas BEST
new—Jacob SHOEMAKER

Guardian for minor children of Peter EDDINGER, Lower Saucon Township—motion of John CURRIE, Esq.:
children—the first 3 over age 14:
Conrad
William
Abraham
Frederich, under age 14
guardian: for all 4 children—Conrad REASLEY

Guardians for minor children of David RHOAD, Bethlehem Township (all under age 14):
widow: Elisabeth
4 children: Adam.....................................................guardian: Ulrich HAUSER
Casper....................................................guardian: Ulrich HAUSER
John.......................................................guardian: Conrad GERMANTOWN
David.....................................................guardian: Conrad GERMANTOWN

**Court on 17 March 1779, continued:**

Estate of Henry ATEN, Mt. Bethel Township—report of inquest by Sheriff Jonas HARTZEL, Esq.:
widow
6 children: Henry, eldest son—accepted the land
securities: John MACK and James CAULY, both of Mt. Bethel Township
12 men:by oath and affirmation—John NELSON, Elisha BARTON, David EARY (AYERS), Thomas CONLY (CONALLY), Robert RITCHY (RICHART), Francis HALBERT, Michael HESS, Christian BENTER, George REYMEL, Robert BEER, Asa EVERETT, James OLIPHANT

Estate of George DEEDTZ, died about 1 year ago, Chestnuthill Township, two tracts—request inquest:
land: total of 75 acres bounded by vacant land and Samuel ROLLINS
widow
8 children: George, eldest son
others not named

Estate of Henry KRATZER, died about 4 months ago, Lower Saucon Township—request inquest:
land: 140 acres bounded by Jacob SLOUGH, Reinhart LAUBAGH, Rudolph OVERLEY, Frederich LAUBAGH, and Ulrich BRINKER
widow
7 children: Henry, eldest son
others not named

New guardians for minor children of Philip FOX, Bethlehem Township:
widow: Sarah—said that last December guardians were appointed but they were not proper persons to be guardians
guardians: former—Simon DREISBACH and Peter FOX (also administrators of estate)
new—Matthias KENIG and Jacob HARTZEL

Estate of William BECK, Moore Township—report of inquest by Sheriff Jonas HARTZEL, Esq.:
6 children: Frederich, eldest son—accepted the land
others not named
securities: Paul FLICK and George JACOBIE, both of Moore Township
12 men:by oath or affirmation—Timothy READ, James ALLISON, John LERCH, Paul KNAUS, Henry BARTHOLOMEW, Jacob BOGER (BOGART), Michael APP, Adam TREISBACH (DREISBACH). William CARR, John CLEPPINGER, George KOCH, John SNIDER (SNYDER)

**Court on 18 March 1779**
**Justices, the Esquires: not named**

Estate of John CHRISTMAN, Upper Milford Township—request sale:
land: 40 acres bounded by Herman NIECE, Michael ANDREW, and Andrew HENRY
administrators: Jacob CHRISTMAN and George CHRISTMAN

Guardian for Peter, over age 14, minor son of Nicholas RIPPLE, Easton:
guardian: Peter KACHLEIN, Esq.

**Court on 18 March 1779, continued:**

Guardian for Catherine, under age 14, only child of John CHRISTMAN, Upper Milford Township:
- widow: Catherine
- guardian: William SHAFER

New guardian for 2 minor children of Benjamin REAGEL:
- guardian: former—Peter SEAN—in very bad state of health
  new—Christopher WAGGONER

Estate of George RYMER, Upper Milford Township—request inquest:
- land: 60 acres bounded by Nicholas STALER, Christian RYMER, Henry HARTZEL, Jacob TROUP, and Stephen TALMAN
- widow
- 7 children: George, eldest son
  others not named

**Court on 25 March 1779**
**Justices, the Esquires: Thomas SILLYMAN, John ARNDT, Abraham BERLIN**

Guardian for Sibilla WALVERT, age 26 years, daughter of Peter WALVERT, now deceased:
- petitioner: Matthias LUDWIG, her step-father, Macungie Township—Sibilla was born deaf and dumb and could not care for herself
- guardian: George WALVERT, her brother

**Court on 26 April 1779**
**Justices, the Esquires: Robert LEVERS, Jacob MORRY, Frederick LIMBACH**

Estate of Casper KEPLER, Lower Saucon Township (had a will, date 1 November 1770)—request sale:
- land: 55 acres adjoining to Simon Jacob DEEL and Jacob Ralph SNYDER
- administrator: John ARNDT, Esq.
- executor: widow, Margaret—now deceased
- administrators: Peter LEITH, alias LLOYD

New guardians for minor children of Philip FOX, Bethlehem Township:
- widow: Sarah
- children: Anna Maria............new guardian: Matthais KENIG
  Mary Margaret............new guardian: Matthais KENIG
  Conrad............new guardian: Henry RHONE
  Peter............new guardian: Henry RHONE
- guardians: former—Matthais KENIG—unwilling to be guardian until a new guardian replaced Jacob HARTZELL; he also desired separate appointments, not joint guardianship; Jacob HARTZEL declined guardianship

**Court on 29 May 1779**
**Justices, the Esquires: Robert LEVERS, Peter TREXLER, Jacob MORRY**

Guardian for John, under age 14, minor child of Peter UHL, Salisbury Township:
- left widow and one child
- guardian: Francis RHOAD, Salisbury Township

**Court on 29 May 1779, continued:**

Estate of George KNAUS, Whitehall Township—follow-up on report of appraisal made in March by Sheriff John JENNINGS:

| | |
|---|---|
| widow | |
| 7 children: | George Frederick, eldest son—took no share because he had been deeded the land in the lifetime of his father and, thus, had already received his share; he did accept the land |
| | Philip |
| | Charlotte |
| | Catherine |
| | Susanna |
| | Margaret |
| | Elisabeth |
| securities: | Francis RHOAD and Adam TORNEY |
| 12 men:not named here | |

**Court on 23 June 1779**

**Justices, the Esquires: Thomas SILLYMAN, Jacob MORRY, John ARNDT, Samuel REA, William McNAIR**

New guardians for minor children of Felix ARNER, Whitehall Township (all under age 14):

| | |
|---|---|
| petitioner: | Peter ANTHONY, step-father of children |
| children: | Felix |
| | William |
| | Dorothy |
| guardian: | former—Daniel SHNYDER, now deceased |
| | new—Joseph BALLIET |

Guardians for 7 minor children of Frederick FRUTCHIE, Lower Saucon Township (were other children):

| | | |
|---|---|---|
| petitioner: | John GADERT, grandfather of children | |
| children: | John, over age 14 | guardian: Peter KUCHLEIN. Esq. |
| | William, over age 14 | guardian: Lewis KNAUS |
| | the remaining 5 children all under age 14: | |
| | Jacob | guardian: Anthony LERCH, Jr. |
| | Matthais | guardian: Anthony LERCH, Jr. |
| | Peter | guardian: Anthony LERCH, Jr. |
| | Anna Mary | guardian: Adam KUKUT |
| | Elisabeth | guardian: Adam KUKUT |

**Court on 24 June 1779**

**Justices, the Esquires: not named**

Guardians for minor children of John HARTZELL, died about 2 years ago, Allen Township:

| | | |
|---|---|---|
| widow: | Barbara | |
| 5 children: | Elizabeth, over age 14 | guardian: Matthias KING |
| | remaining 4 children all under age 14: | |
| | Adam | |
| | Mary | |
| | Susanna | |
| | Leah | |
| guardians: | for younger 4 children—Adam EDELMAN, Lower Saucon Township | |

**Court on 24 June 1779, continued:**

New guardian for Benjamin, under age 14, minor son of Benjamin REEGEL, Lower Saucon Township:
- petitioner: John HAAS, grandfather
- guardian: former—appointed in March, Christopher WAGNER, Esq., refused to serve; new—Michael LAWALL

Complaint of John HASS, grandfather of minor children of Benjamin REEGEL (were other children)—guardians would not pay allowances for children without direction from the court:
- children: Elisabeth REEGEL, age 6 years
  - Benjamin REEGEL, age 1 ½ years
- guardians: Michael LAWALL and Daniel BEIDLEMAN are ordered to pay 40 pounds per year each to the widow

Estate of William BECK, Moore Township—request inquest:
- land: 38 acres 24 perches adjoining to Casper ERB and others
- 6 children: Frederich, eldest son
  - William
  - George
  - Leonard, under age 21
  - Susanna, wife of Casper ALTMAN
  - Eva Elisabetha, wife of Martin ESHBACH

Estate of George DEEDTZ, Chestnuthill Township—report on inquest by Sheriff Jonas HARTZEL, Esq. (Only the valuation was given; nothing was said about the distribution or an heir accepting the estate.):
- 12 men:by oath or affirmation—John GREGORY, John SHERBONTY, Adam SERBER, Nicholas RAMSTEIN, Henry SIGLIN, Henry SHUPP, William SERFAS, George GUNGEL, Lawrence FISHER, John MOYER, Philip KRESSY, Conrad KRESSY

Guardians for minor children of Melgert SIDEL, Heidelberg Township (both over age 14):
- children: Margaret................................................guardian: John KRUM
  - Catherine...............................................guardian: William HOLWIG

**Court on 23 September 1779**
**Justices, the Esquires: Thomas SILLYMAN, Jacob MOREE, Samuel REA, Benjamin DUPUI, William McNAIR, Matthias PROPST**

Estate of Samuel SEELY, Lower Smithfield Township, two tracts—request sale:
- land: 1) 200 acres bounded by Benjamin HANNAH, William JAYNE, and Solomon BUNNEL
  - 2) 300 acres bounded by James BROOKES, Nicholas DUPUI, and others
- administrator: John SEELY

Estate of Nicholas WOLF, Williams Township—request inquest:
- land: 160 acres adjoining Adam MANY, John ECKER, and Jacob WILHELM
- 3 children: Peter
  - Margaret
  - Mary, wife of Casper KLUTTER

**Court on 23 September 1779, continued:**

Estate of Peter ERRET, Bethlehem Township—request inquest:

land: 150 acres bounded by Adam RHOAD, William Henry LAWALT, and Ulrich SLEPPY

4 children, all over age 21:

George, eldest son

others not named

Guardian for 2 minor children of George WEAVER, Lower Saucon Township, also legatees of Casper KEESLER, their grandfather, also deceased (both over age 14) (were other children):

children: John

Susanna

guardian: for both children—John BOYER

Guardians for 2 minor children of Daniel TURNEY, Whitehall Township (both under age 14):

widow: Eve

2 children: Peter.....................................................guardian: George Frederich KNAUSE

Catherine...............................................guardian: Peter GOOD, Jr.

William CONGLETON, a soldier requesting 1/2-pay:

court ordered Lieutenant of the County, Lt. John WETZELL, Esq., to so pay

**Court on 23 December 1779**

**Justices, the Esquires: Thomas SILLYMAN, John ARNDT, Samuel REA, John BYLE, William McNAIR, Abraham BERLIN**

Guardian for Aaron, over age 14, minor child and eldest son of Aaron DUPUI, Lower Smithfield Township:

guardian: Jacob STROWD, Lower Smithfield Township

Guardians for minor children of Philip SCHNYDER, Bethlehem Township:

widow: Elisabeth

children: the oldest 3 are over age 21

John

Margaret

Conrad

Elisabeth, over age 14.............................guardian: Matthias KENIG

Catharine, over age 14............................guardian: Matthias KENIG

the youngest 3 were all under age 14:

Christina

Philip

Eve

guardians: for youngest 3 children—Peter SEIP and Matthias KENIG

Estate of Samuel SEELY, two tracts in Lower Smithfield Township—return of sale:

administrator: John SEELY

sold to: Peter KACHLINE, Esq., Easton

**Court on 23 December 1779, continued:**

Estate of Peter ERRET, Bethlehem Township, 150 acres—report of inquest by Sheriff Jonas HARTZEL, Esq.:
- 4 children: George, eldest son—accepted the land
- securities: Matthias PEIFFER and Conrad KOCHER
- 12 men:by oath or affirmation—John SENTEE, Casper RITTER, Christian NEWMAN, Michael HUBER, George PIFER, Philip HERTZEL, Frederick SAYLER (SAILER), Henry ROHN, Conrad KOCHER, Gotlieb DORNBLESER, John BUSS, Jost KOCHER

**Court on 23 March 1780**
**Justices, the Esquires: Thomas SILLYMAN, John ARNDT, Samuel REA, William McNAIR**

Guardian for 2 minor children of Jacob WEISS, Lower Saucon Township (both under 14) (were other children):
- children: Jacob
  - Catherine
- guardian: for both children—John Philip BAHL

Guardian for 2 minor children of Jacob WEISS, Lower Saucon Township (both over 14) (were other children):
- children: John.......................................................guardian: Jesse JONES
  - Matthais.................................................guardian: John George LUDWIG

Guardians for minor children of Adam FEHLER, Lower Saucon Township:
- widow: Dorothea
- 5 children: older 4 were all over age 14:
  - Dorothy...................................................guardian: Philip BEAHM
  - Anna Margaret.......................................guardian: Philip BEAHM
  - Ann Mary...............................................guardian: Daniel BEIDLEMAN
  - John Adam ............................................guardian: Daniel BEIDLEMAN
  - John George, under age 14......................guardian: Daniel BEIDLEMAN

Estate of Philip KEBLER, died about 18 years ago, Macungie Township—request inquest:
- land: 200 acres bounded by Casper WISTAR, George CURR, John TREXLER, & David SHUTT
- widow: since remarried
- 2 children: George, eldest son
  - other not named

Estate of Conrad FOX, died about 15 months ago, Bethlehem Township—request inquest:
- land: 110 acres adjacent to Henry CRAMER and Philip FOX
- widow
- 5 living children:
  - Peter
  - Nicholas
  - Elisabeth, wife of Mr. KRATZER
  - Anna Maria, wife of Simon DREISBACH
  - Catherine, wife of Conrad FOGLEMAN
- 4 grandchildren, children of deceased son Philip:
  - Conrad
  - Peter
  - Anna Maria
  - Margaret

**Court on 25 March 1780**

**Justices, the Esquires: Robert LEVERS, John ARNDT, Abraham BERLIN**

Guardian for Catherine, over age 14, minor child of Nicholas RIPPLE, Easton (were other children):
guardian: Peter KUCKLEIN, Esq.

**Court on 22 June 1780**
**Justices, the Esquires: Thomas SILLYMAN, Nicholas DUPUI, Jacob MORRY, William McNAIR, Peter MYER, Abraham BERLIN, John BYLE**

Guardians for minor children of Samuel MOOSICK, died in March last, Whitehall Township (both over age 14):
widow: Dorothy
2 children: Margaret............................................guardian: Leonard STENINGER, Whitehall Twp.
Samuel..............................................guardian: George HOFFMAN, Macungie Twp.
(Samuel was unable to choose his own guardian, "...from weakness in his understanding....")

John TAYLOR, Mt. Bethel Township, a soldier requesting 1/2-pay:
John produced a petition dated 1 May 1779 stating that he was a soldier in Cap. Timothy JAYNE'S Company of the Flying Camp. He was taken prisoner at the surrender of Ft. Washington. His health was greatly impaired through the suffering he endured and was now incapable of getting his bread by labor.
Court ordered Lieutenant of the County, Samuel REA, Esq. to so pay.

Estate of Frederich SHOEMAKER—complaint about administration account:
petitioner: Jacob SHOEMAKER on behalf of himself and other heirs
widow: Magdalena, administratrix, now wife of Frederich SHECHLER—accused of leaving out items in the report; she was ordered to appear in September

**Court on 23 June 1780**
**Justices, the Esquires: not named**

Estate of Philip KEBLER—report of inquest by Sheriff Jonas HARTZEL, Esq.:
eldest son: George KEBLER, did not appear to accept the land—remained under advisement

**Court on 21 September 1780**
**Justices, the Esquires: Thomas SILLYMAN, Jacob MORRY, William McNAIR, Peter MYER, Abraham BERLIN, John BYLE**

Guardians for minor children of John EVERETT, Penn Township (both over age 14):
children: John
Thomas
guardian: for both children—John HOSSE, Bethlehem Township

**Court on 1 March 1781**
**Justices, the Esquires: Robert LEVERS, Jacob MORRY, John BYLE**

Estate of Jacob SHYMER, died some years ago, Lower Saucon Township, 2 tracts—request inquest:
land: total of 200 acres adjoining to Anthony OBERLEY, Matthias KETNER, Teeter HELLER, Jacob CHRISTMAN, John OBERLEY, and Lehigh River
widow: since married to Edward SHYMER
3 children: Peter, eldest son (others not named)

New guardian for Samuel, now over age 14, minor child and one son of Jacob SHYMER, Lower Saucon Township:

guardians: former—appointed while he was under age 14, Rudolph OBERLEY and Gratzius LERCH, one of whom was now dead
new—Frederick LAUBACH, Lower Saucon Township

**Court on 22 March 1781**
**Justices, the Esquires: Nicholas DUPUI, Jacob MORRY, Thomas SILLYMAN, William McNAIR, Lewis STACKER, John BYLE, Abraham BERLIN**

Guardians for minor children of Henry BUCHACKER, Upper Saucon Township (both over age 14):

petitioner: Ludwig KOCH, step-father of children
children: Magdalena..............................................guardian: John APPLE
Mary Elisabeth.......................................guardian: Philip BAHL

Estate of Jacob SHYMER, Lower Saucon Township, two tracts of 200 acres total—report of inquest by Sheriff Jonas HARTZEL, Esq.:

widow
3 children: Peter SHIMER—held one tract of 131 acres
other two children—held other tract of 97 acres 90 perches and improvements:
Samuel, under age 21
John, under age 21
securities: none needed
12 men:all by oath—Henry LAWALL, John SENTEE, Matthias KING, Philip ODENWELDER, Conrad OMMENSETLER, John OBERLING, Adam KUKER, Joseph RICHARDS, Jacob SLOUGH, Anthony OBERLING, George MICHAEL, Andrew ULLY

Estate of Conrad FOX, Bethlehem Township, 110 acres—report of inquest by Sheriff Jonas HARTZEL, Esq.:

widow
6 children: Peter, eldest son—accepted the land
others not named
security: Simon DREISBACH
12 men:by oath and affirmation—Michael LAWALL, John SENTEE, Jacob HARTZELL, Adam ROAD, George MICHAEL, Nicholas YOUNG, Michael HUBER, Philip REESER, George BECK, Jacob ESSIG, Conrad BAKER, Jacob MEYER

Estate of Jacob BILDHAUSE, died about 21 years ago, Upper Milford Township—request inquest:

land: 130 acres bounded by John HAESTAND, Michael BISHOP, David ROTHROCK, and Jacob ROTHROCK
widow
3 children: Jacob, eldest son
others not named

Estate of Marks WANNEMACHER, died 3 years ago, Lynn Township, 2 tracts—request inquest:

land: total of 180 acres bounded by Andrew SECHLER, Barnet FULLWEILER, Martin WERTMAN, and Jacob WANNEMACHER, Sr.
widow: Catherine
4 children: Jacob, eldest son
others not named

Guardian for Daniel, over age 14, minor child of Marks WANNEMACHER (were other children):
guardian: Frederich SECHLER

New guardian for Mary Barbara, minor child of George HAFFIN, Heidelberg Township:
guardian: former—Casper SNERR, appointed years ago, about to move out of county
new—Conrad RETTER

Guardians for minor children of Samuel MILLER, deceased, who were also left a legacy by their paternal grandfather who died lately:
petitioner: Alexander MILLER, Mt. Bethel Township, brother of the deceased
6 children: Alexander, over age 14
John, over age 14
the remaining 4 children all under age 14:
Martha
Samuel
Sarah
Mary
guardian: for all 6 children—Alexander MILLER, their uncle

Guardians for minor children of John LATTIMORE, Allen Township (were other children):
administrator: Robert LATTIMORE, Esq.
children: Arthur, over age 14..................................guardian: William McNAIR, Esq.
William, over age 14..............................guardian: John RALSTON, Esq.
John, under age 14..................................guardian: John RALSTON, Esq.

Guardian for John SHIMER, over age 14, minor son of Jacob SHYMER, Lower Saucon Township:
guardian: John BYLE, Esq.

Estate of Jacob SHYMER, Lower Saucon Township—request audit:
petitioners: Frederich LAUBACH, guardian of one child, and Peter SHYMER, eldest son
auditors: Jacob MORRY, Esq., Jesse JONES, Philip BEAHM

**Court on 26 April 1781**
**Justices, the Esquires: Jacob MORRY, Thomas HARTMAN, Jacob HORNER, Peter MEYER**

Rev. John ROSEBOROUGH, a chaplain of the 3rd Battalion of Militia for Northampton County—he was killed January 1777 in Trenton by British Army while in service to the United States:
widow: Jane—requested support, "having suffered much thro the Depreciation of the Continental Money...."
5 small children
court ordered the Lieutenant of the County, Samuel REA, Esq., to pay her 40 pounds Pennsylvania State money for relief and support

Guardians for minor children of William STRAUP, Salisbury Township (both under age 14):
administrator: Daniel HURLOCHER
widow
2 children: William
Mary
guardian: for both children—Daniel TROXEL, Whitehall Township

**Court on 26 April 1781, continued:**

Guardians for minor children of Michael LOWRY, Whitehall Township:

petitioner: Godfrey LOWRY, nearest kin

4 children: Jacob, over age 14....................................guardian: Jacob SHRIVER
Margaret, over age 14..............................guardian: Adam REBER
Elizabeth, under age 14...........................guardian: Jacob SHRIVER
Catherine, under age 14...........................guardian: Adam REBER

George KOCHER, a soldier from Penn Township, "in September last in an Engagement with the Savages in Neskopeck Valley, ...was unfortunately killed;..."—family's request for relief:

widow: Magdalena
2 small children
Court ordered the Lieutenant of the County, Samuel REA, Esq., to pay them 7 pounds, 10 shillings Pennsylvania State Money.

James SCOBY, Whitehall Township, a soldier, "in September last in the Service of the Militia of this County, and in the Engagement with the Savages in Nescopeck Valley had the misfortune to be taken or killed by the Enemy...."—family's request for relief, "...on the Remonstrance of the Overseers of the Poor and Divers of the Freeholders of Whitehall Township...":

widow: Catherine
5 small children
Court ordered the Lieutenant of the County, Samuel REA, Esq., to pay 7 pounds, 10 shillings Pennsylvania State Money.

Guardians for minor children of Christian MILLER, died about 2 years ago:

widow: Mary, now wife of John SWARTZ, Lynn Township

7 children: John, over age 14.............................guardian: Jacob MICKLEY, Whitehall Twp.
Susanna, over age 14.......................guardian: Jacob MICKLEY, Whitehall Twp.
the remaining five children all under age 14:
Elisabeth.........................................guardian: Christian SNIDER, Heidelberg Twp.
Peter...............................................guardian: Christian SNIDER, Heidelberg Twp.
Daniel.............................................guardian: Christian SNIDER, Heidelberg Twp.
Catherine........................................guardian: Nicholas BACHMAN, Weisenberg Twp.
Christian.........................................guardian: Nicholas BACHMAN, Weisenberg Twp.

William CONGLESON, a soldier who was awarded ½ pay on 30 September 1779 but had not drawn it, requested that the court grant him further allowance—awarded 10 pounds, PA State money

**Court on 20 June 1781**

**Justices, the Esquires: Thomas SILLYMAN, Jacob MORRY, William McNAIR, Thomas HARTMAN, Benjamin DUPUI, Abraham BERLIN**

Estate of John LATTIMORE, Allen Township, two tracts—request inquest:

land: total of 192 3/4 acres adjoining John WYNN, Joseph HORNER, & Mary LATTIMORE
widow: Elizabeth
4 children: Robert, eldest son
Arthur
William
John

**Court on 21 June 1781**

**Justices, the Esquires: not named**

New guardian for Susanna BILDHAUSE, under age 14, over her estate on Upper Milford Township:
petitioner: Jacob ERDMAN, step-father, Springfield Township, Bucks County
guardian: former—Jacob ERDMAN
new—John OHLEWEIN, Upper Milford Township

Guardian for George, over age 14, minor son of Felix HOOVER, Salisbury Township:
guardian: Thomas McWHORTER

Guardian for minor children of Nicholas MYER, Whitehall Township (both under age 14) (were other children):
widow: Margaret
children: David....................................................guardian: Jacob MECHLEY
Margaret................................................guardian: Michael COLP

Estate of Nicholas MYER, Whitehall Township, 2 tracts—request inquest:
land: total of 190 acres bounded by Philip Jacob SHREIVER, Jacob MECHLEY, Jacob HARTMAN, and Lehigh River
widow
5 children: John, eldest son
others not named

Estate of Mark WANNAMACHER, Lynn Township, 180 acres—report on inquest by Sheriff Jonas HARTZEL:
widow
4 children: Jacob, eldest son—accepted the land
others not named
securities: Philip ANTHONY and John ANTHONY
12 men:by oath and affirmation—Philip ANTHONY, Philip BROPST, William MOYER (Wilhelm MYER), Conrad BILMAN, John (Johannes) SMITH, Henry HALLER, Andres SECHLER, John BRINER, Andrew MOYER, Adam CREITZ, Engel MOYER, Philip SITLER (SETLER)

Estate of Jacob BILDHOUSE, Upper Milford Township, 130 acres—report on inquest by Sheriff Jonas HARTZEL, Esq.:
widow
3 children: Jacob, eldest son—accepted the land
others not named
securities: Nicholas KOOKEN and John OTT
12 men:by oath and affirmation—John NEWCOMER, John STAHL (STALL), John KOOKEN, Michael HELLIGASS, Jacob HUBER, Adam ENGLEMAN, Henry OTT, Nicholas KOOKEN, George RUCH, Christopher OTT, Adam RODENBERGER, John SHOUT

**Court on 22 June 1781**
**Justices, the Esquires: not named**

Review of circumstances of Mrs. Jane ROSEBOROUGH, widow of Rev. John ROSEBOROUGH, chaplain:
the Lieutenant of the County was to pay her 15 pounds

**Court on 20 September 1781**
**Justices, the Esquires: Nicholas DUPUI, Jacob MORRY, Thomas SILLYMAN, William McNAIR,**

**Samuel REA, Frederick LEIMBACH, Abraham BERLIN**

Estate of Nicholas MYER, Whitehall Township, 190 acres—report of inquest by Sheriff Jonas HARTZELL:
widow
5 children: John, eldest son—accepted the land
others not named
securities: Jacob SHRYVER, Whitehall Township, and Daniel SWARTZ, Allen Township
12 men:by oath and affirmation—Peter BURKHALDER, Jacob SHREIBER, Jacob KERN, Peter BISEL, Daniel SWARTZ, Peter KERN, Wendel HAVER, Peter DESHLER, Adam MILLER, Adam DESHLER, Henry FOUST, George HAAS

Estate of Michael LOWRY, died about 4 years ago, Whitehall Township, 2 tracts—request inquest:
land: total of 80 acres bounded by Jacob MILLER, Philip KNAPPENBERGER, and Michael NEIHART
widow: deceased since death of husband
9 children: Godfried, eldest son
others not named

Estate of Jacob LEYABERGER, Lehigh Township—request inquest:
land: 200 acres bounded by Henry SHEFFER, Conrad SILVIUS, Charles GRASS, and John SEAGER
widow
6 children: Abraham, eldest son
others not named

Estate of Timothy McCARTY, died about 9 years ago, Allen Township—request inquest:
land: 116 1/4 acres bounded by the late Arthur LATTIMORE, William ATTEN, Samuel BROWN, and James McCORD late vacant
widow
7 children: William, eldest son (others not named)

Estate of Henry SMITH, died about 9 years ago, Heidelberg Township, 3 tracts—request inquest:
land: 1) 150 acres in Heidelberg Twp. bounded by Conrad LENTZ, Jacob WEAVER, and Peter MEYER, Esq.
2) 30 acres in Heidelberg Twp. bounded by George SMETHER and vacant land
3) 300 acres in Penn Twp. bounded by John KISTNER, John ZEANER, & vacant land
widow: since remarried
6 children: Christian, eldest son
others not named

Guardian for Hannah, over age 14, minor child of Martin HARBOS, Moore Township:
guardian: Daniel SHWARY, Allen Township

Guardians for minor children of Henry WETZEL, Macungie Township:
widow: has possession of the land
children: Catherine
John, under age 14..................................guardian: William HAINES
Jacob, under age 14.................................guardian: Peter MATTERN
Jeremiah, under age 14............................guardian: Peter MATTERN

**Court on 15 December 1781**

**Justices, the Esquires: John ARNDT, Thomas SILLYMAN, Abraham BERLIN**

Estate of Benjamin RIEGEL, Lower Saucon Township—request sale:

administrators: Johannes ROTHROCK and John HAASE—have sold all moveable property but are still in debt, "...by the Depreciation of the Paper Money, and the heavy Taxes...."

widow: Barbara, administratrix

Estate of George KEMBLE, died about 1774 (had a will):

daughter: Eleanor—was bequeathed 115 pounds to be paid to her at age 21, the interest to be paid to her at age 18

guardians and executors:

Thomas MACHENESS and Nicholas GARRISON—Thomas soon after his appointment, left for England and never returned

Eleanore turned 18 in 1778 and did receive the interest due her but had received no support since. She was now upwards of 20 years and needed more funds. Nicholas GARRISON was cited to appear on 20 December to report.

**Court on 20 December 1781**

**Justices, the Esquires: Thomas SILLYMAN, William McNAIR, Thomas HARTMAN, Lewis STACKER, James VANAKEN, Abraham BERLIN, John BYLE**

Estate of Frederich SHOEMAKER, died without issue—request audit:

widow: Magdalena, administratrix, now wife of Frederich SHECKLER, Moore Township

auditors: Simon TREISBACH, Conrad KREIDER, Neigal GRAY

Estate of Henry SMITH, Heidelberg Township, 150 acres—report on inquest by Sheriff Jonas HARTZELL:

widow

6 children: Christian, eldest son—accepted the land

others not named

securities: Peter MEYER, Esq., Heidelberg Township, and Henry HARTMAN, Lowhill Township

12 men: by oath and affirmation—Michael OHL, Henry NAFF, William MYER, Jacob WEAVER, Adam CREUTZ, Adam GERMAN, John KRUM, Peter MISSEMER, Abraham SHELHAMER, Christian SCHNEIDER, Conrad RIEDIG, Ulrich NEFF

Estate of Michael LOWRY, Whitehall Township, 80 acres—report on inquest by Sheriff Jonas HARTZELL:

9 children: Godfried, eldest son—accepted the land

others not named

securities: Frederick NEYHARD and George FLICKINGER, both of Whitehall Township

12 men: by oath and affirmation—Jacob MILLER, Peter KERN, Philip KNAPEBERGER (KNAPPENBERGER), Peter NEIHART (NAUHART), Martin GRAFF (GROFF), Stophel KERN, Martin MICKELY, David NEYHARD (NEIHART), Jacob LAUP (LAUB), George FLIKENGER, Frederick NEYHARDT, Peter MEYER

**End Volume D**

**Court on 20 December 1781 (cont.)**
**Justices, the Esquires: Thomas SILLYMAN, William McNAIR, Thomas HARTMAN, Lewis STACKER, James VANAKEN, Abraham BERLIN, John BILE**

Estate of Benjamin RIEGEL, Lower Saucon Township—order to sell:
- widow: Barbara
- petitioner: Johannes ROTHROCK
- administrators: the petitioner, John HAASE and the widow

Estate of Jacob LEYABERGER, Lehigh Township—report of inquest by Sheriff Jonas HARTZELL:
- land: 200 acres bounded by Henry SHEFFER, Conrad SYLVIUS, Charles GRESS, and John SEAGER
- widow
- 6 children: Abraham, eldest son—accepted the land
  others not named
- securities: Henry STRAUSE and Henry SHAFER, both of Lehigh Township
- 12 men: by oath and affirmation—Henry STROUSE (STRAUSS), Bernhard KUNTZ, Michael NEYHARD, Henry SHEFFER, John BALLIET, Peter ANTHONY, Frederick NEYHARD, John SEGER, Peter NEYHARD, Jacob ROAD, Tobias GILDNER, Dewald SHEFFER

Estate of Timothy McCARTY, Allen Township—report of inquest by Sheriff Jonas HARTZELL, Esq.:
- land: patented land, 116 1/4 acres, bounded by Arthur LATTIMORE, deceased, William ALLEN, Samuel BROWN, James McCORD
- widow
- 7 children: William, eldest son—accepted the land
  others not named
- securities: George STECKER and Thomas GRIMES, both of Forks Township
- 12 men: James CLYD, Robert BROWN, James HEMPHILL, William KERR, Jr., James KERR, John HUNTER, William KERR, Sr., John SENTEE, Philip SCHLOUCH, Andreas RANTS, George PIFFER, Jacob DECH

Estate of Frederick SHOEMAKER—request audit:
- petitioner: Frederick SHECHLER, Moore Township
- widow: Magdalena, now wife of the petitioner
- children: no issue
- auditors: Simon DREISBACH, Conrad KREIDER, Neigal GRAY

**Court of 19 February 1782**
**Justices, the Esquires: Robert LEVERS, John ARNDT, Abraham BERLIN**

Guardians for minor children of George HOMES (all under age 14):
- children: Barbara
  Eve
  Henry
- guardian: for all 3 children—Samuel SEGER

**Court of 19 February 1782, continued:**

Estate of George HOMES, Whitehall Township along Lehigh River, died sometime ago—request inquest:

| | |
|---|---|
| land: | 70 acres adjoining Adam SERFAS, Conrad LEYSINGRING, Martin GROVES, & river |
| widow: | Barbara |
| 6 children: | Conrad, eldest son |
| | Elisabeth |
| | Jacob |
| | Barbara |
| | Eve |
| | Henry |

**Court on 21 March 1782**

**Justices, the Esquires: Jacob MORRY, Benjamin DEPUI, Jacob HORNER, Thomas HARTMAN, Lewis STACKER, John BILE**

Estate of Benjamin RIEGEL—return of sale:

| | |
|---|---|
| administrators: | John ROTHROCK and John HAAS |
| sold to: | Jacob KRAM, Lower Saucon Township |

Estate of George STEININGER, Macungie Township, two tracts—request inquest:

| | |
|---|---|
| land: | 1) 194 acres adjoining Adam SMITH, Melchior SMITH and others |
| | 2) 10 acres adjoining Valentine MILLER, John FOGEL, and others |
| widow: | now deceased |
| 6 children: | George, eldest son |
| | Christian, under age 21 |
| | Anna Maria, wife of Peter SMITH |
| | Anna Margaretha, wife of Dewalt KOONS |
| | Maria Elizabetha, under age 21 |
| | John, deceased since his father's & mother's deaths while still under age 21, single |

Estate of Jacob WEISS, Lower Saucon Township—request inquest:

| | |
|---|---|
| land: | 100 acres bounded by Jacob LUDWIG, Adam BITSCH, and others |
| widow: | |
| 6 children: | John, eldest son |
| | Jacob |
| | Matthias |
| | Elizabeth |
| | Magdalena |
| | Catherine |

Estate of William GABLE, Penn Township, died about 7 years ago—request inquest:

| | |
|---|---|
| land: | 250 acres adjoining Jeremiah WARDER, Michael OHL, and Joseph CUSTARD |
| widow: | now remarried |
| 7 children: | Joseph, eldest son |
| | Mary |
| | Catherine |
| | Thomas |
| | Israel |
| | Barnet |
| | Elizabeth |

**Court on 21 March 1782, continued:**

Estate of John BEER, Lehigh Township, 3 contiguous tracts—request inquest:

land: total of 250 acres, adjoining Martin SINGLE, Dewalt FAHRINGER, and others
widow: Anna
8 children: Amos
Enoch
Adam
John
Moses, died in lifetime of father, left 4 children, all minors:
Samuel
David
Jacob
Rachel
Samuel, died in lifetime of father, left 2 children, both under age 14:
Ann
Cleora
Elisabeth, wife of William DIETER
Susanna

Guardians for minor children of John DEPUI, Mt. Bethel Township (were other children):

widow: Mary
children: Mary, over age 14....................................guardian: Benjamin VANCAMPEN
Abraham, under age 14............................guardian: Benjamin DEPUI, Esq.
Samuel, under age 14..............................guardian: Nicholas DEPUI, Esq.

Guardians for minor grandchildren of Jacob BÄRR, Lynn Township:

children: John BÄRR, eldest surviving son
Jacob BÄRR, deceased, left 4 minor children, all under age 14:
Daniel
John
Valentine
Magdalena
guardians: for all 4 grandchildren—Martin PROPST and Martin METZER

Estate of Henry FULLERT, Esq., Easton—request sale:

land: tenement and lot on north side of Northampton Street, 50' front x 220' depth
administrator: Abraham BERLIN, Esq.
[note with entry says that it was entered here by mistake and was entered hereafter on 18 April 1782]

Estate of Henry FULLERT, Esq.—request audit by motion of Collinson READ, Esq.:

administrator: Abraham BERLIN, Esq.
auditors: Melchior HAY, Herman SNIDER, and John SPANGENBERG

**Court on 21 March 1782, continued:**

Estate of John George HOMES, Whitehall Township, 70 acres—report of inquest by Sheriff Robert TRAILL:
widow
6 children: Conrad, eldest son—accepted the land
others not named
securities: Martin GROFF and Conrad MARKS, both of Whitehall Township
12 men:by oath—Peter KERN, Christopher KERN, George KEALER, Jacob SHRYBER (SHREIBER), George FLICKINGER, Jacob KERN, Martin MACKLEY, Jacob KOHLER, Conrad MARKS, Peter DESHLER, Adam DESHLER
by affirmation—Martin GROFF

**Court on 25 March 1782**
**Justices, the Esquires: Robert LEVERS, John ARNDT, Abraham BERLIN**

Estate of Henry FULLERT—new auditor appointed:
administrator: Abraham BERLIN
new auditor: John OKELY, Esq.—to replace Herman SNIDER who refused to serve

Estate of Frederick SHOEMAKER—balance of estate to be distributed:
widow: Magdalena, now wife of Frederick SHECHLER

**Court on 18 April 1782**
**Justices, the Esquires: Robert LEVERS, Jacob MORY, John BILE**

Estate of Henry FULLERT, Esq.—request sale:
administrator: Abraham BERLIN, Esq.

**Court on 20 June 1782**
**Justices, the Esquires: Nicholas DEPUI, Jacob MORRY, Thomas SILLYMAN, William McNAIR, Benjamin DEPUI, Abraham BERLIN, John BILE**

Guardians for minor children of Samuel MOOSICH, Whitehall Township:
by first wife: two children—already have guardians
widow: Dorothea, second wife—6 minor children, all under age 14
children: Elisabeth
David
Anthony
Mary Barbara
Eve Catharina
Mary Salome
guardians: for all of Dorothea's children—Gottfridt KNAUSE and Benedict NEIDLINGER

Estate of George STEININGER, Macungie Township, 190 acres—report of inquest by Sheriff Robert TRAILL:
5 children: George, eldest son—accepted the land
others not named
securities: Michael KEGLE and Philip FOGLE, Macungie Township
12 men:all by oath—John TRAXLER, Jr., John FOGLE, Michael SHNYDER, Baltzer SMITH, William HAYNES (HAINTZ), Valentine MILLER, Andrew MILLER, Adam HAVERLEY, Jacob HAMAN, Michael KICHLEY, Joseph SLOUGH, George SLICHER

**Court on 20 June 1782, continued:**

Estate of Jacob WEISS, Lower Saucon Township, 100 acres—report of inquest by Sheriff Robert TRAILL:
widow
6 children: John, eldest son—accepted the land
others not named
securities: Jacob LUDWIG and Adam SNIDER, Upper Saucon Township
12 men: by oath—Philip BOEHM, Christopher HELLER, Michael HELLER, Nicholas EVENROAD, Conrad OMENSETTER, Peter HARRIS
by affirmation—Andrew RICKERT, Valentine KOUP, Daniel HELLER, Francis HARTMAN, George SWENKER, Abraham BACHMAN

Estate of Samuel BOND, Chestnuthill Township, 2 tracts—request sale:
land: 300 acres bounded by Jacob HYPGEE and Jacob EVERET
administrator: Nicholas YOUNG
2 children: Jane, under age 21
Lewis, under age 21

Estate of Henry FULLERT, Esq.—auditors' report:
administrator: Abraham BERLIN, Esq.
(gave a detailed list of money on hand, debts owed, list of creditors—over 60 men listed)

Estate of Henry FULLERT—return of sale:
administrator: Abraham BERLIN, Esq.
sold to: Adam DREISBACH, Sr., Easton

**Court on 21 June 1782**
**Justices, the Esquires: Nicholas DEPUI, Robert LEVERS, Abraham BERLIN**

Application of Mrs. Jane ROSEBOROUGH, widow of Rev. John ROSEBOROUGH for additional support:
50 pounds State Money ordered

Guardians for minor children of Paul BALLIET, Whitehall Township:
children: Paul, over age 14....................................guardian: Jacob WERT
Mary, over age 14...................................guardian: Peter RHOADS

**Court on 19 September 1782**
**Nicholas DEPUI, Jacob MORRY, Thomas SILLYMAN, Thomas HARTMAN, Frederick LIMBACH, Benjamin DEPUI, Abraham BERLIN, John BILE**

Guardian for Mary, over age 14, minor child of James BROWN, late of West Pennsborough Township, Cumberland County:
guardian: James BOYD, Allen Township

Guardian for minor children of Michael NAGLE, Town of Northampton (both under age 14):
children: John
Catherine
guardian: for both children—Matthias RINGLE, Town of Northampton

**Court on 19 September 1782, continued:**

Estate of John LATTIMORE, Allen Township, 2 tracts of 192 acres—report of inquest made in September 1781 by Sheriff Jonas HARTZELL, Esq.:

widow: Elizabeth
4 children: Robert, eldest son—accepted the land
others not named
securities: Peter OBERSHIMER, Allen Township, & Patrick CAMPBELL, Mt. Bethel Twp.; both declined to serve
new securities: Neigal GRAY and Samuel WILSON, both of Allen Township
12 men:by oath and affirmation—John HAYS, Neigal GRAY, John McNAIR, Peter OBERSHIMER, William CRAIG, Adam CLENDINEN, James BOYD, Joseph HORNER, Robert CRAIG, James KERR, James CLYD, James DOAK

Guardians for 5 minor children of Christian RUTH (all under age 14):

petitioners: Daniel SWARTZ and Borgert MEINDER, brothers-in-law of deceased
5 children: Catherine
Christian
Philip
Elisabeth
Jacob
guardians: for first 3 children—Daniel SWARTZ, their uncle
for last 2 children—Valentine SHAFER, their uncle

**Court on 6 January 1783**
**Justices, the Esquires: Samuel REA, Thomas HARTMAN, Abraham BERLIN**

New guardians for 4 minor children of Henry SNYDER:

children: Peter, though over age 14, "...not being present, but supposed to be a prisoner of war at New York...."
Henry, over age 14.................................guardian: John SCHOOK, step-father
Elisabeth, under age 14
Catherine, under age 14
Juliana, under age 14
guardians: former—Lewis KNAUS & Jacob OPP, appointed 24 September 1778; now declined
new, for all (including Peter) but Henry—Henry BARNET and Abraham LABAR

**Court on 3 February 1783**
**Robert LEVERS, Thomas SILLYMAN, Abraham BERLIN**

Estate of Jacob ENGLER, Plainfield Township, died about 5 years ago, two tracts—request inquest:

land: total of 172 acres adjoining Abraham HELLER, Conrad GERMANTOWN, Leonard BUYER, and vacant land
widow: Anna Maria, now wife of Philip ACHENBACH, Easton
6 children: Leonard, eldest son
Jacob
Simon
Susanna
Anna Maria
Adam

**Court of 25 February 1783**
**Robert LEVERS, John ARNDT, Abraham BERLIN**

Estate of Felix ARNER, Whitehall Township, died 6 years ago, 2 contiguous tracts—request inquest:

land: total of 280 acres adjoining Joseph BALLIET, Peter SIGFRIDT, Jacob BERGER, Daniel SCHNYDER, Nicholas SEGER, Jacob KRATZMAN

widow: Elisabeth, now wife of Peter ANTHONY

11 children: Jacob, eldest son
Anna Margaretha
Susanna
Catharina
Elisabetha
Margaret
Salome
John
Felix
William
Dorothy

**Court on 20 March 1783**
**Nicholas DEPUI, Samuel REA, Jacob HORNER, Abraham BERLIN, John BILE**

Guardians for 2 minor children of Gottlieb DORNBLASER, Bethlehem Township, died sometime ago:

children: John, over age 14
Catherine, under age 14

guardian: for both children—William Henry LAWALT

Estate of John BEER, Lehigh Township, 3 contiguous tracts, 250 acres total—report of inquest by Sheriff Robert TRAILL, Esq., referred to a petition in March 1782 by the second son, Enoch BEER:

land: 1) 100 acres of deeded land adjoining River Lehigh and the late Dewalt FAHRINGER and other 2 tracts
2) 50 acres deeded land adjoining Barnet BOWMAN and other two tracts
3) 129 acres adjoining Amos BEER, Martin SINGLE, and the late Moses BEER

widow

8 children: Amos, eldest son—refused the land
Enoch, second surviving son—refused the land
Adam, third surviving son, the petitioner—accepted the land
others not named

securities: Nicholas KERN, Towamensing Township, and George BROWN, Lehigh Township

12 men:all by oath—Jost DREISBACH, Casper ERB, Paul FLICK, Henry STROUSE (STRAUSS), Peter ANTHONY, Tobias GILLNER (GELDENER), Frederick KOONTZ (COONS), Joseph PETTY, William KERN, John (Johannes) KERN, Barnet (Bernhart) BOWMAN, Henry BOWMAN

Guardian for Jacob, one minor children of Jacob LEYABERGER, Lehigh Township, died years ago:

guardian: Frederick NEÜHARD, Whitehall Township

Estate of Theobald FAHRINGER, Lehigh Township, two plantations—request sale:

land: 1) 140 acres in Lehigh Township
2) 100 acres in Towamensing Township

administrator: Herman RUP, acting administrator

**Court on 20 March 1783, continued:**

Estate of Jacob ENGLER, Plainfield Township, 2 tracts of 172 acres total—report of inquest by Sheriff Robert TRAILL, Esq.:

widow

6 children: Leonard, eldest son—accepted the land
others not named

securities: Henry HAUSER and Conrad GERMANTOWN

12 men:all by oath—Casper DOLL, Henry ENGLE, Jacob HELER, Deeter BOWER (BAUER), Abraham HELLER, Conrad GERMANTOWN, Leonard ANDREW, Frederick HAHN, George MUMBOUR (MUMBAUER), Henry HAPPLE, Charles HEIMER, Henry HOWSER (HAUSER)

Estate of William GABLE, Penn Township, died about 7 years ago—request inquest:

land: 250 acres adjoining Jeremiah WARDER, Michael OHL, and Joseph CUSTARD

widow: now remarried

7 children: Joseph, eldest son
Mary
Catherine
Thomas
Israel
Barnet
Elisabeth

Guardians for minor children of Reverend Conrad STEINER, died sometime ago:

widow: Catherine

8 children: Elisabeth, of age
Frederick, minor over age 14...................guardian: Melchior STEINER, Philadelphia, PA
Jacob, minor over age 14.........................guardian: Jacob STEINER, Frederickstown, VA
the remaining 5 children were all under age 14:
Magdalena
John
Catharina
Susanna
Salome

guardian: for younger 5 children—Peter KACHLEIN, Esq., EASTON

Estate of John DEPUI, Mt. Bethel Township, died about 5 years ago—request inquest:

land: 290 acres adjoining John SCOTT, Robert SIMONTON, Henry JACOBI, Derrick LOWE, Joseph MARR

widow: Mary

7 children: Benjamin, eldest son
Elisabeth
Susanna
Sarah
Mary
Abraham
Samuel

**Court on 20 March 1783, continued:**

Estate of John WEBER, Allen Township, died sometime ago, 50 acres—request sale:
administrators: Elisabeth ROGERS and William McCARTHY

Guardian for Gerardus SWARTWOOD, over 14, grandson of Bernardus SWARTWOOD, Delaware Tp.:
petitioner: Thomas HEYSHAM, next friend
guardian: Emanuel GONZALEZ, Delaware Township

New guardian for 2 minor children of Felix ARNER, Whitehall Township (both now over age 14):
children: Felix
William
guardian: former—Joseph BALLIET
new—Jacob WERT, Whitehall Township

**Court on 31 March 1783**
**Justices, the Esquires: not named**

Guardians for 4 minor children of John WEBER, died sometime ago (all under age 14):
administrator: William McCARTHY
4 children: Catherine
Salome
Henry
John
guardians: "Whereupon the court do appoint..."—not named [rest is blank]

**Court on 17 April 1783**
**John ARNDT, Frederick LEIMBACH, Abraham BERLIN**

Guardian for 2 of the minor children of Peter BEISEL, Allen Township, died lately (both over age 14):
petitioner: Peter BEISEL, next friend
children: Daniel
Frederick
guardian: for both children—Simon DREISBACH, Allen Township

**Court on 20 June 1783**
**Thomas HARTMAN, Benjamin DEPUI, Jacob HORNER, William McNAIR, James VAN AKEN, Abraham BERLIN, John BEYL**

Guardians for minor grandchildren of Lewis GORDON, Esq.:
petitioner: Thomas AFFLECK, widower, City of Philadelphia, cabinet maker, on behalf of his children, the grandchildren of Lewis GORDON
child: Isabella, deceased, late wife of Thomas AFFLECK; daughter of Lewis GORDON
grandchildren: Lewis AFFLECK
Thomas AFFLECK, Jr.
Mary AFFLECK
Margaret AFFLECK
John AFFLECK
William AFFLECK
guardian: for all 6 children—their father, Thomas AFFLECK

**Court on 20 June 1783, continued:**

Guardians for minor grandchildren of Lewis GORDON, Esq.:

petitioner: John GORDON, uncle and next friend
child: Elizabeth, daughter of GORDON, the late wife of James TAYLOR, Esq., both now deceased
grandchildren: George TAYLOR, over age 14
Ann TAYLOR, over age 14
Mary TAYLOR, over age 14
Thomas TAYLOR, under age 14
James TAYLOR, under age 14
guardian: for all 5 children—Thomas AFFLECK, City of Philadelphia, and Henry ALLSHOUSE, Northampton County, gentleman

Estate of George TAYLOR, Esq., (had a will) grandfather of minor children of James TAYLOR, also deceased—request for reimbursement of funds spent on maintenance of grandchildren:

executors: Robert LEVERS, Robert L. HOOPER, Jr., and Robert TRAILL, all Esquires—these men had the 2 minor children of James TAYLOR, deceased, in their care. James was the husband of Elizabeth, daughter of Lewis GORDON, Esq. The executors requested money from the guardians appointed for the children for the expenses they had in caring for these 2 children.

**Court on 19 June 1783 (out of order)**
**Justices, the Esquires: not named**

Guardians for 6 minor children of William TOWNSEND, Bethlehem Township, died lately:

widow: Susanna
6 children: Susanna, over age 14................................guardian: Joseph RICHARD
the remaining 5 children were all under age 14:
Mary
Elisabeth
Joseph
Sarah
Hannah
guardian: for 5 younger children—Joseph KIDD

Guardian for minor sons of William MILLER, Mt. Bethel Township (both over age 14):

children: Joseph
William
guardian: for both sons—Joseph MARTIN

Guardian for minor children of Alexander MILLER, Plainfield Township:

petitioner: Samuel MILLER, next friend
children: Thomas, over age 14
Elisabeth, over age 14
Isabel, under age 14
guardian: for all 3 children—Alexander FORESMAN

Guardian for Margaret, over age 14, minor daughter of Andrew BERLIP, Chestnuthill Township:

guardian: Abraham SMITH, Chestnuthill Township

**Court on 19 June 1783 (out of order), continued:**

Estate of John DEPUI, Mt. Bethel Township, 290 acres—report of inquest by Sheriff Robert TRAILL:
widow
7 children: Benjamin, eldest son—accepted the land (others not named)
securities: Benjamin DEPUI, Esq., and Samuel REA, Esq.
12 men:all by oath—William McFARREN, Robert SYMENTON, Garret (Gerrit) MIDDAGH, James BEARD, Henry JACOBI, Joseph MARTIN, Michael NEIGH, William MOORE, James MOORE, William MASON, Adrijan (Adrieÿaen) ATTEN, Derrick LOW

**Court on 1 August 1783**
**Thomas SILLYMAN, John ARNDT, Abraham BERLIN**

Estate of William GABLE, Penn Township, 250 acres—report of inquest by Sheriff Robert TRAILL:
widow
7 children: Joseph, eldest son—accepted the land (others not named)
securities: Joseph BALLIET, Heidelberg Township, and Leonard BALLIET, Penn Twp.
12 men:all by oath—Michael OHL, Thomas EVERET (EVERITT), Philip MOSER, Peter MISSEMER, David GORTNER, Jacob WERTMAN, Martin SHUCK, George GILBERT, Leonard ZIMMERMAN, Adam ZEANER, Tobias EBERT, John KRUM (KRAM)

**Court on 20 March 1783 (out of order—a return to this date)**
**Justices, the Esquires: as named before**

Estate of Felix ARNER, Whitehall Township, 2 tracts of 280 acres total—report of inquest by Sheriff Robert TRAILL, Esq.:
widow
11 children: Jacob, eldest son—accepted the land
others not named
securities: Stephen BALLIET, Whitehall Township, and Peter ANDREAS, Heidelberg Township
12 men:by oath—Samuel SEAGER, Jacob MILLER, Peter REACH, Frederick KUNTZ, Michael RINGER, Henry SHAFFER (SHEFFER), Joseph BALLIET, Peter SHLOSSER, Henry BAST, Tobias GILTNER
by affirmation—Frederick NEIHART, Nicholas SEAGER

**Court on 19 June 1783 (out of order—a return to this date)**
**Justices, the Esquires: as named before**

Estate of Samuel MEYER, Upper Milford Township, died, "some considerable time since"—request inquest:
land: 50 acres bounded by Henry SCHLEIFFER, Thomas MECHLIN, Henry LORASH, and others
widow: Elisabeth, now wife of Jacob SCHLEIFFER
3 daughters: Mary, wife of Philip HESS—Philip wished to accept the land
Esther, deceased, the late wife of Abraham FUNCK, Bucks County—left issue, one male child, John, under age 14
Eve, of age

**Court on 19 September 1783**
**Justices, the Esquires: Nicholas DEPUI, Thomas SILLYMAN, Samuel REA**

Soldier's pay: referred to an order made 21 June 1782 to Lieutenant of County to pay 50 pounds State Money to Mrs. Jane ROSEBOROUGH, widow of Rev. John ROSEBOROUGH. So far none of the money had been paid. The court rescinded the order and issued a new order for the Treasurer of the County to pay her 200 pounds.

**Court on 16 December 1783**
**Thomas SILLYMAN, William McNAIR, Thomas HARTMAN, Abraham BERLIN, John BEIL**

Guardian for John, over 14, minor child of Henry WETZEL, Macungie Township, died about 7 years ago (there were 3 other children):
petitioner: William SMITH, step-father of child
guardian: Baltzer SMITH, Macungie Township

Estate of Benjamin GILBERT, Penn Township, 5 tracts—request for partition; the widow asked the court if it "...would be pleased to appoint Michael OHL, Philip MOSER, Borick MOSER, Francis BAILER, Daniel WARNER, Nathan WARNER, John SNIDER, Josiah THOMAS, gentleman, or some other four or more of them to make the said partition....":
widow: Elisabeth, now of Philadelphia County
children: Joseph, eldest son
Benjamin
John
Joshua
Caleb
Jesse
Rachel, wife of William WALTON
Abigail, wife of Benjamin WALTON
Sarah, wife of Daniel WALTON
Abner, minor child
Rebecca, minor child
Elisabeth, minor child
guardian: for 3 minor children, already appointed—Jacob COMLY

**Court on 18 December 1783**
**Justices, the Esquires: not named**

Estate of Samuel MEYER, Upper Milford Township, 50 acres—report of inquest by Sheriff Robert TRAILL:
widow
3 daughters: Mary, wife of Philip HESS—Philip accepted the land
others not named; one deceased
securities: Anthony LERCH and Conrad FOGLEMAN
12 men:all by oath—Frederick MARTIN, Michael HETTINGER (HEDINGER), Christopher ANDREAS, George DOODT, Nicholas MILLER, Simon HEIN, Adam GEPHART, Philip YENTER (YENDERN), John JACOBIE (JACOBY), Matthias MILLER, Jost WENTZ, Henry LARASH (LAROSS)

Guardian for Louisa, over age 14, minor daughter of Peter SNELL, Lower Smithfield Township:
guardian: Henry HAUSER, Plainfield Township.

**Court on 18 December 1783, continued:**

Guardian for Abraham, under age 14, minor son of George DERR, Lower Saucon Township (other children):

guardian: Jacob DERR.

Estate of Zacharias HOLLER, Lynn Township, lately died—request inquest:

| | |
|---|---|
| land: | 250 acres bounded by Thomas EVERET, George PROBST, Michael BUCK, Bernard FULLWYLER, Jacob WANNEMAKER |
| widow: | Anna |
| 10 children: | John Adam, eldest son |
| | Henry |
| | Christian |
| | Zacharias |
| | Daniel |
| | John |
| | Elisabeth |
| | Susanna |
| | Barbara |
| | Christina |

Estate of Charles BRIGGS, Williams Township, died several years ago—request inquest:

| | |
|---|---|
| land: | 200 acres adjoining Isaac STOUT, Abraham ARNDT, George KNIGHT, Conrad MILLER |
| widow: | Mary |
| 2 children: | Joseph, eldest son |
| | Sarah, wife of John DYER |

Estate of Michael NARREGANG, Lower Saucon Township—request inquest:

| | |
|---|---|
| land: | 70 acres bounded by Peter LLOYD, Stophel RAUCH, Adam ENGLEMYER, Henry SHAFER |
| widow: | Elisabeth |
| 5 children: | John, eldest son |
| | Catherine, wife of Peter GRUVER, Springfield Township, Bucks County |
| | Peter |
| | George |
| | Magdalena |

Soldier's pay: William CONGELTON appeared, "sometime since," and obtained relief from the court on account of half-pay. He was at present in needy circumstances and requested further allowance. The court ordered the Lieutenant of the County to pay him 20 pounds.

**Court on 18 March 1784**
**Thomas SILLYMAN, Samuel REA, Thomas HARTMAN, Lewis STECKER, Abraham BERLIN**

Guardian for Elisabeth, over age 14, one child of Christian ROOT, Macungie Township:
guardian: Adam HAVERLY, Jr.

Estate of Henry NELICH (had a will)—audit requested:

| | |
|---|---|
| petitioner: | Christian WIRTH, Whitehall Township, one heir |
| executor: | John HUNSECKER |
| auditors: | George GROFF, John LERCH, Andrew BACHMAN |



Estate of George REX, Heidelberg Township—request audit of estate of George KNAUS, also deceased;

George KNAUS , as a guardian, had received monies on behalf of Catherine REX for which he never accounted:

petitioners: Dewalt PETER and his wife Catherina, daughter of George REX
administrator: for George REX's estate—William REX
guardian: for Catherine, appointed earlier—George KNAUSE, Whitehall Township, now deceased
administrator: for George KNAUSE's estate—George Frederick KNAUSE, son of George KNAUSE
auditors: Jacob WIRTH, Jacob SHRIVER, Peter KERN

Estate of Anthony SNYDER, Allen Township—request sale:

land: 120 acres bounded by Peter SHILP, George FASS, and others, "part of the Manor of Fermor commonly called the dry land."
widow: Margaret, now wife of George RISHELL
5 children: not named; the youngest is 9 years old

Estate of Michael NORAGONG, Lower Saucon Township—request sale:

land: 75 acres adjoining Engle MYER, Henry SHAFER, Peter LLOYD, Stophel RAUCH
widow: Elisabeth, administratrix
5 children

Guardian for Lewis, over age 14, one child of Samuel BOND, Chestnuthill Township, died sometime ago (there were other children):

guardian: George GAUER, Hamilton Township.

Guardians for 2 minor children of John FRITZ, Plainfield Township, died about 5 years ago (both under age 14):

petitioners: John FRITZ and George INSLEE, next friends
children: Conrad
Louisa
guardian: for both children—Ulrich HAUSER, Plainfield Township

Estate of Philip SNIDER, died about 5 years ago, Bethlehem Township—request inquest:

land: 150 acres, part of the Manor of Fermor commonly called the Dryland Tract, bounded by George SCHNABEL, Michael LAWALT, Frederick SOEHLER and John SNIDER (eldest son of deceased)
widow: Elisabeth
8 children: John, eldest son
Conrad, second son (wished to accept the land)
Philip
Margaret
Elisabeth
Catherine, wife of John HARTZELL, Bethlehem Township
Christina
Eve

**Court on 25 March 1784**

**Justices, the Esquires: Thomas HARTMAN, Lewis STECKER, Abraham BERLIN**

Estate of John SCHIFFERSTEIN, died sometime ago, Weisenberg Township—request sale:

| | |
|---|---|
| land: | 47 acres bounded by John Adam DIEL, George SHOEMAKER, Valentine CRAMLEY |
| widow: | Mary Magdalena, now wife of Mr. FRITZ |
| 2 children | |

Guardians for 3 minor children of Peter BÄR, died sometime ago (had a will), Heidelberg Township:

| | |
|---|---|
| children: | Hans Jacob, petitioner, brother of children, and next friend |
| | Mary Catharina, over age 14....................guardian: Samuel WOODRING |
| | Anna Margaret, over age 14.....................guardian: John BÄR |
| | Anna Apolonia, under age 14...................guardian: Samuel WOODRING |
| guardians: | both were from Whitehall Township |

**Court on 25 March 1784 (continued)**
**John ARNDT now present in place of Lewis STACKER as Justice**

Estates of George DIETZ, the younger, and George DIETZ, the elder, both of Chestnuthill Township, both deceased, both estates concerning land of George, the elder—request sale:

| | |
|---|---|
| land: | 2 tracts of 75 acres total bounded by vacant land and Samuel ROLLINS |
| administrator: | of George, the younger—Lewis STACKER, Esq. |
| administrator: | of George, the elder—George DIETZ, the younger |
| situation: | *George, the elder, died sometime before his son, George, the younger |
| | *George, the younger, had requested an inquest into partitioning his father's land |
| | *George, the younger, planned to accept the land but could not produce securities |
| | *then George, the younger, died |
| | *Lewis STACKER appeared in court to request permission to sell the property |

**Court on 15 May 1784**
**Justices, the Esquires: Robert LEVERS, John ARNDT, Thomas SILLYMAN**

Estate of Zacharias HOLLER, Lynn Township—referred to petition of 18 December 1783; John Adam, eldest son, requested permission to rectify a mistake he had made in that earlier petition—request inquest:

| | |
|---|---|
| widow: | Anna |
| 10 children: | John Adam, eldest son |
| | Henry |
| | Christian |
| | Zacharias |
| | Daniel |
| | John |
| | Elisabeth |
| | Susanna |
| | Barbara |
| | Christina |
| correction: | Estate involves 150 acres bounded by Thomas EVERET, George PROPST, Michael BUCK and others, plus 4 tracts of woodland in Lynn Township: |
| | 1) 11 acres bounded by Daniel OSWALT, Thomas EVERET, George PROPST |
| | 2) 34 acres bounded by Daniel OSWALT, Michael BUCK |
| | 3) 125 acres bounded by George ENNES, George HARMANY, Thomas EVERET |
| | 4) 125 acres bounded by Michael PROPST, Frederick LIESER, Thomas EVERET |

**Court on 23 June 1784**

**Peter RHOADS, Abraham BERLIN, John BEYL, Peter KOHLER**

Guardian for Samuel Frederick BADER, minor child of Peter Paul BADER, "late a Missionary among the Negroes in the Island of Jamaica in the West Indies, died in the said Island sometime ago leaving no other child...," leaving an estate in the, "Island of Jamaica and in some parts of Europe.":

| | |
|---|---|
| guardian: | Joseph HORSEFIELD, Bethlehem |

Guardian for 5 minor children of James HALL, Bethlehem (all under age 14):

| | |
|---|---|
| widow: | Anna Mary |
| children: | John |
| | James |
| | Christian |
| | Elisabeth |
| | Joseph |
| guardian: | for all 5 children—Andrew BORHOEK, Bethlehem |

**Court on 24 June 1784**
**Justices: not named**

Estate of Michael NORAGONG, Lower Saucon Township—return of sale:

| | |
|---|---|
| widow: | Elisabeth, administratrix |
| sold to: | Peter LEIDT |

Estate of Anthony SCHNYDER, Allen Township—return of sale:

| | |
|---|---|
| widow: | Margaret, administratrix, now wife of George RISHELL |
| sold to: | John BINGAMAN |

Estate of Martin KARG—citation for administrator to appear to explain why he had not settled the estate:

| | |
|---|---|
| administrator: | Bartholomew MILLER |
| widow: | Margaret, now wife of Michael HERBST |

**Court on 25 June 1784**
**Justices: not named**

Soldier William CONGLETON appeared and requested additional funds for support:
Lieutenant of the County, Thomas CRAIG, Esq., was ordered to pay 5 pounds in gold and silver.

Estate of Christian ROOT—complaint about guardians of the 5 minor children:

| | |
|---|---|
| widow: | Anna Mari, now wife of Michael MICHEL, the petitioners, who have maintained the children for 2 years. |
| guardians: | Valentine SHAFFER and Daniel SWARTZ, who are "managing the Estate of the deceased very improperly, renting it for less than a third of its value and intirely refusing to pay any thing towards the maintenance of the said children." |

**Court on 22 July 1784**

**Justices, the Esquires: Robert LEVERS, Abraham BERLIN, John BEYL**

Guardians for 5 minor grandchildren of Maria Elisabeth HEYBRUCH, late widow of John George SCHOMACKER, deceased, late of the "City of Hamburgh in Europe" (Maria Elisabeth had a will):

child: Daniel SCHOMACKER, petitioner:

grandchildren, all children of Daniel:

John George, of age

Maria Elisabeth, over age 14...............guardian: Sebastian WERLIN, Weisenberg Twp.

Anna Maria Barbara, over age 14........guardian: Henry KREGLO, Lowhill Tp.

Maria Margaretha, over age 14...........guardian: Johannes SIEGER, Weisenberg Twp.

John Henry, under age 14....................guardian: Henry STEIGERWALD, Lynn Twp.

Johannes, under age 14........................guardian: Matthias PROBST

examiner: Matthias PROBST, Esq., was asked by the court to examine the choices of the three older minors to make certain that they had chosen these men as guardians.

**Court on 31 July 1784**
**Peter RHOADS, John BEYL, Peter KOHLER**

Estate of John SCHIFFERSTEIN, Weisenberg Township—return of sale:

widow: Mary Magdalena, administratrix, now wife of Mr. FRITZ

sold to: Tobias STAYRY

Guardians for 2 minor children of Philip LERCH, Lower Saucon Township, died about 2 years ago (both under age 14):

next friend: Gratius LERCH

children: John

Henry

guardian: for both children—John BEYER, Lower Saucon Township

**Court on 21 September 1784**
**Justices, the Esquires: Peter RHOADS, John BEYL, Peter KOHLER**

Guardians for 4 minor children of Frederick HAINTZ, the elder, died sometime ago, Macungie Township (had a will) (all under age 14):

next friend: William HAINTZ

children: Mary......................................................guardian: Andrew EISENHARD,

Frederick................................................guardian: Andrew EISENHARD,

Jacob.....................................................guardian: Philip WALTER

Michael..................................................guardian: Philip WALTER

guardians: both men were from Macungie Township

**Court on 23 September 1784**
**Justices, the Esquires: Peter RHOADS, John BEYL, Peter KOHLER, Benjamin DEPUI, Frederick LEIMBACH**

Guardian for Katherine, over age 14, minor daughter of David WANAKER, died about 7 years ago, Delaware Township (were other children)—Katherine now lived with her brother-in-law, Peter CORSA, Shawonese Township, Northumberland County, PA:

guardian: Peter CORSA

**Court on 23 September 1784, continued:**

Estate of Philip SNIDER, Bethlehem Township; referred back to an inquest ordered last March where son Conrad wanted to accept the land—report of inquest by Sheriff Robert TRAILL, Esq.:

land: 150 acres bounded by George SCHNABEL and others
widow
8 children: John, eldest son—now wanted to accept the land
Conrad, 2nd son—wanted to accept the land but could not provide securities and declined to accept it at the valuation made
others not named
securities: John ERHART and John BUSS, both of Bethlehem Township
12 men: all by oath—William Henry LAWALT, John BUSS, George SNABLE, Nicholas MICHAEL (MICHEL), John FRY, Frederick SAYLOR (SEILER), Frederick WAGNER (WAGGONER), Conrad KOCHER, Casper NULF, Conrad EDLEMAN, George ERET (EHRET), Philip ZIMMERMAN

Estate of Henry SHOENER, died sometime ago, Allen Township—request inquest:

land: 140 acres adjoining George NEUHART, Sarah WISTAR, Peter MENIG, and Lehigh River
widow: Eve, now wife of George ROUDENBUSH
11 children: Peter, 4th son—wanted the land
Matthias
George
Martin
Henry
Adam
John
Clara
Catharina
Susanna
Elisabeth

Guardian for Jacob, over age 14, minor son of John HAAS, died sometime ago, Lower Saucon Township (had a will):

guardian: William Henry LAWALT, Bethlehem Township

New guardian for Frederick, now over age 14, minor son of George WEAVER, Lower Saucon Township:

other children: Catherine
Mary
guardian: former—John NEWCOMER, Sr., appointed in 1772, for Frederick (then under age 14) and his sisters, Catherine and Mary
new—Jacob ROAD, Lower Saucon Township

Guardian for 3 minor children of Henry SHOENER, died several years ago, Allen Township (all over 14):

children: Adam.....................guardian: George YUND, Whitehall Twp.
Elisabeth.....................guardian: George YUND, Whitehall Twp.
John .....................guardian: Peter RHOADS, Esq.

**Court on 23 September 1784, continued:**

Estate of Zacharias HOLLER, Lynn Township—report of inquest by Sheriff Robert TRAILL, Esq.:

widow

10 children: John Adam—could not secure securities earlier but now had them
others not named

securities: Peter BEISEL and Abraham LEVAN, both of Allen Township

12 men: by oath—Michael POBST (BOBST), Thomas EVERET, Philip MOSER, George HARMONY, Andrew SECHLER, Adam CREÜTZ, Martin PROPST (PROBST) George PROPST (PROBST), Philip SITLER, Samuel EVERED (EVERETT)
by affirmation—Michael BUCK, Barnet FULWEILER

**Court on 27 October 1784**
**Justices, the Esquires: John BEYL, Benjamin DEPUI, Frederick LIMBACH**

Estate of Benjamin GILBERT, Penn Township, 5 tracts, referred to petition 16 December 1783—request sale:

tracts: 1) tract called the Old Place, 329 ½ acres
2) 92 acres of barrens
3) tract called the White Oak Tract, 260 acres
4) tract called the Saw Mill Tract, 111 acres
5) 150 acres warranted land

administrators: John GILBERT and Joshua GILBERT

widow: Elisabeth

children: none of the children, "encline to take the said Lands at the said Appraisement...."
Joseph
Benjamin
John
Caleb
Jesse
Rachel, wife of William WALTON
Abigail, wife of Benjamin WALTON
Sarah, wife of Daniel WALTON
Rebecca
Abner, minor child
Elisabeth, minor child

guardian: for 2 minor children, already appointed—Jacob COMLY, Byberry Township, Philadelphia County

8 men: by oath—Philip MOSER, Borick MOSER, John SNIDER
by affirmation—Michael OHL, Francis BAILER, Daniel WARNER, Nathan WARNER, Josiah THOMAS

[Not known why there were only 8 men instead of 12, but they were requested by the family rather than chosen by the sheriff—"being eight substantial Men of said County...," qualified before Jacob HORNER, Esq.]

**Court on 22 December 1784**
**Justices, the Esquires: Peter RHOADS, John BEYL, Peter KOHLER, Benjamin DEPUI, Frederick LIMBACH**

Guardian for George, over age 14, minor son of Michael SHICK, Lowhill Township:

guardian: Leonard ZIMMERMAN, Penn Township

**Court on 22 December 1784, continued:**

Guardian for Susanna, over age 14, one minor child of Philip HALL, Upper Saucon Township:
guardian: Adam ROMIG, Upper Saucon Township

Guardian for minor children of Jacob GINTNER, died sometime ago, Mt. Bethel Township (all under age 14):
widow: Sarah, administratrix
4 children: Charles....................................................guardian: Jacob BECK, Mt. Bethel Twp.
Mary......................................................guardian: Jacob BECK, Mt. Bethel Twp.
Jacob.....................................................guardian: Christian EIDENBERGER
John......................................................guardian: Christian EIDENBERGER

Estate of Henry SHOENER, Allen Township, 140 acres—report of inquest by Sheriff Peter EALER, Esq.:
widow
11 children: Matthias, eldest son—refused land
George, 2nd son—refused land
Martin, 3rd son—refused land
Peter, 4th son—accepted the land
others not named
securities: Adam REBER, Allen Township, and Christopher JANSEN, Upper Saucon Twp.
12 men:all by oath—David DESHLER, Daniel SWARTZ (SCHWARTZ), Michael BEAVER (BEIBER), William DANIEL, Peter DESHLER, Robert YOUNG, Nicholas FOX, Valentine WALTMAN, Nicholas REMMEL (RIMMEL), Adam REBER, Abraham ALBERT, Michael GANGWEHR (GANGWER)

**Court on 23 December 1784**
**Justices, the Esquires: not named**

Guardians for 2 minor children of John SPERING, Town of Easton, cordwainer (both over age 14); "John SPERING stands attainted of High Treason against the Commonwealth of Pennsylvania, by means whereof all his Estate Real and Personal became lawfully vested in the said Common Wealth; and that by act of General Assembly of the Common Wealth passed the twenty second day of November in the Year one thousand seven hundred and eighty two, the Estate was again Vested in Four of the children of the said John SPERING....":
petitioners: John ARNDT, Esq., and Andrew KACHLEIN
children: Henry
John
Jane, "bounded as a Servant by the Overseers of the Poor unto...John ARNDT"
Elisabeth, bounded "unto the said Andrew KACHLEIN"
guardians: for Jane—John ARNDT
for Elisabeth—Abraham LABAR

Estate of Peter BEISEL, Allen Township—request audit:
administrator: Peter BEISEL
widow and children
auditors: Jacob SHRIVER, John FREDERICK, John HAYS

**Court on 23 December 1784, continued:**

Estate of Benjamin REEGEL, died "considerable time since," Lower Saucon Township—request inquest:

| | |
|---|---|
| land: | 370 acres bounded by Jacob CRUM, John ROTHROCK, John BEYL |
| widow: | Barbara, now wife of George Adam WEAVER, Lower Saucon Township |
| 7 children: | Matthias, eldest son |
| | John |
| | Jacob |
| | Margaret |
| | Benjamin |
| | Catharine |
| | Elisabeth |

**Court on 24 December 1784**
**Justices, the Esquires: not named**

Estate of Peter LONG, Upper Milford Township—request audit:

| | |
|---|---|
| executor: | Abraham MOYER, cited to appear to settle the accounts which appeard to be "imperfect and unsatisfactory" |
| widow: | Elisabeth |
| auditors: | Thomas MECHLIN, Frederick MARTIN, Sebastian DRUCKENMILLER |

Estate of Henry BRUNNER, Upper Saucon Township (had a will)—request for money; the will set aside funds for the care of Henry's son, "put out at interest and the interest thereon duly paid unto the said Magdalena until the year 1777, from whence, until the present time, the payment thereof hath totally ceased, as the petitioners believe, thro the negligence or mismanagement of her co-executors.":

| | |
|---|---|
| petitioners: | Peter LAUTENSTEIN and his wife Magdalena, late Magdalena BRUNNER |
| executors: | Jacob MORRY, Esq., and George PLANK—ordered to appear next March |
| son: | Henry, a lunatic, "totally helpless and void of understanding" |

**Court on 10 January 1785**
**Justices, the Esquires: John BEYL, Benjamin DEPUI, Robert LEVERS**

Estate of Dewalt FAHRINGER, deceased, who was the administrator for Moses BEER, deceased, Lehigh Township; Dewalt had exhibited an administration account in March 1776 but not all of Moses's debts were satisfied—request audit:

| | |
|---|---|
| administrator: | of FAHRINGER estate, Herman RUPP |
| auditors: | Peter KOHLER, Esq., William McNAIR, Esq., John LERCH |

Estate of Christian RUTH—citation issued for guardians of minor children to appear in court in March; repeat of complaint made on 25 June 1784:

| | |
|---|---|
| petitioners: | Michael MICHEL and his wife Anna Maria, widow of RUTH |

**Court on 18 January 1785**

**Justices, the Esquires: Robert LEVERS, William McNAIR, Thomas HARTMAN**

Guardians for minor children of Philip ROOFNER, "died some little time past," Moore Township (had a will):
executor: Peter OBESHIMER, the petitioner
children: Simon, over age 14
Mary, over age 14
Henry, under age 14
Anthony, under age 14
Philip, under age 14
Margaret, under age 14
Joseph, under age 14
guardians: for Simon and Mary—Paul FLICK, Moore Township
for younger 5 children—John KUCKUS, Moore Township

**Court on 22 March 1785**
**Peter RHOADS, John BEYL, Peter KOHLER, Thomas HARTMAN, Lewis STACKER, Benjamin DEPUI, William McNAIR**

New guardian for Gerardus SWARTWOOD, age 19 years, minor grandson of Bernardus SWARTWOOD, Delaware Township—by motion of William Moore SMITH, Esq.:
guardian: former—Emanuel GONZALES, "having declined acting"
new—Peter SCHOONOVER

Guardians for minor children of James NEIGH, died sometime ago, Mt. Bethel Township (all under age 14):
4 children: John
Richard
Margaret
Jacob
guardian: for all 4 children—Michael NEIGH, their grandfather

**Court on 23 March 1785**
**Peter RHOADS, John BEYL, Peter KOHLER, Benjamin DEPUI, Thomas HARTMAN, William McNAIR**

Estate of Benjamin GILBERT—return of sale:
administrators: John GILBERT and Jonas GILBERT
sold to: Isaac LONGSTRETH and Abraham DUFFIELD, Township of Mooreland, Montgomery County, tanner and innkeeper, and Joseph LONGSTRETH, Southampton Township, Bucks County

Guardian for 2 minor grandchildren of John Isaac KLEIN, Lower Salford Township, Philadelphia County (both over age 14):
executor: George KLEIN, surviving executor—"who hath unjustly deprived the petitioners of part of the benefit intended for them"
father: Thomas DENHART
petitioners, the children:
Henry DENHART
Sophia DENHART
guardian: for both grandchildren—John PUTTON, their half-brother

**Court on 23 March 1785, continued:**

Guardian for minor children of James NEIGH—a repeat of a petition made on 22 March 1785

Estate of Peter SHOP, "died considerably in debt," Weisenberg Township—request sale:
land: 200 acres adjoining Jacob HOLWIG and Jacob BACHMAN
administrators: Barbara MESER (late Barbara SHOP); and Jacob BACHMAN
guardian: of minor children, already appointed—John BARE
debt owed: to estate of Martin SHOP

Guardian for Elizabeth Barbara, over age 14, minor daughter of Michael SHICK, Penn Township:
guardian: Christian SCHNEIDER, Heidelberg Township

**Court on 24 March 1785**
**Justices, the Esquires: not named**

Daniel St. CLAIR, late a drum major with the 11th Pennsylvania Regiment, discharged—requested $15 pension: Treasurer of County, Jacob ARNDT, Esq., was ordered to pay Daniel "out of the moneys in the said Treasurers Hands appropriated to the Use of the United States," a three months pension allowed him by Act of General Assembly of 31 January 1783.

Estate of Benjamin RIEGEL, Lower Saucon Township, 370 acres—inquest report by Sheriff Peter EALER:
widow
7 children: Matthias, eldest son—accepted the land
others not named
securities: John BEYL, and John ROTHROCK, both of Lower Saucon Township, Esquires
12 men: by oath—Andrew (Andreas) OHL, John BYER (Johannes BEYER)
by affirmation—Anthony LERCH, Sr., Francis (Frantz) HARTMAN, Frederick LAWBACK (LAUBACH), Andrew (Andreas) HELLER, John APPLE, Carl Ludwig KOCH, Andrew RICHART (Andreas RICHERT), Samuel KAUFFMAN, Daniel HELLER, Christopher HELLER

Estate of Christian BACHMAN, Lower Saucon Township, grist mill plantation and 2 tracts—request inquest:
land: 1) 300 acres bounded by John APPLE, Christopher WAGNER, David OWEN and others
2) 60 acres woodland bounded by Peter SEAN and Christopher HELLER
widow: Barbara
10 children: Abraham, eldest son
John
George
Henry
Mary, wife of Christian SHICK
Christian
Jacob
Joseph
Solomon
David

Guardian for Sarah, age 15, minor daughter of Alexander MILLER, Mt. Bethel Township, died in 1781:
guardian: Alexander MILLER, Mt. Bethel Township

**Court on 24 March 1785, continued:**

Estate of Adam SHULER, died about 2 years ago, Upper Milford Township, 219 acres—request inquest:

| | |
|---|---|
| widow: | Opalone |
| 13 children: | Peter, eldest son |
| | Michael |
| | John Adam |
| | John Abraham |
| | John George, under age 21 |
| | Elisabeth, wife of Andrew OHLWEIN |
| | Eve, wife of Matthias KERN |
| | Barbara, wife of George HAAS |
| | Catharine, wife of Henry ARDT |
| | Margaret, wife of George MILLER |
| | Ann Maria |
| | Elisabetha, wife of Christian FISHER |
| | Magdalena, under age 21, wife of John FISHER |

Estate of Philip LARCH, Lower Saucon Township—request audit:

| | |
|---|---|
| widow: | Elizabeth, now wife of Peter SHYMER—Elizabeth had renounced administration to her father-in-law, Gratius LERCH, but said there were several mistakes in his administration account. |
| children | |
| auditors: | Peter SIEN, Jacob GROSS, Daniel BEIDELMAN |

Guardian for 8 minor children of Michael HILLEGASS, Upper Saucon Township:

| | |
|---|---|
| petitioner: | John WAGNER, step-father |
| 8 children: | Ann Margaret, over age 14......................guardian: Jacob GARY, Upper Hanover Township, Montgomery County |
| | Rebecca, over age 14..............................no guardian since she did not appear |
| | the remaining 6 children were all under age 14: |
| | John |
| | Elizabeth |
| | Michael |
| | Eve |
| | Catharina |
| | Mary |
| guardians: | for John, Elizabeth, and Mary—Daniel COOPER, Upper Saucon Township |
| | for younger 3 children—John NEWCOMER, the elder, Upper Saucon Township |

Guardian for Christina SHOEMAKER, over age 14, one child of ____________ [not named--left blank]:

| | |
|---|---|
| guardian: | Jacob ERB |

Estate of Michael ANDRES, Upper Milford Township, 80 acres had been sold to Henry MYER—will of 17 December 1782 stated that his widow would lose her legacy of 15 pounds if she remarried:

| | |
|---|---|
| widow: | Ann Elisabeth, now wife of George KLEIN—petitioned to retain her widow's legacy despite her remarriage; court reversed her loss. |

**Court on 25 March 1785**

**Justices, the Esquires: Peter RHOADS, John BEYL, Peter KOHLER, Benjamin DEPUI, William McNAIR**

William CONGLETON, soldier, "at present in needy circumstances," requests further aid:
Col. Henry WALDEGRAVE, Archer Lieutenant of County, ordered to pay him 7 pounds, 10 shillings

Estate of Henry SHENER, Allen Township
petitioner: George ROUDEBUSH, step-father of children—had purchased the shares of 5 of the children
children: Peter—accepted the land (did not sell his share)
Matthias
George
Clora
Martin
Henry
clerk: Robert LEVERS, Esq.—to deliver the bonds for the shares to the petitioner

Care of Henry, lunatic, a child of Henry BRUNNER, Upper Saucon Township—referred back to petition of last December; case dismissed because complainants did not appear in court:
widow: Magdalena, now wife of Peter LAUTENSTEIN—last December they had complained to the court that the executors were not providing proper support to son Henry
executors: Jacob MORRY, Esq., and George PLANK

Estate of Dewalt FAHRINGER, deceased, who was administrator for estate of Moses BEER, deceased, Lehigh Township—auditors' report:
widow was granted funds for three years to raise younger children and given an allowance for rent

Estate of Peter LONG, Upper Milford Township—auditors' report:
executor: Abraham MOYER, administrator

**Court on 12 April 1785**
**Justices, the Esquires: Peter RHOADS, John BEYL, William McNAIR**

Guardians for minor children of Christian BACHMAN, died some years ago, Lower Saucon Township (were other children):
children: Abraham, petitioner
Christian, over age 14..............................guardian: Philip BAHL
Jacob, over age 14..................................guardian: George BACHMAN, Sr.
Joseph, over age 14................................guardian: John BACHMAN, Sr.
Solomon, under age 14............................guardian: Philip BAHL
David, under age 14................................guardian: Philip BAHL
guardians: all from Upper Saucon Township

Guardians for minor BEER children, both over age 14:
children: David, son of Moses BEER, Lehigh Township
Ann, daughter of Samuel BEER, Towamensing Township
guardians: for David—George BROWN, Lehigh Twp.
for Ann—Enoch BEER, Lehigh Twp.

**Court on 12 April 1785, continued:**

Estate of Michael NAROGANG, Lower Saucon Township—distribution and guardian for son:
widow: Elizabeth, administratrix—asked for direction on dividing the balance of estate
5 children: John
Catherine
Peter
George, who "hath been from his infancy and continues Non Compos, so that he cannot possibly earn his living"
Magdalena
guardian: for George—Daniel BEIDLEMAN, Lower Saucon Township

**Court on 26 April 1785**
**Justices, the Esquires: John BEYL, Robert LEVERS, William McNAIR**

Guardian for John George, over age 14, youngest son of Adam SHULER, Upper Milford Township:
guardian: Peter SHULER, Upper Milford Township

New guardian for 2 minor children of Christian BACHMAN, Lower Saucon Township (both under 14):
children: Solomon
David
guardian: former—Philip BAHL, Upper Saucon Township, appointed 12 April 1785, declined because he also was appointed as guardian for Christian, another son
new—Charles Lodowick KOCH, Upper Saucon Township

Estate of John STEIN, Lynn Township—request sale:
land: 150 acres bounded by Christian MILLER, George Michael KUNTZ, Burkhart MOSER, and others
administrator: Ludwig STEIN
widow: Elizabeth, administratrix, now wife of Mr. SHNYDER
5 children, all under age 14:
William
John
Henry
Catharine
Eve

**Court on 23 June 1785**
**Justices, the Esquires: Peter RHOADS, Peter KOHLER, Benjamin DEPUI**

Estate of Christian BACHMAN, Lower Saucon Township, gristmill and two tracts of 300 acres and 60 acres—report of inquest by Sheriff Peter EALER, Esq.:
widow
10 children: Abraham, eldest son—accepted the land (others not named)
securities: Peter KACHLEIN, Esq., Easton, and Christopher WAGNER, Lower Saucon Tp.
12 men:by oath—Michael HELLER, Jacob ROTH, Daniel BEIDLEMAN (BEUTELMAN)
by affirmation—Christopher WAGNER, John (Johannes) ROTHROCK, John BEYL, Christopher HELLER, Daniel HELLER, John APPLE, Carl Lodowick (Ludwig) KOCH, Andrew (Andreas) RICHERT, Andrew (Andreas) HELLER

**Court on 23 June 1785, continued:**

Estate of Adam SHULER, Upper Milford Township, 219 acres—inquest report by Sheriff Peter EALER:
widow
13 children: Peter, eldest son—accepted the land
others not named
securities: William SHAFFER and Daniel GOOD, both of Upper Milford
12 men:by oath—William SHAFFER, Daniel GOOD, George DUT, Frederick MARTIN, Henry LARASH (LAROS), Anthony STAHLER, George SEIDER
by affirmation—Michael SHAFFER, Andrew (Andreas) ENGLEMAN, Jacob DELLENGER (DILLINGER), Herman NIESS, Thomas MECHLIN

Estate of Jost SWALM, Macungie Township—request inquest:
land: 157 acres bounded by Harman RUPP, Dewalt KUNTZ, Leonard MYER
widow: Dorothy
2 daughters: Catherine, eldest daughter and heiress at law, wife of John LANG
Christina, wife of Peter SHAFFER

Estate of Jacob TANNER, Macungie Township—request inquest:
land: 1) 165 acres of which 115 acres were deeded land bounded by George SHAFFER, Leonard KOON, Jacob HERMAN, Godfrey DIFFENDERFER
2) 55 acres of woodland bounded by Frederick ROMICH and Christian RUTT
widow: Christina
7 children: Deeter, eldest son
Elisabeth
Jacob
Catharine
Leonard
Christina
Melchior

Guardian for Adam, over age 14, minor son of Adam BAKER, Salisbury Township:
guardian: John BEYL, Esq.

Estate of Peter SHOP, Weisenberg Township—return of sale:
administrator: Barbara MESER (late Barbara SHOP), and Jacob BACHMAN
sold to: Jacob BÄHR, Weisenberg Township

Estate of Frederick SHAFFER—motion on behalf of John NEWCOMER, purchaser of tract in Hamilton Township, 100 acres, sold to him by Christian WILLAUER, administrator of SHAFFER estate:
sale was previously permitted by the court but it was not yet recorded in the Record Book by Lewis GORDON, Esq., clerk. The administrator had made the deed. The clerk was ordered to enter the sale upon receipt of money not yet paid.

**Court on 24 June 1785**
**Justices, the Esquires: not named**

Daniel St. CLAIR, drum major, 11th Pennsylvania Regiment—request for pension:
Jacob ARNDT, Treasurer of County, ordered to pay Daniel $15 for 3 months pension.

**Court on 21 September 1785**

**Justices, the Esquires: Peter RHOADS, John BEYL, Peter KOHLER, Frederick LIMBACH**

Estate of Christian RUTH—referred to citation made in January against guardians of children; request audit:

| | |
|---|---|
| widow: | Anna Maria, now wife of Michael MICHEL |
| guardians: | Daniel SWARTZ and Valentine SHAFER, already appointed |
| auditors: | Peter RHOADS, Peter KOHLER, Frederich LIMBACH, Esquires |

Guardians for minor children of Paul BROAD, Lower Saucon Township:

| | |
|---|---|
| next friend: | Barnet MILLER |
| widow | |
| 10 children: | first 4 were minors over age 14: |
| | Mary |
| | Barnet |
| | Frederick |
| | Conrad |
| | younger 6 were all under age 14: |
| | Michael |
| | Margaret |
| | Rosina |
| | Catharine |
| | Jacob |
| | Susanna |
| guardians: | for Mary, Frederick and Conrad—Jacob LERCH, Lower Saucon Township |
| | for Barnet—Michael BROD |
| | for Michael, Margaret, and Catharine—Anthony LERCH, Jr. |
| | for Rosina, Jacob, and Susanna—Benedict LUTZ |

New guardian for 4 minor children of Jacob GINTNER, Mt. Bethel Township (all under age 14):

| | |
|---|---|
| widow: | Sarah |
| 4 children: | Charles |
| | Mary |
| | Jacob |
| | John |
| guardians: | former—Harman DILDINE & Jacob BECK, appointed last December, refused to serve |
| | new—Jacob GOOD, Mt. Bethel Township |

Daniel St. CLAIR, drum major, 11th Pennsylvania Regiment:

order drawn on Treasurer of County, Jacob ARNDT, Esq. to pay him 15 pounds for 3 months pension

**Court on 12 July 1785 (out of order)**
**Justices, the Esquires: Robert LEVERS, Peter KOHLER, Benjamin DEPUI**

Guardian for Melchior, minor child over age 14, one child of Jacob TANNER, "died near one year since," Macungie Township (were other children):

| | |
|---|---|
| guardian: | Jacob HARMAN, Macungie Township |

**Court on 23 December 1785**

**Justices, the Esquires: Peter RHOADS, John BEYL, Peter KOHLER, Benjamin DEPUI, Lewis STACKER, Thomas HARTMAN**

Guardian for minor children of Philip HERTZOG, the younger, Upper Milford Township (all under 14):
petitioner: Paul HERTZOG, brother of the deceased
4 children: Jacob
Catherine
Philip
Mary
guardian: Thomas MECHLIN, Upper Milford Township, farmer

Estate of Philip HERTZOG, the elder, Upper Milford Township, two tracts—request inquest:
land: 1) 108 acres bounded by William SHAFFER, Simon SHNYDER, Jacob WEISS, Conrad MYER, Nicholas HITTLE
2) 37 acres bounded by Nicholas STAHLER, Rudolph WEISS, Stephen DALMAN
widow
6 children: Paul, eldest son
Catherine, wife of Jacob SEEGER
Elizabeth, wife of Michael JACOBIE
Margaret, wife of Adam RODEBURGER
Gertrude, wife of David HEIMBACH
Christina, wife of Vandle WEEANT
grandchildren: 4 children of deceased son Philip (see preceding entry):
Jacob
Catherine
Philip
Mary

Guardian for Frederick, over age 14, eldest son of Frederick NAGLE, Moore Township (were other children):
guardian: John HUGHES, Moore Township, farmer

Estate of Lawrence HOOD, died about 10 years ago, Chestnuthill Township—request sale:
land: 60 acres bounded by Jacob SMITH, deceased, and vacant land
administrator: George HOOD
widow: now remarried
one child: Eve

**Court on 22 September 1785 (out of order)**

**Justices, the Esquires: Peter RHOADS, John BEYL, Peter KOHLER, Benjamin DEPUI, William McNAIR**

Estate of Jacob TANNER, Macungie Township, 165 acres plus 55 acres woodland—report of inquest by Sheriff Peter EALER, Esq.:

widow
7 children: Deeter, eldest son—accepted the land
others not named
securities: Jacob HARMAN and George SHAFER, both of Macungie Township
12 men:by oath—William HAINTZ, George BREINIG, Peter TREXLER, Jr., Jacob HARMAN (HERMAN), Jeremiah TREXLER, Jacob SWARTZ, Daniel SMEYER, Jacob (John Jacob) STEPHEN, Andrew EISENHART (Andreas EISENHARD); Conrad MEITZLER (MAITZLER)
by affirmation—Henry KNAPPENBERGER, Godfrey DIFFENDERFER

**Court on 23 December 1785 (continued)**
**Justices, the Esquires: as before**

Estate of Michael ANDREW, Upper Milford Township (had will)—motion of Robert TRAILL, Esq., regarding a citation against executors:

executors: George SYDER and Jacob STAHL—commanded to appear in office of John ARNDT, Register, in February
guardians: of minor children of Frederick HAINTZ (already appointed), heirs of ANDREW—Philip WALTER and Andrew EISENHART

Guardian for George, under age 14, minor son of Lawrence ROSS, Heidelberg Township:

petitioner: Peter WENG (written in over the surname is REEG)—father-in-law of deceased
guardian: Peter KUHNS, Lehigh Township

Guardians for minor children of Ulrich BRINKER, Lower Saucon Township (were other children):

administrator: John BYER
children: Jacob, over age 14..................................guardian: John OBERLY
Adam, over age 14.................................guardian: Adam KUCHER
John, under age 14..................................guardian: John OBERLY
John George, under age 14 .....................guardian: Adam KUCHER
guardians: both from Lower Saucon Township

New guardian for Catharine, over age 14, minor child of Christian RUFF, Macungie Township:

guardian: former—Daniel SWARTZ
new—Jacob SHWARTZ, Macungie Township

Estate of Michael SHICK, Lowhill Township—request audit:

widow: Barbara, now wife of Philip SLICKER, both as administrators
children
auditors: Jacob HORNER, Michael BOBST, Andrew BUCHMAN

**Court on 17 January 1786**

**Justices, the Esquires: Peter RHOADS, Robert LEVERS, Thomas HARTMAN**

Estate of Daniel RECKNER, died about 20 years ago, Bethlehem Township—request inquest:
- land: 200 acres, which were part of the Dry Land Tract, bounded by Casper RITTER, Abraham YOUNG, John GEARINGER, Francis SMITH
- widow: now wife of John LOWREY
- 5 children, all of age:
  - Daniel, eldest son
  - Catherine
  - Elizabeth
  - John
  - Mary

Estate of John SHADE (had will)—request audit:
- executors: Elizabeth Catharine SHADE and Samuel SEEGER
- auditors: Peter KOHLER, Esq., Peter BURKHALTER, Esq., and Jacob SHRIVER

**Court on 18 January 1786**
**Justices, the Esquires: not named**

Daniel St. CLAIR, late drum major in the 11th Pennsylvania Regiment—request for support:
He submitted a certificate signed on 11 November 1783 by Baron STEUBEN, Inspector General of the Army of the United States, stating that Daniel was unfit for any further duty.
Awarded $5 per month pension.

Henry LOVE, a soldier in the Pennsylvania Regiment of Artillery in the Corps of invalids—request for support:
He submitted a certificate signed by Baron STEUBEN stating that he was unfit for further duty, "having lost his left leg at the seize of York." Awarded $4 per month pension.

**Court on 6 February 1786**
**Justices, the Esquires: John BEYL, Thomas HARTMAN, Lewis STACKER**

Estate of Daniel RECKNER, Bethlehem Township, 200 acres, part of tract called Dry Lands—report of inquest by Sheriff Peter EALER, Esq.; final disposition was kept under advisement:
- widow: Catharine, now wife of Mr. LOWRY—objected to the confirmation of the land and premises to the eldest son, "alledging that the said two hundred acres of land...were surveyed to her after the decease of...husband, in order to agree with her for the same in her own right, and further, that she paid the chief of the debts...out of her own labors...as well as having made considerable improvements on the premises at her own expense...."
- children: Daniel, eldest son—was to accept the land until objection was made
- securities: Michael RITTER and Jacob BALLIET, Bethlehem Township
- 12 men: by oath—William Henry LAWALL, Philip SCHLAUCH, Francis SMITH, Casper RITTER, Peter SHILP, Michael HUBER, Daniel RITTER, Nicholas (John Nicholas) FOX, Nicholas PAUL, Jacob BALLIET
  by affirmation—George SHURTZ, Frederick FOGLE

## Court on 2 March 1786
## Justices, the Esquires: John BEYL, Robert LEVERS, Thomas HARTMAN

Estate of Philip ZIMMERMAN, died about 1 year ago, Bethlehem Township—request for sale and guardian appointment:

land: 125 acres, which were part of Dry Land Tract, bounded by Conrad SNIDER, Dewalt KRAHTWOHL, John KAMERER, Hans KNECHT
administrator: Nicholas MICHAEL
widow: Mary, administratrix
one child: Sarah, under age 14..................................guardian: William Henry LAWALT, Bethlehem Township, tavern keeper

## Court on 21 March 1786
## Justices, the Esquires: Peter RHOADS, John BEYL, Peter KOHLER, Benjamin DEPUI, William McNAIR, Thomas HARTMAN

Estate of Daniel RECKNER—motion of Daniel CLYMER, Esq., concerning the objection raised last March by the widow, Catharine, now wife of Mr. LOWREY:

The court ruled that, "the lands had been surveyed to her after the deceased of the said Daniel RECKNER, her former husband, in trust...." The court ordered that the valuation and appraisement "be and remain firm and stable forever." Eldest son, Daniel, was awarded the land.
securities: Matthias KENNIG and Jacob BALLIET, both of Bethlehem Township

Estate of Peter BEISEL, died about 3 years ago, Allen Township, 2 tracts—request inquest:

land: 1) 300 acres confirmed by patent adjoining Jacob FROCH, Christian FENSTERMACKER, Wendel HAUER
2) 90 acres, part of Dry Land Tract, adjoining the other tract and Jacob BEISEL
widow: Catharine
6 children: Peter, eldest son
Jacob
Susanna, wife of Peter DREISBACH
John, since deceased
Daniel
Frederick

Estate of Christian MILLER, died about 7 years ago, Lynn Township, 3 tracts—request inquest:

land: 1) 150 acres deeded land adjoining Nicholas BACHMAN, George Michael KUNTZ, and William HELWIG
2) 32 acres adjoining the first
3) 54 acres adjoining the other tracts
widow: Maria, now wife of John SWARTZ, Lynn Township, farmer
7 children: John, eldest son
Susanna
Elizabeth
Peter
Daniel
Catharine
Christian

**Court on 21 March 1786, continued:**

New guardians for 4 minors, legatees of Henry KUHN, Salisbury Township (had will) (all now over 14):
petitioner: Peter KAESS, Lehigh Township, father of the children
4 children: Mary KAESS
Peter KAESS
John KAESS
Magdalena KAESS
guardian: former—Peter RHOADS, Esq., who wanted to be discharged
new—Peter KAESS, their father

New guardians for 4 minors, legatees of Henry KUHN, Salisbury Township (had will) (all now over 14):
petitioner: Henry ECKENROTH, Macungie Township, father of the children
4 children: Henry ECKENROTH
John ECKENROTH
George ECKENROTH
Catharine ECKENROTH
guardian: former—Henry HAGENBACH, Town of Northampton, tavern keeper
new—Henry ECKENROTH, their father

**Court on 22 March 1786**
**Justices, the Esquires: not named**

New guardian for Catharina, now over age 14, daughter of Benjamin REEGLE, Lower Saucon Township:
guardian: former—Daniel DIEHL
new—Anthony LERCH, Jr., Lower Saucon Township

Guardians for minor children of Christian SMITH, lately died, Heidelberg Township (all under age 14) (were other children) :
petitioners: Abraham LEINBERGER and John ALSPACK
children: Barned
Elizabeth
Susanna
guardian: for all 3 children—Peter HANDWERG, Heidelberg Township

Guardian for 3 children of Christian FISHER, Upper Milford Township (all under age 14) (12 children in all):
widow: Magdalena, now wife of John MORRITZ, Whitehall Township
children: Maria
Anthony
Magdalena
guardians: Jacob SHRIVER and Godfridt KNAUS, Whitehall Township

New guardians for 4 minor children of Ulrich BRINKER, Lower Saucon Township (were other children):
children: Adam, over age 14
Jacob, over age 14
George, under age 14
John, under age 14
guardians: former—Adam KUCHER and John OBERLY, appointed last December; refused
new—for Adam: Frederich LABACH, Lower Saucon Township, farmer
for Jacob: John REEL, Williams Township, farmer
for George and John: Michael BOYER, Bethlehem Township, farmer

**Court on 22 March 1786, continued:**

New guardians for minor KAESS children, the grandchildren of Henry KUHN, Salisbury Township (had will)—left legacies to the children of his daughter, Margaret, wife of Peter KAESS:

petitioner: Peter RHOADS, Esq.
guardian: Peter RHOADS, appointed earlier, "that some of the Monie belonging to the said children came into his hands as Guardian before and since the late war...is very desirous to have his account finally adjusted or at least as far as the depreciation operated on the monies in his hands..." and wanted the court to appoint new guardians for the children, "in order to settle and adjust the account of the said petitioner, relative to his guardianship...."
new guardian: for all minor children under age 14 (not named), Casper SHOENEBRUCH

Estate of Jacob HAFELFINGER, tract of Indian Land in Lehigh Township—request inquest:

land: 200 acres bounded by Ludwig KLIPPINGER, Martin SWOAB, John DREISBACH, James HUTCHINSON
petitioners: Michael FABEYON, Springfield Township, Bucks County and his wife Gertrude, one daughter of the deceased
8 children: Henry, eldest son
Catharine, wife of William SYLVIUS
Elizabeth, widow of Jacob FRIED (mother of 10 children)
Esther, wife of Andrew MOYER
Barbara, wife of Conrad SYLVIUS
Mary, wife of Casper FABEYON
John
Gertrude, wife of Michael FABEYON

**Court on 23 March 1786**
**Justices, the Esquires: not named**

Estate of John SHADE (had will)—auditors' report:

executors: Elizabeth Catharina SHADE and Samuel SEEGER
debt due to: John BERLIP (for clothes)

Guardians for 5 minor children of Jacob ZELLNER, Lowhill Township (all under age 14):

administrators: Andrew BUCHMAN and Jacob BACHMAN, Lowhill Township
5 children: Henry
Jacob
Peter
Catharina
Barbara
guardians: for all 5 children—Jacob HORNER and John KNERR, Lowhill Township

Estate of Michael SHICK, Lowhill Township—auditors' report:

widow: Barbara, now wife of Philip SLICKER, administrators
children: a son
a daughter
a daughter, deceased 23 January 1786

**Court on 23 March 1786, continued:**

Guardian for Christian NAGLE, Moore Township, who "has been for four years past non compos mentis, incapable of taking care of his person and estate":

petitioner: Frederick NAGLE, his brother and next friend
guardians: Paul FLICK and Henry STROUSS

Citation against guardian of one daughter of Henry SMITH—motion of Collison READ, Esq.:

daughter: Margaret, now wife of Casper MADENY
guardian: Andreas OHL—to appear in court next June to settle his account of guardianship

Estate of Philip HERTZOG, the elder, Upper Milford Township, 2 tracts of 108 acres and 37 acres—report of inquest by Sheriff Peter EALER, Esq.:

widow
7 children: Paul, eldest son—accepted the land
others not named
securities: David HEIMBACH and Simon SCHNEIDER, upper Milford Township, farmers
12 men:by oath—John WETZEL, Ludwig STAHLER, Adam SHULER, William SHAFFER, Simon SHNYDER, Peter SHAFFER, Joseph KOKEN, Nicholas HITTLE, George HAMAN, Christian FISHER
by affirmation—Michael SHAFFER, Joseph SEWITZ

**Court on 24 March 1786**
**Justices, the Esquires: not named**

Estate of Paul BALLIET, Whitehall Township (had will made 15 March 1777)—request audit:

petitioner: John BARR in right of his wife Susanna, daughter of the deceased
children: Susanna, wife of John BARR
Stephen, the executor
auditors: Michael SHNYDER, George BREINIG, Esq., William HAINTZ

**Court on 25 March 1786**
**Justices, the Esquires: not named**

William CONGLETON, Allen Township, age 50 years+, served as private man in 1st Battalion of Militia of Northampton commanded by Col. Stephen BALLIET in September 1777; at Battle of Brandywine, he was appointed to drive wagons in the service of the army, "the horses taking fright he was thrown down and received a contusion in his right shoulder which has forever disabled him from the use of that arm and rendered his incapable of getting his livelihood by labor." He had applied to the court at various times for support, two orders were still unsatisfied. The court ordered and decreed to him ½ pay of a private soldier from 1 October 1779 less any amount he had already received.

**Court on 2 May 1786**
**Justices, the Esquires: Benjamin DEPUI, William McNAIR, Robert LEVERS**

Estate of Leonard WELSCH, died about 5 days ago, Forks Township—request sale:

land: 163 acres, part of Dry Land Tract, bounded by Peter SEIP, Nicholas MICHAEL, Casper NOLF, Michael LAWALL
administrators: Jacob WELSCH and Anthony LERCH, Jr.
5 children

**Court on 2 May 1786, continued:**

Estate of Arnold BILLIG, died about 1 year ago, Penn Township—request inquest:

| | |
|---|---|
| land: | 100 acres adjoining Michael WEAVER, one SHELHIMER and one BAUMAN |
| widow: | Peternella, now wife of George ZIMMERMAN, Penn Township |
| 9 children: | Anthony, eldest son |
| | Magdalena, wife of Dewalt PEELMAN, Northumberland County |
| | Christina, wife of Michael BUCK, Lynn Township |
| | Henry |
| | Emanuel |
| | Eva Catharina, wife of William NICHOL, Fayette County |
| | Maria, under age 14 |
| | Peternella, under age 14 |
| | John, under age 14 |

Estate of John STINTON, Allen Township (had will)—citation for guardian to appear and render account:

| | |
|---|---|
| petitioners: | David COCHRAN and wife Elizabeth, one daughter of deceased |
| executor: | William OLIPHANT |
| guardians: | John LATTIMORE, now deceased, & Neigal GRAY, about to leave state |

**Court on 23 December 1785 (out of order)**
**Justices, the Esquires: not named**

Estate of Christian RUTH—further action on citation against guardians of minor children; request audit:

| | |
|---|---|
| petitioners: | Michael MICKEL and wife Anna Maria, widow of RUTH |
| guardians: | Daniel SWARTZ and Valentine SHAFER |
| auditors: | George GRAFF, John ROMICH, George SHREIBER |

**Court on 20 June 1786**
**Justices, the Esquires: Peter RHOADS, Peter KOHLER, Jacob MORRY, Thomas HARTMAN, George BREINIG, Jacob ROSECRANZE**

Guardian for Robert, minor over age 14, one child of Robert HANNAS, Lower Smithfield Township:

| | |
|---|---|
| guardian: | Elias DEALY, Mt. Bethel Township |

New guardian for Mary, minor over age 14, one child of George WEAVER, Lower Saucon Township:

| | |
|---|---|
| guardian: | former—John NEWCOMER |
| | new—Isaac SHYMER, Lower Saucon Township |

Guardian for minor children of Arnold BILLING, died about 1 year ago, Penn Township (all over age 14) (were other children):

| | |
|---|---|
| widow: | Eleanore, now wife of George ZIEGLER |
| children: | Mary |
| | Eleanore |
| | John |
| guardian: | for all 3 children—Henry MILLER, Penn Township |

**Court on 21 June 1786**
**Justices, the Esquires: not named**

Estate of Philip ZIMMERMAN—return of sale:
administrators: Mary ZIMMERMAN and Nicholas MICHAEL
sold to: Leonard FRANKENFIELD, Bethlehem Township

Estate of Christian RUTH—auditors' report; rent for the estate was sufficient but the guardians were indebted to the MICKELS for maintenance of the children:
petitioners: Michael MICKEL and wife Anna Maria, widow of RUTH
guardians: Daniel SWARTZ and Valentine SHAFER

Estate of Ulrich BRINKER, died about 1 year ago, Lower Saucon Township—request inquest:
land: 150 acres bounded by Henry KRATZER, George HUBNER, Andreas OHL
6 children: Andrew, eldest son
Margaret, wife of Simon HAWK
Jacob
Adam
John
George

**Court on 22 June 1786**
**Justices, the Esquires: not named**

Barnet SCHLAUCH, age 29 years, late a soldier in Cap. Henry SHADE's Company in 1st Pennsylvania State Regiment in service of United States—on 2 January 1777, he was wounded in the leg at Battle of Princetown; his leg was lost. Request pension.
Awarded $3 per month pension from last 31 May, having received assistance until then.

Estate of Jacob HAFELFINGER, Lehigh Township, 200 acres—report of inquest by Sheriff Peter EALER, Esq.:
12 men:all by oath—Conrad CREIDER (KREITER), Abraham LEVAN, John LERCH, Christian HAGENBACH, George SEAME, Frederick BECK, Michael (George Michael) BASTIAN, Paul KNOUSE (KNOUSS), Andrew LILLY, George REES (RIESS), George EDLEMAN, Leonard LILLY

Estate of Jacob HAFELFINGER, Lehigh Township, 200 acres—Motion of Collinson READ, Esq. on behalf of John HAFELFINGER, one child of Jacob HAFELFINGER:
John thought he was entitled to the land from the partition issued on 22 March last on petition of Michael FABEYON. He wanted the Court of Common Pleas to try the title of the land.

Estate of Christian MILLER, Lynn Township—report of inquest by Sheriff Peter EALER, Esq.:
land: 150 acres patented land, plus two tracts of 32 acres and 54 acres
widow
7 children: John, eldest son—accepted the land
others not named
securities: Henry HARTMAN, Lowhill Township, and John SWARTZ, Lynn Township
12 men:all by oath—Michael OHL, Michael BOBST, Philip MOSER, Barnet SHNYDER (SCHNEIDER), George Michael KUNTZ, Burkhart MOSER, Philip SHUCK (SHUK), Michael FENSTERMACHER, Jacob HANS, Jacob WERTMAN, John SHUCK (SHUK), Peter WEISS

**Court on 22 June 1786, continued:**

Estate of Peter BEISEL, Allen Township—report of inquest by Sheriff Peter EALER, Esq.:
land: 1) 300 acres adjoining Jacob FRACH, Christian FENSTERMACHER, Wendel HAUER
2) 90 acres of Dry Land Tract adjoining other tract and Jacob BEISEL Jacob HAFELFINGER, Lehigh Township
3) 200 acres
widow
6 children: Peter, eldest son—accepted the land
John, died intestate, unmarried but of age
others not named
securities: William Henry LAWALL, Bethlehem Township, tavern keeper, and John GRIESSEMER, Whitehall Township, farmer
12 men:by oath—John HAYS, David DESHLER, Abraham LEVAN, James CARR (KERR), Jacob FRACH, Joseph LAROSCH, Christian HAGENBACH
by affirmation—John SIEGFRIED, Nicholas HAUER, Frederick KLIPPINGER, George HAAS, Henry BEIL

Estate of Leonard WELSH, Forks Township 163 acres—return of sale:
administrators: Jacob WELSCH and Anthony LERCH, Jr.
sold to: Thomas HARTMAN, Esq.

Johannes LEIBY, age 43 years, Lynn Township, late a private in Cap. John KRUM's Company, 3rd Pennsylvania Battalion, Northampton County Militia commanded by Col. Jacob STROWD—request support:
While in service, he was at the house of Isaac SUMMONY in North Wales Township, now Montgomery County, on 26 April 1778. He was wounded by the British enemy in 27 places; one wound cut by a cutlass on each hand and one on the ankle rendered him disabled. Awarded a monthly pension.

**Court on 19 September 1786**
**Justices, the Esquires: Peter RHOADS, Peter KOHLER, Benjamin DEPUI, Thomas HARTMAN, Jacob MORRY, Benjamin VAN CAMPEN**

Estate of Jonas PETTIT—remained under advisement:
administrator: Godfrey GREENSWEIG

**Court on 20 September 1786**
**Justices, the Esquires: not named**

Estate of Ulrich BRINKER—inquest report by Sheriff Peter EALER, Esq.; remained under advisement:
eldest son: Andrew, "does not attend, the valuation of the said Real Estate is not now confirmed by the court"

**Court on 21 September 1786**
**Justices, the Esquires: not named**

Guardian for 2 minor children of George SHICK, died about 10 years ago, Plainfield Township (both under 14) (were other children):
executor: Ulrich HAUSER
children: John

Philip
guardian: for both children—William FREEMAN, Plainfield Township, farmer

**Court on 21 September 1786, continued:**

Estate of Christian RUTH—court ordered an attachment issued against the guardians for not obeying court order:

petitioners: Michael MICKEL and wife Anna Maria, widow of RUTH
guardians: Daniel SWARTZ and Valentine SHAFER, "have refused to pay obedience to a certain order of this court"

Estate of George WEAVER, Lower Saucon Township (wrote will on 28 July 1770, then died soon after)—complaint against former guardians of 3 minor children:

executor: Valentin OPP
widow: Barbara, now wife of Anthony STOCK
children: Catherine, wife of John MOYER
Valentine................................................guardian: Jacob ROAD
Mary......................................................guardian: Isaac SHYMER
guardians: former, appointed on 7 March 1772—John NEWCOMER and Gratius LERCH; John had not paid shares to the three children; both men were cited to appear

Guardians for 5 minor children of Benjamin KRATZER, Mt. Bethel Township (all under age 14) (were other children):

children: Philip, eldest son, of age, the petitioner
John
Jacob
David
Magdalena
Christina
guardian: for all 5 minor children—Nicholas MILHENBERGER, Lehigh Township, farmer

Estate of Paul BALLIET (had will)—auditors' report (auditors met at house of Michael SCHNEIDER, Whitehall Township):

executor: Stephen BALLIET

Estate of George WEAVER, Lower Saucon Township [repeat of above]

**Court on 18 December 1786**
**Justices, the Esquires: Peter RHOADS, William McNAIR, Robert LEVERS**

Estate of George WEAVER, Lower Saucon Township—request audit (repeated names of children and guardians):

auditors: John BEYL, Joseph HORSFIELD, George GRAFF

Estate of Christian RUTH—refers back to attachments made against guardians on 21 September last:

guardians: Daniel SWARTZ and Valentine SHAFER—they appeared and paid into the hands of the clerk, Robert LEVERS, Esq., 24 pounds in specie for Michael MICKEL and wife Anna Maria, the widow of Christian RUTH; the guardians were then discharged by the court

**Court on 19 December 1786**
**Justices, the Esquires: Peter RHOADS, Peter KOHLER, Peter CONRAD**

Guardian for Archibald, age about 3 years, only child of Henry MILLER, died a few months ago, Macungie Township:
administrator: Frederick MARTIN
widow
guardian: Peter HAAS, Macungie Township

**Court on 21 December 1786**
**Justices, the Esquires: not named**

Estate of George DIETZ, the younger, deceased, Chestnuthill Township, who was the administrator for his father, George DIETZ, the elder—return of sale:
administrator: Lewis STECKER, Esq.
sold to: Emanuel DERSHIMER, Plainfield Township

**Court on 23 December 1786**
**Justices, the Esquires: Peter RHOADS, Peter KOHLER, Thomas HARTMAN**

Estate of Philip RUTH (had will), who was one administrator of the estate of Christian RUTH (served with Michael MICKEL and wife Anna Maria, the widow of Christian RUTH)—request audit:
executor: Daniel SWARTZ
auditors: George BREINIG, Peter TREXLER, Esquires, and John ROMIG, Macungie Township

**Court on 22 January 1787**
**Justices, the Esquires: Robert LEVERS, Lewis STACKER, Thomas HARTMAN**

Estate of Ulrich BRINKER, Lower Saucon Township, 150 acres—inquest report by Sheriff Peter EALER:
6 children: Andrew, eldest son—accepted the land
others not named
securities: John BOYER, Lower Saucon Twp., & Leonard BEIDLEMAN, Bethlehem Twp.
12 men:by oath—Adam OHL, Andrew KOOCHERT (Andreas KOCKERT), Adam EDLEMAN, Christian RUCH, Jacob LERCH, Jacob OBERLY, Adam WEAVER (WEBER), Henry OHL, Henry KRATZER
by affirmation—Gratius LERCH, Benedict LUTZ, Jacob DÖRR (DERR)

**Court on 19 March 1787**
**Justices, the Esquires: Peter KOHLER, Benjamin DEPUE, Thomas HARTMAN**

New guardian for 3 minor children of Michael HILLEGAS, Upper Saucon Township (all under age 14):
children: Eve
Catharine
Mary
guardian: former—John NEWCOMER, now declined
new—Francis HARTMAN, Upper Saucon Township

Estate of Jacob GINTNER, Mt. Bethel Township—request audit:

petitioner: Jacob GOOD, children's guardian
widow: Sarah, now wife of Mr. SMITH
auditors: Samuel REA, Major John NELSON, Henry JACOBIE, Mt. Bethel Township

**Court on 19 March 1787, continued:**

Estate of Henry WETZEL, died about 10 years ago, Macungie Township—request inquest:

land: 150 acres patented land bounded by Jacob SWARTZ, William HAYNES, Melchior SMITH, Reuben HAYNES
widow: now wife of William SMITH
4 children: John, eldest son
Catharine, wife of Michael STEINER
Jacob
Jeremiah

**Court on 20 March 1787**
**Justices, the Esquires: Peter RHOADS, Peter KOHLER, Lewis STECKER, William McNAIR, Jacob MORRY, Peter KACHLEIN**

New guardian for minor children of Philip HERTZOG, the younger (all still under age 14):

children: Jacob
Catharine
Philip
Mary
guardian: former—Thomas MECHLIN, now deceased, Upper Milford Township (appointed 23 December 1785) (his administrator was Jacob LERCH)
new—George KRIEPEL, Upper Milford Township

Estate of Bernardus SWARTWOOD (had will)—motion of Samuel SITGREAVES, Esq. requesting citation against surviving executor, Benjamin DEPUE, Esq.:

DEPUE was cited to appear in court and exhibit an account

**Court on 10 April 1787**
**Justices, the Esquires: Peter KACHLEIN, Christopher WAGGONER, Robert LEVERS**

Estate of Jonathan NILSON, died sometime ago, Mt. Bethel Township—request inquest:

land: 350 acres bounded by David LOCKART, Alexander KILPATRICK, Joseph SMITH, and others
widow: Sarah
3 children: John, only son
Rebecca, wife of Samuel REA
Eleanor, wife of William McVICKERS
5 grandchildren, children of deceased daughter Sarah, late wife of Thomas SILLYMAN:
Jane SILLYMAN
William SILLYMAN
Mary SILLYMAN
Sarah SILLYMAN
Elisabeth SILLYMAN

**Court on 20 June 1787**
**Justices, the Esquires: Peter RHOADS, Peter KOHLER, William McNAIR, Benjamin DEPUE, Thomas HARTMAN, Peter KACHLEIN**

Estate of Jacob YEANTZER, Weisenberg Township, 2 tracts—request sale and audit:
land: 1) 130 acres in Wesisenberg Township bounded by Jacob GREENEWALT, George KRIM, Godfrey BOGER
2) 100 acres in Lynn Township bounded by Henry NODSTINE, Christopher SUNDAGH, Jacob BACHERT
widow: Sarah, administratrix
auditors: Jacob HORNER, Esq., Matthias PROBST, Philip MOSER

Estate of Ulrich REESER, Upper Milford Township (had will)—request audit:
executors: Casper REESER, George KRIEBEL
children: Andrew, found errors in administration account
others not named
auditors: Peter TREXLER, Jr., John ROMIG, Nicholas KLOTZ

Guardians for minor children of John REINSMITH, Heidelberg Township (all under age 14):
administrator: George HOLDER
children: Henry
Leonard
Maria
guardians: for all 3 children—Andrew MILLER, Lynn Township, and Henry HOFFMAN, Heidelberg Township

Estate of Jonas PETTIT, land in Towamensing Township—refers to petition on 19 September last. Since then, the court learned that Jonas died in Hunterdon County, New Jersey where John BRAY had administered the estate. Godfrey, was "to produce from the surrogate of the said county of Hunterdon a certificate that" John BRAY had settled the administration account there. Moore FURMAN, a surrogate of Hunterdon County, signed such a certificate on 9 May last:
land: 100 acres bounded by Conrad MERKAM, Abraham SMITH, and others
administrator: Godfrey GREENSWEIG—could now sell the property

Estate of Bernardus SWARTWOOD (had will)—auditors appointed:
executor: Benjamin DEPUI, Esq. (surviving executor), appeared under citation and exhibited the administration account
auditors: Jacob ROSENKRANTZE, Esq., Emanuel GONZALEZ, John CHAMBERS

Estate of Henry WETZEL, Macungie Township, 150 acres—report of inquest by Sheriff Peter EALER:
widow
4 children: John, eldest son—accepted the land (others not named)
securities: Jeremiah TREXLER and Peter HAAS, both of Macungie Township
12 men:by oath—George BREINIG, Esq., Peter TREXLER, Esq., William HAYNES (HAINTZ), Jacob SCHWARTZ, Daniel SMYER (SCHMEYER), Andrew ISENHART (EISENHARD), Leonard SCHLAUGH, Herman RUP, Peter HAAS, John TREXLER, Jeremiah TREXLER
by affirmation—John (Johannes) ROMIG

**Court on 20 June 1787, continued:**

Estate of Jonathan NELSON, Mt. Bethel Township, 350 acres—inquest report by Sheriff Peter EALER:
widow
4 children: John, only son—accepted the land
others not named
securities: David LOCKART and Hugh McCRACKEN, both of Mt. Bethel Township
12 men:all by oath—William McFARREN, John NELSON (NEILSON), David LOCKART, Thomas CONNELLY, Hugh McCRACKEN, Michael KAESTER, Garret (Gerrit) MIDDAGH, James ROSS, Adam DEEHL (DEEL), John WILLIAMS, William McFARREN, Jr., Philip KAESTER

**Court on 21 June 1787**
**Justices, the Esquires: not named**

Estate of Arnold BILLIG, Penn Township, 100 acres—report of inquest by Sheriff Peter EALER, Esq., was made on 22 June 1786 but eldest son was not ready to provide securities then:
widow
9 children: Anthony, eldest son—now ready to provide securities (others not named)
securities: John SIGFRIDT, Allen Township, tavern keeper, and Adam BROUSE, Macungie Twp.
12 men:by oath—Philip MOSER, Jacob HAUSER, Philip SHUK, Andrew (Andreas) MILLER, Jacob WERTMAN, John (Hanns) SHUK, George GILBERT, Leonard ZIMMERMAN, Michael OHL, Jr., Cornelius KLINGEMAN, Henry MILLER
by affirmation—Daniel OSWALD

**Court on 17 September 1787**
**Justices, the Esquires: Peter RHOADS, Jacob HORNER, George BREINIG, William McNAIR**

Guardian for 2 minor children of William TOWNSEND, died some years ago, Bethlehem Township (both under age 14) (were other children):
petitioner: Joseph RICHARD, next friend
2 children: Elisabeth
Joseph
guardian: for both children—Jonas HARTZELL, Bethlehem Township, tavern keeper

Guardian for 2 minor sons of Nicholas DEPUE, died "some considerable time ago," (both over age 14) (were other children):
widow: Elisabeth, now wife of Mr. VANCAMPEN
2 sons: Benjamin
Elijah
guardian: for both sons, Daniel SHOEMAKER, Lower Smithfield Township, farmer

Estate of Jacob GENTNER, Mt. Bethel Township—request for new audit because first one did not include everything (same auditors assigned):
petitioner: Sarah SMITH, late GENTNER, administratrix
guardian: already appointed, Jacob GOOD

**Court on 19 September 1787**
**Justices, the Esquires: Peter RHOADS, Peter KOHLER, William McNAIR, Lewis STACKER, George BREINIG, Thomas HARTMAN, Peter KACHLEIN**

Guardian for Jacob, over age 14, minor son of Jacob KENNEL, Whitehall Township:
guardian: Nicholas SAEGER, the younger, Whitehall Township

Guardian for minor children of Henry OTT, Upper Milford Township (both over age 14):
children: Susanna..........................................guardian: Valentine PAUL, Up. Saucon Twp.
Eve................................................guardian: Jacob KOEHLER, Up. Milford Tp.

Estate of Henry OTT, died about 2 years ago, Upper Milford Township, 2 tracts—request inquest:
land: 1) 250 acres bounded by George ENGLEMAN, Simon WALTER, George HALL
2) 97 acres bounded by George ENGLEMAN and Jacob ZERFINK
widow
11 children: Christopher, eldest son
Michael
Henry
George
Jacob
Elisabeth, wife of Nicholas SAMSEL
Mary, wife of John OLINGER
Catharine, wife of George WORMAN
Margaret, wife of Michael RUDOLPH
Susanna
Eve

Jane ROSBROUGH, Allen Township, widow of Rev. John ROSEBROUGH, who died while in service of the United States of America in 1777 when chaplain to a Battalion of Militia under the command of John SIGFRIDT, then a major—requested support for herself and her 5 small children:
remained under advisement

**Court on 13 November 1787**
**Justices, the Esquires: Robert LEVERS, Peter KACHLEIN, Thomas HARTMAN**

Estate of Jacob BRAUCHER, died about 2 months ago, Weisenberg Township—request sale; auditors appointed:
land: 75 acres bounded by Paulus PAUL, Lawrence HOLWIG, George KRAMLICH
administrators: George BRAUCHER and Valentine GRAMLICH
widow: Margaret
2 children: Anna Maria, minor over age 14
Mary, minor over age 14
auditors: Michael BOBST, Jacob HORNER, Esq., Frederick SEIBERLING

**Court on 18 December 1787**
**Justices, the Esquires: Peter RHOADS, Peter KOHLER, Benjamin DEPUE, George BREINIG, Jacob HORNER**

Estate of Jacob KUNTZ, Lynn Township, 3 contiguous tracts—request sale; auditors appointed:
land: 1) 113 acres bounded by Jacob GERBER, Adam MILLER, the late Conrad REIN, George Michael KUNTZ, and Sylvester HOLBEY
2) 25 acres bounded by 1st tract & Michael FENSTERMACHER, Jacob HANTZ
3)11 acres patented land bounded by other tracts and the great road leading to Philadelphia
administrators: George Michael KUNTZ and Jacob HANTZ
children
auditors: Jacob HORNER, Esq., Philip MOSER, Mathias PROBST

**Court on 20 December 1787**
**Justices, the Esquires: not named**

Estate of Bernardus SWARTWOOD (had will)—motion of Samuel SITGREAVES, Esq., referred to petition on 20 June last when auditors were appointed; request new auditors:
executor: Benjamin DEPUE, Esq.
auditors: former—Jacob ROSENKRANTZE, Esq., Emanuel GONZALES, John CHAMBERS
new—Nicholas DEPUI, Esq., John SMITH, Daniel SHOEMAKER

Estate of Jacob BRAUCHER, Weisenberg Township—auditors' report; sale approved:
administrators: George BRAUCHER and Valentine GRAMLICH

Estate of Godfrey KNOUSE, Whitehall Township—request audit:
administrators: George Frederick KNOUSE, Philip KNOUSE, Gottfried KNOUSE, and Paul KNOUSE, administrators de Bonis non
auditors: Peter KOHLER, Esq., John ROMIG, Joseph HORSFIELD

**Court on 20 March 1788**
**Justices, the Esquires: Peter KOHLER, Benjamin DEPUE, George BREINIG**

Guardian for Christian RUTH, now age 14, one child of Christian RUTH, died 1 year ago, Macungie Township (were other children):
guardian: Adam HEVERLY, Whitehall Township

Guardians for 4 minor children of Thomas MECHLIN, Upper Milford Township (all under age 14):
petitioner: Anthony OBERLY, step-father of children
4 children: John
Ann
Barbara
Peter
guardians: for John and Ann—Frederick LAUBACH, Lower Saucon Township
for Barbara and Peter—Anthony LERCH, Lower Saucon Township, miller

Estate of Jacob KUNTZ, Lynn Township, 3 tracts—auditors' report; permission to sell:
administrators: George Michael KUNTZ and Jacob HANTZ
children

**Court on 20 March 1788, continued:**

Guardians for 6 minor children of Peter HARTMAN, Heidelberg Township (all under age 14):
petitioner: Henry HARTMAN, one administrator
6 children: Eve
Susannah
Philip
Andrew
Catharina
Peter
guardians: for all 6 children—John HARTMAN and Nicholas MILLER

Estate of Jacob YEANTZER, Weisenberg Township, 2 tracts—auditors' report (found that the widow had sold one tract of 100 acres in Lynn Township bounded by Henry NODSTEIN, Christopher SUNDAGH, Jacob BARKET and used the money to pay some debts); permission to sell remaining land:
widow: Sarah, administratrix

Guardians for 5 minor children of George REICHERT, Lower Saucon Township (had will) (were other children):
executors: Michael REICHERT and George REICHERT
5 children: Andrew, over age 14................................guardian: Michael REICHERT
John, over age 14....................................guardian: Michael REICHERT
Jacob, over age 14..................................guardian: George REICHERT
George William, under age 14................guardian: Anthony LERCH, Jr., same place
Catharina, under age 14..........................guardian: Anthony LERCH, Jr., same place

Estate of Peter HARTMAN, died about 1 year ago, Heidelberg Township, 2 tracts—request sale; auditors appointed:
land: 1) 119 acres bounded by Jacob HARTMAN, Henry HOFFMAN, John EVERT, Simon WARE
2) 27 acres bounded by Jacob HARTMAN, Christian HARTMAN, Jacob GREASLE
administrators: Henry HARTMAN and Andrew KNERR
widow: Eve
6 children: Eve
Philip
Susanna
Andrew
Peter
Catharine
auditors: Mathias PROBST, Andrew BUCKMAN, Michael OHL

Estate of Moses BEER, died about 13 years ago, Lehigh Township—request inquest:
land: 80 acres bounded by Frederick KUNTZ, Jacob KESTER, John LEIENBERGER, Adam BEER
widow: now wife of William SMITH, now of New York
4 children: Samuel, eldest son
David
Jacob

Rachel, "the two last being at present prisoners with the Delaware Indians"

**Court on 25 March 1788**
**Justices, the Esquires: Robert LEVERS, Peter KACHLEIN, Thomas HARTMAN**

Estate of Henry RUMFELD, Upper Saucon Township—request sale; auditors appointed (10 children, all of age):
land: 200 acres deeded land bounded by John NEWCOMER, John BACHMAN, Felix LYNN, John STAHL
administrators: John RUMFELD and Casper RUMFELD
10 children: Margaret
Catharine
John
Jacob
Henry
Casper
George
Philip
Hannah
Susannah
auditors: Christopher WAGNER, Esq., John ROTHROCK, Sr., John NEWCOMER, Sr.

Estate of Peter HARTMAN, Heidelberg Township, 2 tracts—auditors' report; permission to sell:
administrators: Henry HARTMAN and Andrew KNERR
debt owed to: John EBERT (original report listed wrong amount; correction made)

**Court on 2 April 1788**
**Justices, the Esquires: Robert LEVERS, Peter KACHLEIN, Robert TRAILL**

Guardian for John David, over age 14, minor son of John Wolfgang MICHLER:
guardian: John SCHROPP, Nazareth

**Court on 1 May 1788**
**Justices, the Esquires: Robert LEVERS, Peter KACHLEIN, Thomas HARTMAN**

Estate of Henry RUMFELD, Upper Saucon Township—auditors' report; permission to sell:
administrators: John RUMFELD and Casper RUMFELD (sons)

Estate of Moses BEER, Lehigh Township, 80 acres—report of inquest by Sheriff George GRAFF, Esq.:
widow
4 children: Samuel, eldest son—refused to accept the land
David, 2nd son—accepted the land
others not named
securities: Enoch BEER, Esq., and George BROWN, both of Lehigh Township
12 men: all by oath—Frederick KUNTZ, Peter ANTHONY, Henry (Henrich) SHNEIDER, Leonard HEISLY, Joseph PETY (BETY), George LEIBENGOOD, George SENGLY (SINGLI), Jacob GEISSEL, Henry PEST (Henrich BËST), Michael PEST (BEST), Nicholas SHNEIDER, Jacob KESTER (KÜSTER)

**Court on 17 May 1788**

**Justices, the Esquires: William McNAIR, Thomas HARTMAN, William HENRY**

Mrs. Jane ROSEBRUGH, widow of Rev. John ROSEBRUGH, killed by enemy in Trenton—court ruled that she should receive ½ pay due her by right of her husband, deducting funds already received.

**Court on 20 June 1788**

**Justices, the Esquires: Peter KOHLER, William McNAIR, William HENRY**

Estate of Bernardus SWARTWOOD—auditors' report:

| | |
|---|---|
| executor: | Benjamin DEPUE |
| debts owed to: | Christopher DENMARK |
| | Nealty SWARTWOOD |
| | Anthony SWARTWOOD |
| | Benjamin SWARTWOOD |
| | Gradus SWARTWOOD |
| | Jarnity CORTRIGHT |

Estate of Jacob GENTNER (KENTNER), Mt. Bethel Township—auditors' report; return of sale:

| | |
|---|---|
| widow: | Sarah, now wife of Mr. SMITH, administratrix |
| guardian: | for minor children, already appointed—Jacob GUTH |
| sold to: | Adam OYER and Christian ILLENBERGER—land which had been purchased from Abraham LUKENS by the deceased |
| father-in-law: | Christian ILLENGERGER, "Extraordinary to be allowed to Christian ILLENBERGER for adjusting his Daughter's Administratrix,"and "Christian ILLENBERGER in behalf of his daughter now Sarah SMITH" |
| funds paid to: | Joseph FORGEMAN, Charles FLEMING, Arthur MITCHEL, Philip STYNE, George Henry KNEGHT, John KLING, Moses PHENIX, Thomas PARRY |

Estate of Casper RUMMAGE, Lower Smithfield Township—request audit:

| | |
|---|---|
| petitioner: | Jacob STROWD, Esq., guardian for 2 minor children |
| widow: | Mary, now wife of Jacob SCHÄFFER, administratrix |
| auditors: | Nicholas DEPUE, Samuel DRAKE, Benjamin SHOONOVER |

John TAYLOR, soldier, Mt. Bethel Township, was granted order for ½ pay from Lt. of County, Samuel REA, Esq., on 22 December 1780, which he never received, "petitioner having been taken Prisoner at the Surrender of Fort Washington and his Health so greatly Impaired...."—remained under advisement.

**Court on 21 June 1788**

**Justices, the Esquires: not named**

Estate of Samuel MUSICK, died about 12 years ago, Whitehall Township—request inquest:

| | |
|---|---|
| land: | warranted land of 150 acres bounded by Casper WISTAR, Lawrence GOOD, Adam GOOD, John LARR, Leonard STAININGER |
| widow: | now wife of Andrew KNEDLER |
| 8 children: | Samuel, eldest son |
| | David |
| | Anthony |
| | Margareth |
| | Elizabeth |
| | Barbara |
| | Catharine |
| | Salome |

**Court on 25 June 1788**
**Justices, the Esquires: Lewis STACKER, Thomas HARTMAN, William HENRY**

Estate of John OBITZ, Plainfield Township, 2 tracts—request sale (except for mansion house and 30 acres to include meadow ground and orchard):
land: 1)125 acres patented land adjoining Jacob EYERLY, Jr., Nicholas SEYFRIED, Christian BREION?, John SCHAFFER, and others
2)190 acres warranted land and one moiety of 2 warrants for 400 acres adjoining Durst ALLEMAN, Gottlieb DEMUTH, and others
administrators: Jacob EYERLY, Jr., and George HAHN

**Court on 17 September 1788**
**Justices, the Esquires: Peter RHOADS, George BREINIG, Peter KACHLEIN, William HENRY**

Guardian for Ann Mary, under 14, one child of Jacob HOLTZHAUSEN, Upper Milford Township:
petitioner: Jacob STAHL, one executor
guardian: George KRIEBEL, Upper Milford Township

**Court on 18 September 1788**
**Justices, the Esquires: Christopher WAGNER, present in room of Mr. KACHLEIN**

Guardian for 2 minor children of George DOLL, Hamilton Township:
widow: Hannah, now wife of Adam BEIDELMAN
2 children: Elizabeth, over age 14
John, under age 14
guardian: for both children—Valentine METZ, Plainfield Township

**Court on 18 September 1788**
**Justices, the Esquires: Peter RHOADS, George BREINIG, Christopher WAGNER, William HENRY**

Citation against guardian of minor daughter of Henry FRIEDLY—motion of Robert TRAILL, Esq.:
child: Elizabeth
guardian: George BREINER—cited to report to court and make account of his guardianship

Estate of John MUSCH, Easton—request sale; auditors appointed:
land: 27 acres warranted land in Lower Saucon Township bounded by Frederick ERNST, Adam KUCKER, Jacob LERCH
widow: Anna Catharina, administratrix
auditors: Robert TRAILL, Esq., Jacob ARNDT, Jr., Peter SCHNYDER

Estate of William LABAR, Mt. Bethel Township—request audit:
administrator: William LABAR, perceived there were mistakes in the administration account
auditors: George A. BAKER, Alexander FORSEMAN, Derrick ATTEN

Guardians for 3 minor children of Leonard WELSCH, Forks Township (all under age 14):
3 children: John

Anna
Mary
guardian: for all 3 children—Anthony OBERLY, Lower Saucon Township

**Court on 19 September 1788**
**Justices, the Esquires: Peter RHOADS, Peter KACHLEIN, Thomas HARTMAN, Jacob HORNER, William HENRY**

Estate of John OBITZ, Plainfield Township, 3 tracts—return of sale:
administrators: Jacob EYERLY, Jr., and George HAHN
sold to: 1) 36 acres, 144 perches patented land to Joseph HILL
2) 51 acres, 85 perches patented land to Dorst ALLEMAN
3) 24 acres, 130 perches warranted land to Joseph HILL
4) 104 acres, 38 acres warranted land to Joseph HILL
5) 64 acres, 68 perches warranted land to Christian Henry BEK
6) one moiety of 2 warrants to Joseph HILL

**Court on 10 October 1788**
**Justices, the Esquires: Thomas HARTMAN, Peter KACHLEIN, William HENRY**

Estate of Henry FRIEDLY—George BREINER, guardian for Elizabeth FRIEDLY, appeared on citation; auditors appointed:
"alledges that all the monies he had in his hands for the said Elizabeth was in Bills Emitted by the Congress of the United States of America."
auditors: Jacob HORNER, Esq., Mathias PROBST, Michael BOBST

Estate of Henry MILLER, Macungie Township—request sale; auditors appointed:
land: land messuage and tenement on 2 acres lot of land, Miller's Town, Macungie Township bounded by Christian FISHER and Michael SHÄFFER
petitioners: Catharine RAWN (late Catharine MILLER) and Frederick MARTIN, administrators
auditors: John WETZEL, Esq., James GILL, Andrew GIERING

Estate of John MUCSH, Easton—auditors' report; permission to sell:
widow: Anna Catharine, administratrix
debts owed to: George PALMER, Michael OPP, John MYER (were not included in admin. account)

**Court on 29 October 1788**
**Justices, the Esquires: Peter KOHLER, Peter KACHLEIN, William HENRY, Jacob HORNER**

Estate of Peter HARTMAN, Heidelberg Township—return of sale:
administrators: Andreas KNERR and Henry HARTMAN
sold to: 1) 115 acres land adjoining John EBERT, Henry HOFFMAN, Jacob HARTMAN and others—to Lewis LUKE
2) 27 acres adjoining Jacob HARTMAN, Jacob GRESSLY, & others—to Lewis LUKE
3) 57 acres in Lowhill Township adjoining John HARTMAN, Henry KRACOLO, Simon GEORGE, & others—to Christian SMITH

Estate of Henry MILLER, Macungie Township, 2 acres lot in Miller's Town—auditors' report; permission to sell:
administrators: Catharine RAWN (late Catharine MILLER) and Frederick MARTIN

Estate of Henry FRIEDLY—auditors' report:

guardian: George BREINER (for minor daughter Elizabeth FRIEDLY)

funds to: Jacob WELCHER (funds which George said was the same money he had received from Bertholomus HUBER, money which Bertholomus had borrowed from Henry FRIEDLY)

**Court on 29 October 1788, continued:**

Estate of Paul BROD, died about 5 years ago, Lower Saucon Township—request inquest:

land: 180 acres bounded by Conrad REASLY, George DREIBLE, John LADEMACKER, and Andrew SICKAFOOSE

widow: now wife of William GROOVER

10 children: Barnet, eldest son
Frederick
Conrad
Michael
Jacob
Mary
Margaret
Catharine
Rosina
Susannah

**Court on 14 November 1788**
**Justices, the Esquires: Peter RHOADS, Peter KOHLER, George BREINIG**

Estate of Christian RUTH—in reference to citation for Daniel SWARTZ, late guardian of minor children, to appear and account for monies and effects of guardianship; Daniel asked for more time:

children: Christian
Catharina

guardian: Adam HERBERLE

**Court on 15 December 1788**
**Justices, the Esquires: Thomas HARTMAN, Peter KACHLEIN, William CRAIG**

Estate of Philip DRUM, Moore Township; Philip was guardian to Frederick, a son of Henry DIEHL; Frederick now of full age and wanted his share of the estate, but there was dispute respecting different currencies—request audit:

executor: Henry STRAUSS, petitioner

auditors: Conrad IHRIE, Jr., Esq., John HERSTER, Peter SHNYDER

**Court on 16 December 1788**
**Justices, the Esquires: Peter KACHLEIN, William HENRY, William CRAIG**

Estate of Philip DRUM, late guardian of Frederick DIEHL—auditors' report:

Frederick is due 15 pounds, 15 shillings, 4 pence specie in hand

**Court on 17 December 1788**
**Justices, the Esquires: Peter RHOADS, Peter KOHLER, George BREINIG, William HENRY**

Guardian for Conrad, over age 14, one minor child of Philip FOX:

guardian: Simon DREISBACH, Esq.

Estate of Jacob KUNTZ, Lynn Township—return of sale:
- 2 tracts sold: 1) 11 acres, 76 perches patented land
  2) 153 acres, 20 perches warranted land
- sold to: Michael BOBST

**Court on 17 December 1788, continued:**

Estate of Frederick BERKENSTOCK, died about 17 years ago, Upper Milford Township—request inquest:
- land: 200 acres adjoining Michael OTT, Andrew ENGLEMAN, Adam ENGLEMAN, of which 100 acres were sold by order of the court
- widow: now wife of Adam ENGLEMAN
- 2 children: John, eldest son
  Abraham

Estate of Michael ENDRES, Upper Milford Township—citation against executors to make account of estate:
- executors: Jacob STAHL and George SYDER, who had refused to render an account
- guardians: Philip WALTER and Andreas EISENHART, the guardians of minor children of Frederick HAINTZ, deceased, Macungie Township, legatees of ENDRES estate

**Court on 18 December 1788**
**Justices, the Esquires: Peter KOHLER, George BREINIG, Jacob HORNER**

Estate of Christian RUTH—guardians of minor children gave an accounting; balance distributed:
- children: Christian
  Elizabeth
  Catharine
  Philip
  Jacob
- guardians: Daniel SWARTZ and Valentine SHÄFFER
- cash paid to: Adam HEBERLY
  Jacob SHUCK
  Frederick MARTIN
  Mess-r SMITH and CLYMER (for advice)
- debts owed to: Joseph EISENHART
  George KNOP
  Isaac HANCOCK
  Jacob WELSCH
  Anthony MOLL
  Frederick BERND
  George GILBERT

**Court on 18 December 1788**
**Justices, the Esquires, now present: Peter KOHLER, Thomas HARTMAN, William HENRY**

Guardian for Peter, over age 14, minor son of Philip FOX:
- guardian: Jacob EYERLY, Jr., Nazareth

## Court on 18 December 1788
**Justices, the Esquires, now present: Peter RHOADS, Peter KOHLER, Lewis STACKER, Thomas HARTMAN, Jacob HORNER, William HENRY**

Estate of Henry OTT, Upper Milford Township, 2 tracts, 250 acres and 97 acres—report of inquest by Sheriff Peter EALER, Esq.; refers to 17 December 1787 when eldest son could not provide securities:

widow
11 children: Christopher—accepted the land
securities: George WARMAN and Michael OTT, Upper Milford Township
12 men: by oath—Simon WALTER
by affirmation—Adam ROMICK, George BACHMAN, Daniel COOPER, John (Hannes) BACHMAN, John (Johannes) GEISSINGER, Abraham GEISSINGER, Andrew (Andreas) ENGLEMAN, Nicholas DIETZ, George RUCH, Stoffel LIEGLER (ZIEGLER), Jacob HUBER

## Court on 19 December 1788
**Justices, the Esquires: Peter RHOADS, Peter KOHLER, Lewis STACKER, Peter KACHLEIN**

Estate of Simon HELLER, died about 3 years ago, Hamilton Township (had will)—request for citation against executor to make an account:

petitioners: Henry HAUSER and Conrad GERMANTON, 2 heirs of the estate
sole executor: Anthony HELLER, son—never exhibited any inventory

Estate of John MUSCH—return of sale:

administratrix: Anna Catharine MUSCH
sold to: John BEYER, Lower Saucon Township

Estate of Paul BRODT—Sheriff George GRAFF, Esq. ready to report inquest; remained under advisement:

eldest son: Barnet BRODT, did not appear

Estate of William LABAR, Mt. Bethel Township—auditors' report (lists names of over 30 men):

widow
6 children: William, eldest son—administrator

## Court on 9 January 1789
**Justices, the Esquires: Peter KACHLEIN, William CRAIG, Jacob ABEL**

Guardian for John Jost, over age 14, minor son of Philip DRUM, Moore Township:

guardian: Simon DRUM

## Court on 18 March 1789
**Justices, the Esquires: Peter RHOADS, Peter KOHLER, Christopher WAGNER, William HENRY**

Guardians for 2 minor children of Abraham DEPUE, Lower Smithfield Township (both over age 14):

2 children: Moses.................................................guardian: Nicholas DEPUE, L. Smithfield Tp.
Abraham..............................................guardian: Henry SHOEMAKER, same

Guardian for Daniel, under age 14, minor child of Frederick SMITH, Lower Saucon Township (were other children):

petitioner: John APPLE, one administrator
guardian: Philip BAHL, Upper Saucon Township

**Court on 18 March 1789, continued:**

Guardian for Frederick KERN, over age 14, of Upper Milford Township (father not named):

guardian: Mathias KERN, Upper Milford Township

**Court on 18 March 1789**
**Justices, the Esquires: Thomas HARTMAN now present with the others**

Guardians for 3 minor children of Daniel STAMBACH, died about 5 years ago, Lynn Township (all under 14):

petitioner: Jacob GREENEWALT, next friend
3 children: Daniel....................guardian: Jacob MANTZ, Lynn Township
Philip....................guardian: George CUSTARD, Lynn Township
Elizabeth....................guardian: Philip MOSER, Lynn Township

Estate of Jacob YEANTZER, Weisenberg Township—return of sale:

administratrix: Sarah YEANTZER
sold to: 1) 230 acres in Weisenberg Township—to George KRIM
2) 100 acres in Lynn Township—to Jacob BILLMAN

**Court on 18 March 1789**
**Justices, the Esquires, now present: Peter RHOADS, Peter KOHLER, Lewis STACKER, Lewis STÄHLER**

Guardians for minor children of Philip SCHÄFFER, Heidelberg Township:

children: Adam, over age 14....................guardian: George BROWN, Lehigh Township, innholder
Philip, over age 14....................guardian: George BROWN, as above
Anthony, under age 14....................guardian: Anthony SCHÄFFER, Heidelberg T.

Estate of William McCARTY, Allen Township—request sale; auditors appointed:

administrators: Elizabeth McCARTY, Thomas GRIMES, Hugh HORNER
land: 2 tracts, a total of 216 acres, bounded by Robert BROWN, Jesse JONES, Henry BERGER, John SILVIES
auditors: John BONN of Christian's Brunn, gentleman, John RALSTON, Robert BROWN, the last two of Allen Township

**Court on 19 March 1789**
**Justices, the Esquires: Peter RHOADS, Peter KOHLER, William HENRY, Lewis STÄHLER**

Estate of Paul BRODT, Lower Saucon Township, 180 acres—report of inquest, held over from December, by Sheriff George GRAFF, Esq.:

widow
10 children: Barnet, eldest son—now appeared and accepted the land
others not named
securities: Barnet MILLER, Williams Township, and John ODENWELDER, Forks Township

12 men:by oath—Anthony LERCH, Jr., Michael ERNST, John LADEMACHER (LATEMACHER), Henry BACHMAN, George FREIBLY (FREIBEL), Jacob FEAHR (FEHR), Christian RUCH, Peter SEEHN (SEAN)
by affirmation—Frederick LAUBACH, Conrad REICHLY (REICKLE), Peter LERCH, Benedict LUTZ

**Court on 19 March 1789**
**Justices, the Esquires, now present: Peter RHOADS, Peter KOHLER, Thomas HARTMAN, William HENRY**

New guardian for John, over age 14, minor son of John KNECHT, Bethlehem Township:
guardian: former—Peter SEIP
new—John Nicholas HOWER, Allen Township

Guardian for 3 minor children of Peter WEISS, died about 2 years ago, Weisenberg Township (all under 14):
children: Christian, the petitioner
Elizabeth
Christina
Susanna
guardians: for all 3 minors—Andrew MILLER and George CUSTARD, Lynn Township

Guardians for minor children of Baltzer STIEL, died about 5 years ago, Mt. Bethel Township (all under age 14) (were other children):
petitioner: Christian WOLF, step-father
children: Peter
Adam
Andreas
Baltzer
guardian: for all 4 children—Ulrich HOUSER, Forks Township

Guardian for 2 minor children of Baltzer STIEL (both over age 14):
2 children: John
Eve Christina
guardian: Adam SAND, Forks Township

**Court on 21 March 1789**
**Justices, the Esquires: Peter RHOADS, Peter KOHLER, William CRAIG**

Estate of Andrew STAHLNECKER, Upper Saucon Township—request audit:
administrator: Jacob STAHLNECKER
land: 80 acres bounded George KORSHNER, David OWEN, George HAHN, Jacob MOLAX
auditors: Andrew GIERING of Emmaus, John STAHL, Upper Saucon, Anthony STÄHLER, Upper Milford Township

**Court on 19 March 1789 (out of order)**
**Justices, the Esquires: Peter RHOADS, Peter KOHLER, Thomas HARTMAN, William HENRY**

Estate of Frederick BERKENSTOCK—report of inquest by Sheriff George GRAFF, Esq.:
"John BERKENSTOCK the within named petitioner requested that I should not Proceed....":

Estate of Michael ENDRESS—referred to citation of last December against executors to make an adm. account:
executors: Jacob STAHL and George SEYDER

register: John ARNDT—reported that they had now made an admin. account

Estate of Simon HELLER—referred to citation of last December against executor to make an adm. account:
executor: Anthony HELLER
register: John ARNDT—reported that he had now made an admin. account

**Court on 26 March 1789**
**Justices, the Esquires: Peter KACHLEIN, William CRAIG, Jacob ABEL**

Estate of Andrew STAHLNECKER—auditors' report; necessary to sell the land (the report was written and signed in German):
petitioner: Jacob STAHLNECKER

**Court on 30 March 1789**
**Justices, the Esquires: Peter RHOADS, Peter KOHLER, Christopher WAGNER**

Estate of John MILLER, Town of Northampton, carpenter—request sale; auditors appointed:
administrator: Jacob NEWHART
land: 1) 92 acres in Whitehall Township adjoining the late William Allen, Esq., and others
2) 2 acres meadow near the town adjoining Jacob MECHLEY
3) house and lot on Hamilton and James Streets on northeast corner, 60' X 230' deep
4) house and lot on Allen Street

Guardians for 2 minor daughters of George SCHNEPF, Town of Northampton, died sometime ago:
petitioner: John ERHARD, next friend
widow
2 daughters: Catharina, over age 14.............................guardian: Abraham ALBERT, of same, potter
Mary Elizabeth, under age 14..................guardian: Peter HAUCK, of same, cordwainer

**Court on 3 April 1789**
**Justices, the Esquires: Peter KACHLEIN, Thomas HARTMAN, Jacob ABEL**

Estate of Michael BISCHOFF, Upper Milford Township—request audit:
administrator: Jacob BISCHOFF
land: 90 acres, the great part in Upper Milford Township but an 8 acre part in Lower Milford Township, Bucks County, bounded by Jacob WITMER, Jost ERDMAN, John HIESTAND, Adam SHERER
auditors: John NEWCOMER, Daniel COOPER, John GEISSINGER, Upper Saucon Township

**Court on 14 April 1789**
**Justices, the Esquires: Peter RHOADS, George BREINIG, Lodowick STÄHLER**

Estate of Michael BISCHOFF, Upper Milford Township—auditors' report; permission to sell:
administrator: Jacob BISCHOFF

Estate of Michael BISCHOFF, Upper Milford Township—consideration of surety:
administrator: Jacob BISCHOFF—to give other security
surety: "hath since depart this life"

Estate of Henry RUMFELD—return of sale:
administrators: John RUMFELD and Casper RUMFELD, his sons
sold to: John NEWCOMER

**Court on 25 April 1789**
**Justices, the Esquires: Peter KACHLEIN, William CRAIG, Jacob ABEL**

Estate of Michael BISCHOFF, 90 acres mostly in Upper Milford Township but 8 acres in Lower Milford Township, Bucks, County—return of sale:
administrator: Jacob BISCHOFF
sold to: Henry HUBER, Upper Milford Township

**Court on 23 May 1789**
**Justices, the Esquires: Benjamin DEPUE, Thomas HARTMAN, Peter KACHLEIN**

Estate of Philip DRUM, late guardian to the petitioner—auditors' report; request for citation against executor:
petitioner: Frederick DIEHL—found that "a payment was made to the said DRUM on account of the Petitioner of a sum far exceeding the amount so awarded...whereof unless the said award is reconsidered the Petitioner will be defrauded of the little Patrimony which he is entitled...."
executor: Henry STRAUSS—to appear in June and answer the charges

**Court on 16 June 1789**
**Justices, the Esquires: Peter RHOADS, Peter KOHLER, Jacob ABEL**

Guardians for minor grandchildren of John SHAAD, Whitehall Township (had will which bequeathed money to the wife of the petitioner):
petitioner: John FUHR, on behalf of his minor children
daughter: Mary Margaret, wife of John FUHR, the petitioner
grandchildren, children of the daughter Mary Margaret:
John FUHR, age 18
Catharine FUHR, age 16
Barbara FUHR, age 15
Elizabeth FUHR, age 10
guardian: for 3 older children—John FUHR, their father, as long as he provided security
for Elizabeth—John BEAR, Whitehall Township

Estate of William McCARTY, Allen Township, 2 tracts totaling 216 acres—auditors' report; permission to sell:
administrators: Elizabeth McCARTY, Thomas GRIMES, Hugh HORNER

Guardians for 3 minor children of David SCHNYDER, died some years ago, Upper Saucon Township (all under age 14):
petitioner: Abraham SCHNYDER, their uncle
3 children: Jacob
Catharine
John
guardians: for all 3 children—John HIESTAND, Abraham BACHMAN, blacksmith, both of Upper Saucon Township

Estate of Philip DRUM, late guardian for Frederick DIEHL—referred to citation issued 23 May last against

Henry STRAUSS, executor of DRUM estate; court ordered auditors to re-examine the account

**Court on 17 June 1789**
**Justices, the Esquires: Peter RHOADS, Peter KOHLER, William McNAIR, Benjamin DEPUE, George BREINIG, William HENRY, Jacob ABEL**

Guardians for 4 minor children of Jacob BAST, died sometime ago (all under age 14):

| | |
|---|---|
| petitioner: | Casper RITTER, Allen Township |
| 4 children: | Jacob |
| | John |
| | Regina |
| | Martin |
| guardian: | for all 4 children—Jonas HERTZEL, Nazareth Township, Esq. |

New guardian for Casper, now over age 14, one minor child of David ROTH, Bethlehem Township:

| | |
|---|---|
| guardian: | former—Ulrich HAUSSER |
| | new—Leonard SCHWEITZER, Bethlehem Township |

Estate of Lawrence HARTMAN, Chestnuthill Township—request for new audit because the audit rendered in 1780 "by reason of the then fluctuating state of the paper currency, and the receipts and payments by them since that time had and made, in paper and hard money agreeable to the scale of depreciation fixed by the Legislature of this State has so deranged their said account that the same ought to be resettled":

| | |
|---|---|
| auditors: | George GOLHORSLEY, of Christian's Brunn, John YOUNGBERG, of Nazareth, Christian Friederick STEINMAN, of Gnadenthal |

Estate of Abraham FUNK, Springfield Township, Bucks County—request inquest:

| | |
|---|---|
| land: | 55 acres in Upper Milford Township, bounded by land "now or late of" Abraham MYER, Thomas MACHLING, Henry SLEIFER, [blank here but as Gabriel in entry on 17 March 1790] BOBEMEIER, Jacob STAHL on which was a sawmill |
| widow: | Mary |
| children: | Henry, now age 21 |
| | Anna |
| | Jacob |
| | John |
| | Catharine |
| | Elizabeth |
| | Susanna |

**Court on 18 June 1789**
**Justices, the Esquires: Peter RHOADS, Peter KOHLER, George BREINIG**

Guardians for 2 minor children of Leonard GEBHARD, died sometime ago, Upper Milford Township:

| | |
|---|---|
| petitioner: | Killean WEISS, uncle of the children |
| 2 children: | Leonard, over age 14..............................guardian: Killean WEISS, Up. Milford Twp. |
| | John, under age 14..................................guardian: Jacob PROBST, same |

**Court on 18 June 1789**
**Justices, the Esquires, now present: Peter RHOADS, Peter KOHLER, Christopher WAGNER, Jacob ABEL**

Estate of Michael ANDRES—motion of Colinson READ, Esq., of behalf of the guardians of the minor children of Frederick HAINTZ, deceased:

the executors were ordered to shew cause in court next July why they have not given security to the guardians for the children's shares of the estate

**Court on 19 June 1789**
**Justices, the Esquires, now present: Peter RHOADS, Peter KOHLER, Christopher WAGNER, Jacob ABEL**

Estate of Henry RUMFELD, Upper Saucon Township—motion of Robert TRAILL, Esq.:

one heir: daughter Catharine, wife of Michael SMITH

administrators: John RUMFELD and Casper RUMFELD—ordered to appear in court next September to shew cause why the confirmation of the sale of real estate of Henry RUMFELD should not be set aside

**Court on 2 July 1789**
**Justices, the Esquires: Peter KACHLEIN, William HENRY, William CRAIG, Jacob ABEL**

Estate of Michael ANDRES, Upper Milford Township (had will)—request for citation against his executors:

petitioners: George KLEIN and wife Anna Elizabeth, widow of deceased—referred to petition made 24 March 1785 concerning the widow's legacy, which ANDRES's will stated she would lose if she remarried; the court then said she could keep the legacy if she released any claim on the real estate

executors: George SEIDER and Jacob STAHL—had refused to accept a release by the petitioners or pay obedience to a court order; they were cited to appear and shew cause

**Court on 24 August 1789**
**Justices, the Esquires: William McNAIR, William CRAIG, Jacob ABEL**

Estate of Henry RUMFELD—motion of Robert TRAILL, Esq. requesting subpoenas to be issued for witnesses to appear in court in September to testify about a citation issued against the administrators:

administrators: John RUMFELD and Casper RUMFELD

witnesses: Jacob RUMFELD, Jacob BITTENBENDER, John STAHL

**Court on 3 September 1789**
**Justices, the Esquires: Thomas HARTMAN, William HENRY, William CRAIG**

Estate of John HANDWERCK, Heidelberg Township (had will)—motion of Abraham JONES, Esq. regarding a citation against executor:

executor: Peter HANDWERCK—to appear and explain why he had not yet exhibited an account

**Court on 23 September 1789**
**Justices, the Esquires: Peter RHOADS, Peter KOHLER, William HENRY, Jacob HORNER, George BREINIG, Jacob ABEL, Lewis STACKLER**

Estate of Lawrence HARTMAN, Chestnuthill Township, had a mill (had will)—auditors' report:

executors: George HARTMAN, Adolph HARTMAN

land sold to: Peter HORBACH

brother: George HARTMAN, debt owed to him, "to be deducted he having advanced his brother Lawrence said sum in gold and silver before the war"

legacies due to: widow
John HARTMAN

bond: against George DREISBACH, "included in Jacob REEDY's opposite debt"

deed poll to: Jacob REEDY

doctor's fee to: Dr. KENEDY
4 children

**Court on 23 September 1789, continued:**

Estate of Michael ENDRES—motion of Colinson READ, Esq. of behalf of guardians of minor children of Frederick HAINTZ:
executors: George SEIDER and Jacob STAHL—citation issued for them to appear

Estate of Henry RUMFELD—regarding citation issued against administrators; motion of S. SILGREAVES, Esq., to postpone the matter for further consideration:
administrators: John RUMFELD and Casper RUMFELD

Estate of John MILLER, Town of Northampton, carpenter—return of sale:
administrator: Jacob NEWHART
sold to: 1) 92 acres in Whitehall Township to Daniel RHOADS
2) 2 acre meadow near town to Casper WEAVER
3) house and lot on Hamilton Street to George RAUDENBUSH

Estate of John MILLER, Town of Northampton, carpenter—request sale of house and lot on Allen and Andrew Street; permission given:
administrator: Jacob NEWHART—stated that, despite sale of other land, there was still not enough money to pay all the debts
infant child: in need of maintenance and support

**Court on 25 September 1789**
**Justices, the Esquires: Peter RHOADS, Peter KOHLER, Jacob HORNER, Lewis STACKLER**

Guardians for minor children of Henry NEFF, died some years ago, Heidelberg Township (all under age 14):
widow: Catharine, administratrix, now wife of Mr. OSWALD
children: John
Peter
guardian: for both children—Conrad NEFF, Weisenberg Township

Estate of Abraham FUNK—Sheriff George GRAFF, Esq. concerning the inquest for partition:
since the heirs did not attend court, the inquest was kept under advisement

**Court on 25 September 1789**
**Justices, the Esquires, now present: Peter RHOADS, Peter KOHLER, Jacob ABEL**

Jean (Jane) ROSEBRUGH, Allen Township, widow of Rev. John ROSEBRUGH, killed in January 1777—request for support:
Jean presented a certificate signed by John CLYDE and George REIKART, Overseers of the Poor, of Allen Township, and by James CLYD, William MAFFET, and Johannes MICHAEL, freeholders and inhabitants of that township, certifying that Jane and her 5 children, the eldest now 22 and the youngest 13, "being deprived entirely of the support which they derived from the Profession of Mr. ROSEBRUGH and having suffered greatly by receiving part of his Estate in depreciated Money and the widow advanced in years...." She had already received funds from the Lt. of County, Samuel REA, in Continental Money, from Robert LEVERS, Esq., from John HAYS, and from David RITTENHOUSE, Esq. John CRAIG, Lt. of County, was to pay her further funds.

**Court on 26 October 1789**
**Justices, the Esquires: Peter RHOADS, and associates**

Estate of Henry RUMFELD, Upper Saucon Township—complaint heard concerning sale of real estate:
executors: John RUMFELD and Casper RUMFELD—had not given sufficient public notice of the time and place of the sale, therefore, the sale was set aside and declared void; the executors were to pay all court costs

**Court on 23 December 1789**
**Justices, the Esquires: Peter RHOADS, Peter KOHLER, Christopher WAGNER, William HENRY**

Estate of John MILLER, Town of Northampton, carpenter—return of sale:
administrator: Jacob NEWHARD
sold to: George RHOADS

Estate of George SHICK, died about 15 years ago, Plainfield Township—request inquest:
land: 80 acres bounded by Adam ENGLER, John ROHN, Jacob RADD, and others
widow: since deceased
8 children: Jacob, eldest son
George
Elizabeth, wife of Michael RIPPLE
Anna Katharine
Mary Margaret, wife of Abraham MILLER
Anna Barbara
John
Philip

Estate of Reinhard LAUBACH, died sometime ago, Lower Saucon Township—request inquest:
land: 150 acres land formerly of Jacob SHLAUGH, bounded by Gratius LERCH, Jacob HERTZEL, Adam EDELMAN, Rudolph OBERLY, George SEVITZ (conveyed to him by Jacob SHLAUGH and Ann Mary, his wife)
widow
6 children: John, eldest son
Susanna
John George
Elizabeth
Leonhard
Sarah

Estate of Leonard GEBHARD, Upper Milford Township (had will)—request audit:
petitioners: Jacob BROBST and Kilean WEISS, guardians for minor children
executor: Anthony STÄHLER, surviving executor
auditors: George KRIEBEL and James GILL of Upper Milford Township, and Peter TREXLER, Jr., Esq., Macungie Township

Estate of John ALBREGHT, died about 19 years ago, Macungie Township—request inquest:
land: 184 acres bounded by Jacob SWARTZ, Dewalt SHUTT, Jeremiah TREXLER, & others
widow: now wife of John TREXLER
4 children: Jacob, eldest son
Susannah

Catharine, wife of Joseph ALBREGHT
Gerthraut, wife of Christopher STERNER

**Court on 23 December 1789, continued:**

New guardian for John, now over age 14, minor child of George DOLL, Hamilton Township:
guardian: former—Valentine METZ, Plainfield Township
new—Jacob LERCH, Lower Saucon Township

Estate of Henry RUMFELD, Upper Saucon Township—request inquest:
petitioner: John, eldest son

**Court on 24 December 1789**
**Justices, the Esquires: not named**

Estate of Michael ENDRESS—referred to citation issued against executors issued last 23 September; the sheriff only served the citation on George SEIDER; George, along with two freeholders, was to execute and deliver bonds to the guardians :
executors: George SEIDER and Jacob STAHL

Estate of John YOUNG, died sometime ago, Bethlehem Township—request inquest:
land: 125 acres, part of Manor of Fermor commonly called the Dry Land Tract, "with a right of Premption to the same," bounded by lands in tenure of Michael HUBER, Peter SHILP, Michael RITTER, Michael EBENREITER, Philip NEWHART
widow: since deceased
5 children: Abraham, eldest son
Barbara, wife of John ESHELMAN
Elizabeth
Mary, wife of Jacob HOFFMAN
Magdalena

**Court on 19 January 1790**
**Justices, the Esquires: Thomas HARTMAN, Lewis STACKER, Jacob ABEL**

Estate of John GRIESEMER, Whitehall Township—request inquest:
land: 1) 272 acres in Whitehall Township bounded by Casper SHENEBRUK, Peter RHOADS, and ALLEN's land
2) 228 acres in Salisbury Township adjoining 1st tract and John GABLE, George TUTT, and others
3) 100 acres of Woodland in Salisbury Township bounded by Rudolph SMITH, Godhart MORRY, John KECK
widow
8 children: John, eldest son
Felix
Ann Mary, wife of Godfrey KNAUSS
Catharine, wife of Paul KNAUSS
Gertraut, wife of Peter BEYSEL
Elizabeth, wife of George BLANK
Abraham
Isaac

**Court on 19 January 1790, continued:**

Estate of Frederick SMITH, died about 12 years ago, Lower Saucon Township—request inquest:

| | |
|---|---|
| land: | 140 acres bounded by Philip BAHL, Andreas HELLER, the late Christian BACHMAN |
| widow: | now wife of David MARSH |
| 4 children: | Jacob, eldest son |
| | Catharine |
| | Elizabeth |
| | Daniel |

**Court on 15 March 1790**
**Justices, the Esquires: Peter RHOADS, Peter KOHLER, George BREINIG**

Estate of Peter EVERHARD, Upper Milford Township—request inquest:

| | |
|---|---|
| land: | 200 acres bounded by and adjoining Jacob KEHLER, Henry EVERHARD, John GRIESEMER, church land, Henry OTT, Jacob EVERHARD |
| widow: | now deceased |
| 5 children: | Conrad, eldest son |
| | Christina, wife of Peter SHNYDER |
| | Abraham |
| | David |
| | John |

Guardians for 5 minor children of Jacob KUNTZ, Lynn Township (all under age 14):

| | |
|---|---|
| petitioner: | George Michael KUNTZ, brother of deceased |
| 5 children: | Catharine |
| | Susanna |
| | Jacob |
| | Daniel |
| | Magdalena |
| guardians: | for all 4 children—Burkhard MOSER and William MEYER, Lynn Township |

Guardian for Abraham, over age 14, minor son of Peter EVERHARD (were other children):

| | |
|---|---|
| guardian: | Peter SHNYDER, Rockhill Township, Bucks County |

**Court on 17 March 1790**
**Justices, the Esquires: Peter RHOADS, Peter KOHLER, William HENRY, Lewis STACKER, George BREINIG, Jacob HORNER, Thomas HARTMAN**

Estate of Abraham FUNK, Upper Milford Township, saw mill on 55 acres—report of inquest by Sheriff George GRAFF, Esq.:

| | |
|---|---|
| widow | |
| 7 children: | Henry, eldest son—accepted the land |
| | others not named |
| security: | Jacob KRAM, Lower Saucon Township, miller |
| 12 men: | by oath—Jacob MILLER, Philip WALTER, Adam GEBHARD (KEHARD), Adam REINHARD, Mathias MILLER, Frederick KEMERER, Henry LAROSS, Gabriel BOBBENMEIER, Jacob MARSTELLER |
| | by affirmation—John JANTZ, Daniel GREATER (GRETER), Jacob JANTZ (SCHANTZ) |

**Court on 17 March 1790, continued:**

Estate of George HOFFMAN, Whitehall Township, 3 contiguous tracts—request inquest:
land: 170 acres, total, all patented, bounded by and adjoining Leonard STEININGER, Jacob HAMAN, Jacob MEYER, John KREGLO, Nicholas LITZENBERGER
widow: Ann Mary
8 children: George, eldest son
Jacob
Elizabeth
Maria, wife of Andrew RUPP
Henry
Magdalena
Christian
Catharine

Estate of Peter WEISS, died about 3 years ago, Weisenberg Township—request inquest:
petitioner: Andrew MILLER, Lynn Township, one guardian of the minor children
land: 268 acres deeded land bounded by and adjoining Michel FENSTERMACHER, George BRAUCHER, Nicholas BACHMAN, Christian HOFFMAN, and others
widow: Elizabeth
8 children: Christian
Mary, wife of George CUSTARD
Catharine, wife of Frederick SEIBERLING
Barbara, wife of Abraham GRÜNEWALD
Magdalena
Elizabeth
Christina
Susanna

Estate of Conrad SCHNYDER, Bethlehem Township—request sale, auditors appointed:
land: 125 acres bounded by John SNYDER, George SNABEL, Leonard FRANKENFIELD, Jacob BURNSTEIN
administrators: Elizabeth WOLF, John SCHNYDER, Adam SAND
auditors: Joseph HORSEFIELD, Bethlehem, gentleman, Mathias KRESS, Bethlehem Township, Jacob SHOEMAKER, Forks Township

Guardian for John, under age 14, only child of Conrad SHNYDER, Bethlehem Township:
petitioner: John SHNYDER, brother of deceased
guardian: Mathias KRESS, Bethlehem Township, weaver

Guardians for 8 minor children of Jacob HUNSIKER, Heidelberg Township:
petitioner: John HUNSIKER, father of deceased
8 children: Elizabeth, over age 14............................guardian: Casper HUNSIKER, of same place
John, over age 14..................................guardian: Joseph HUNSIKER, of same
the remaining 6 children are all under age 14:
Susanna................................................guardian: Joseph HUNSIKER, of same
Catharine..............................................guardian: John HUNSIKER
Magdalena.............................................guardian: John HUNSIKER
Jacob....................................................guardian: Casper HUNSIKER
Henry....................................................guardian: Henry HUNSIKER

Mary......................................................guardian: Henry HUNSIKER

**Court on 17 March 1790, continued:**

Estate of John YOUNG, Bethlehem Township, 125 acres—report of inquest by Sheriff George GRAFF, Esq.:
5 children: Abraham, eldest son—accepted the land
others not named
securities: Michael HUBER, Bethlehem Township, and Stephen KOCHLER, Allen Township
12 men:by oath—Michael HUBER, Nicholas FOX, Casper RITTER, Jr., Henry YOUNG, Henry HUBER, Stephen KOCHLER, John KLESS, Valentine (Felte) KLESS, John KLESS, Jr., John SMITH
by affirmation—Michael SHURTZ (as George SHORTZ in list of signatures), Frederick FOGLE

Estate of Reinhart LAUBACH, Lower Saucon Township, 150 acres—inquest report by Sheriff George GRAFF:
widow
6 children: John, eldest son—accepted the land
others not named
sureties: Edward FREEMAN and Michael LAUBACH, Lower SauconTownship
12 men:by oath—Andrew OHL, Jacob ROTH, Jacob GROSS, Adam EDELMAN, Jacob LERCH, Peter KNECHT, Christian RUCH, Anthony KRATZER
by affirmation—John BEYL, John ROTHROCK, Anthony LERCH, Gratius LERCH

**Court on 18 March 1790**
**Justices, the Esquires: Peter RHOADS, Lewis STACKER, William HENRY, Thomas HARTMAN, George BREINIG, Jacob HORNER, Christopher WAGGONER, Jacob ABEL, William JACKSON**

Estate of John ALBRECHT, Macungie Township, 184 acres —report of inquest by Sheriff George GRAFF:
widow
4 children: Jacob, eldest son—accepted the land
others not named
sureties: Jeremiah TREXLER, Macungie Township, innholder, and John ALBRECHT, same, miller
12 men:all by oath—John BUTZ, George YOHE, William HAYNS (HAINTZ), John WETZEL, George STEININGER, Andrew EISENHARD, Nicholas KRAMER (GRAMMAR), Jacob KACKLY (KICHLE), Deiderich (Dieter) DANNER, George WALBERT, Michael KISKY (KIRGE), John (Hannes) ALBRECHT

**Court on 18 March 1790**
**Justices, the Esquires, now present: Peter RHOADS, Lewis STACKER, William HENRY, Thomas HARTMAN, Christopher WAGGONER, Jacob ABEL**

Estate of John GREISEMER, Whitehall Township, 3 tracts in Whitehall and Salisbury Townships, 270 acres, 228 acres, 100 acres—report of inquest by Sheriff George GRAFF, Esq.:
widow
8 children: John, eldest son—declined to accept the land
Felix, 2nd son—accepted the land
others not named
sureties: George Adam BLANK and Lawrence KLEIN, Salisbury Township
12 men:by oath—George Frederick KNAUSS, Adam TORNEY (DORNEY), George Adam BLANK, Conrad MARCK, Michael KORLACHEN, John (Johannes) ROTH, Daniel RHOADS, Lawrence KLEIN, George KLICK (GLUECK), John (Johannes) RITTER

by affirmation—John GABLE (Hannes GOEBEL), Lawrence (Lorentz) NEWHARD

**Court on 18 March 1790, continued:**

Estate of George HAFF, died some considerable time ago, Heidelberg Township, 2 tracts—request inquest:
land: 1) 114 acres on which building erected bounded by George BLOSS, George REX, and others (other were listed on 23 June 1790 as William PETER, Conrad READER, Peter SEIDEL)
2) 27 acres bounded by Martin HERTER and others (listed on 23 June 1790 as Baltzer SHNYDER, Christian LANEGENOR)
widow: Mary, now wife of Abraham SHELLHAMMER
only child: Catharine, wife of Henry HUNSIKER

Estate of George SHICK, Plainfield Township—Sheriff George GRAFF, Esq. reported that he needed more time to make inquest on partition:
eldest son: Jacob

Estate of Henry RUMFELD—report of inquest by Sheriff George GRAFF, Esq.:
Since only 11 jurors had signed the inquisition, a new writ was issued

Estate of Michael ENDRESS—court issued an attachment on executor to compel compliance with court order:
executor: George SEIDER—was to deliver bonds to guardian of minor children of Frederick HAINTZ, but "he hath made default in complying"
by oath:Philip WALTER served notice on SEIDER last January

Estate of Frederick SMITH—report of inquest by Sheriff George GRAFF, Esq., remained under advisement:
eldest son: Jacob—did not attend

**Court on 25 March 1790**
**Justices, the Esquires: Benjamin DEPUE, Thomas HARTMAN, Jacob ABEL**

Estate of Frederick SMITH, Lower Saucon Township, 140 acres—report of inquest by Sheriff George GRAFF:
widow
4 children: Jacob, eldest son—accepted the land
others not named
sureties: Jacob ROTH and Henry SCHAEFFER, Lower Saucon Township
12 men:by oath—Andrew OHL, Jacob ROTH
by affirmation—Philip BAHL, John (Johannes) ROTHROCK, Christopher HELLER, Henry (Henrich) BACHMAN, Samuel KAUFFMAN, John BACHMAN, Henry SHAEFFER (Henrich SCHAFFER), George BOWMAN, Andrew (Andreas) HELLER, Andrew RICKARD (REIKERT)

Estate of Conrad SCHNYDER, Bethlehem Township, 125 acres—auditors' report; permission to sell:
administrators: Elizabeth WOLF, John SCHNYDER, Adam SAND

**Court on 6 April 1790**
**Justices, the Esquires: Thomas HARTMAN, William HENRY, Jacob ABEL**

Estate of Jacob WIETMER—request citation against administrator:
petitioner: Jacob EBERSOHL, husband of Magdalena, daughter of deceased
administrator: Henry FUNK, late of this county—never rendered an account

**Court on 29 April 1790**
**Justices, the Esquires: William CRAIG, Christopher WAGNER, Jacob ABEL**

Guardian for George, under age 14, minor child of John SMITH, Upper Milford Township:
petitioner: Peter LYNN, next friend
guardian: Philip WINDT, Upper Saucon Township

**Court on 21 June 1790**
**Justices, the Esquires: Peter RHOADS, Peter KOHLER, Christopher WAGNER, George BREINIG, Jacob ABEL**

Estate of George SHICK, Plainfield Township, 80 acres—report of inquest by Sheriff George GRAFF, Esq.:
8 children: Jacob, eldest son—accepted the land
others not named
sureties: Martin MEYER, Plainfield Township, and John REISWIG, Moore Township, miller
12 men:all by oath—Jacob HELLER, Henry ENGLE, Peter OVERSHYMER (OBERSHEIMER), Abraham HELLER, Henry BUSH, Jacob YOHE, Adam ENGLER (ENGLERT), Diderick BOWER (Dietrick BOUER), George ENSSELY (ENNSSLIN), Peter SEAGLE (SIEGEL), Jacob SHNYDER (SCHNEIDER), Jacob WERNER

Sheriff George GRAFF—return an attachment; a new writ of attachment issued:
says "he could not attach the Body of George SEIDER as he was therein commanded"

**Court on 21 June 1790**
**Justices, the Esquires: Peter RHOADS, Peter KOHLER, George BREINIG, Christopher WAGNER**

Estate of George HOFFMAN, Whitehall Township, 170 acres patented land—report of inquest by Sheriff George GRAFF, Esq.:
widow
8 children: George, eldest son—accepted the land
others not named
sureties: Peter EALER, Esq., Whitehall Township, and Philip KNAUSS, Macungie Township
12 men:all by oath—Peter EALER, George Frederick KNAUSS, Adam TORNEY (DORNEY), Leonard STEININGER, Casper SHENEBRUCH, George KLICK (GLUECK), George STEININGER, Philip KNAUSS, Jacob HAMAN, Jacob SHANTZ, Henry MORTZ (MERTZ), Nicholas LITZENBERGER

Guardian for Jacob, over age 14, minor son of Mathias OX, Upper Milford Township:
guardian: Jacob DILLINGER, Upper Milford Township

Guardian for John, over age 14, one minor child of Daniel VAN ETTEN, Lower Smithfield Township:
Guardian: John JAYNE, Upper Smithfield Township

**Court on 23 June 1790**
**Justices, the Esquires: Peter RHOADS, Peter KOHLER, Lewis STACHER, George BREINIG, Christopher WAGNER, Jacob HORNER, Thomas HARTMAN, Ludowick STÄHLER**

Estate of George HAFF, Heidelberg Township, 2 tracts of 112 acres and 26 acres—report of inquest by Sheriff George GRAFF, Esq.:
widow
daughter: only surviving child, Catharine, wife of Henry HENSIKER—accepted the land
sureties: George BLOSS and Jacob PETER, Heidelberg Township
12 men: by oath—George HORN, Tobias EBERT, Henry HOFFMAN, Lowrence WEHR, George BLOSS, Daniel BLOSS, Christopher RES, Adam SMITH, Jacob BRANDSTETTER, Peter SEIDEL
by affirmation—William FENSTERMACHER, William REX

Estate of Philip DRUMM—auditors' report on the account of the guardian of minor child Frederick DIEHL: found that Frederick's claims were unfounded

Guardians for 8 minor children of Thomas RUCKMAN, Lower Mt. Bethel Township (all under age 14):
widow: Elizabeth
8 children:
Rachel......guardian: Samuel REA, Low. Mt. Bethel Tp.
Mary......guardian: Samuel REA, Low. Mt. Bethel Tp.
Elizabeth......guardian: Thomas CONOLLY, same place
Hannah......guardian: Thomas CONOLLY, same place
Susanna......guardian: Samuel MILLER, Mt. Bethel Tp.
Isabel......guardian: Samuel MILLER, Mt. Bethel Tp.
John......guardian: James DEPUE, same place
Thomas......guardian: James DEPUE, same place

Guardians for 4 minor children of Andrew STAHLNECKER, Upper Milford Township (all under age 14) (were other children):
petitioner: Adam STAHLNECKER, brother of deceased
4 children:
George......guardian: Jacob KEHLERG, Up. Milford Tp.
Eve......guardian: Jacob KEHLERG, Up. Milford Tp.
John......guardian: Michael OTT, same place
Andrew......guardian: Michael OTT, same place

Estate of Leonhard GEBHARD—auditors' report:
administrator: Anthony STÄHLER, surviving executor
guardians: appointed earlier—Jacob PROBST and Killian WEISS, had complaint

Estate of Christian STEININGER—motion of Collinson READ, Esq. on behalf of Adam STEININGER; request audit:
executors: Martin RITTER and Ludwig RISHEL
auditors: Peter KOHLER and Peter EALER, Whitehall Township, Esquires, and George KRIEBEL, Upper Milford Township

**Court on 24 June 1790**
**Justices, the Esquires: Peter RHOADS, Peter KOHLER, Christopher WAGNER, Jacob HORNER, Jacob ABEL, Ludowick STACHLER**

Estate of Thomas RUCKMAN, Lower Mt. Bethel Township--request inquest:

| | |
|---|---|
| land: | 368 acres bounded by River Delaware, William MASON, Adrian ATTEN, James BEARD, Samuel REA, George BUTZ |
| widow: | Elizabeth |
| 10 children: | William, eldest son |
| | Sarah, wife of John JACOBY |
| | Rachel |
| | Mary |
| | Elizabeth |
| | Hannah |
| | Susanna |
| | Isabel |
| | John |
| | Thomas |

Estate of Conrad SCHNYDER, Bethlehem Township, 125 acres—return of sale:

| | |
|---|---|
| administrators: | Elizabeth WOLF, John SCHNYDER (SCHNEIDER), Adam SAND |
| sold to: | George WOLF, Allen Township |

Estate of Samuel WERT, died about 14 years ago, Weisenberg Township—request inquest:

| | |
|---|---|
| land: | 170 acres bounded by J. Michael PLYENER, Christian MARBURGER, Bastian WERLY, Jacob GRENEWALT |
| widow | |
| 4 children: | Peter, eldest son |
| | others not named |

New guardian for 4 minor children of Rev. Conrad STEINER:

| | |
|---|---|
| widow: | Catharine, now wife of Jacob EBERTH |
| 4 children: | Magdalena |
| | John |
| | Catharine |
| | Susanna |
| | Salome, now deceased |
| guardian: | former—Peter KACHLEIN, Esq., appointed 20 March 1783, now deceased |
| | new—Jacob ARNDT, Jr., Easton |

Estate of Henry RUMFELD—report of inquest by Sheriff George GRAFF remained under advisement:

| | |
|---|---|
| eldest son: | John—did not attend court |

Estate of Peter EVERHARD—report of inquest by Sheriff George GRAFF remained under advisement:

| | |
|---|---|
| eldest son: | Conrad—did not attend court |

Estate of Peter WEISS—report of inquest by Sheriff George GRAFF remained under advisement:
none of the parties concerned attended court

**Court on 15 July 1790**
**Justices, the Esquires: William HENRY, Thomas HARTMAN, Jacob ABEL**

Jean ROSBRUGH, widow of Rev. John ROSEBRUGH, Allen Township—request for support:
In 1776, John was officiating minister of the gospel. He entered the field as chaplain with a battalion of militia near the end of 1776 under the command of John SIEGFRIED. He was mortally wounded on 2 January 1777 by the British Enemy near Trenton, New Jersey and died the same day. He was then about 55 years old. Had 5 small children; court awards her ½ pay in right of her husband, from May 1788 to May 1790

**Court on 21 September 1790**
**Justices, the Esquires: Peter RHOADS, Peter KOHLER, William HENRY, George BREINIG**

Estate of Thomas RUCKMAN, Lower Mt. Bethel Township, 368 acres—report of inquest by Sheriff George GRAFF, Esq.:
widow
10 children: William, eldest son—accepted the land
others not named
sureties: Joseph MARTIN, William MASON, Lower Mt. Bethel Township
12 men:all by oath—William McFARREN, Samuel REA, William JONSTON, John NELSON (NEILSON), Daniel (Nathaniel) BRITTEN, Gerret MIDDAGH, Adrian ATTEN (Adrieyain ATEN), Robert MILLER, Lowrence LAMOSON (LANBERSON), Andrew NEIGH, James SIMONTON, Ephraim SIMONTON

Estate of Michael ENDRES—sureties appointed for the executor:
executor: George SEIDER, one executor
sureties: John WETZEL, Macungie Township, Esquire, & Michael FLORES, Upper Milford Township—to ensure the legacies to minor children of Frederick HAINTZ

**Court on 21 September 1790**
**Justices, the Esquires, now present: Peter KOHLER, William McNAIR, Christopher WAGNER**

Estate of William McCARTY, Allen Township, 2 tracts totaling 216 acres —return of sale:
administrators: Elizabeth McCARTY and Hugh HORNER
sold to: John MULHALLEN, Sr., Allen Township, turner

**Court on 21 September 1790**
**Justices, the Esquires, now present: Peter KOHLER, William McNAIR**

Estate of Peter EVERHARD, Upper Milford Township, 200 acres—report of inquest by Sheriff George GRAFF, Esq.:
5 children: Conrad, eldest son—accepted the land
others not named
sureties: Philip EVERHARD and George RUCH, Upper Milford Township
12 men:by oath—Jacob SMITH, John REESER, Christian HUBER, Daniel SMITH, Jacob STAHLNECKER, Michael OTT, George HORNER (HERNNER)
by affirmation—Andrew (Andreas) ENGELMAN, Nicholas DIETZ, Adam ENGELMAN, George WURMAN, Peter BUSH

**Court on 22 September 1790**
**Justices, the Esquires: Peter RHOADS, Peter KOHLER, William HENRY, John SHAW, William WILLS**

Estate of Michael STRIEBY, died last May, Lynn Township—request inquest:
land: 224 acres deeded land bounded by William MYER, Charles HORNBERGER, Adam ARNDT, and others
no widow
11 children: Jacob, eldest son
Michael
Paul
Leonard
Sarah, wife of Henry FISHER
Elizabeth, wife of John UNRUE
Susannah
John
Adam
George
Catharine

Estate of Pete WEISS, Weisenberg Township, 223 acres—report of inquest by Sheriff George GRAFF, Esq.:
widow
8 children: Christian, eldest son—accepted the land
others not named
sureties: Michael BOBST, Weisenberg Township, shop keeper, and Philip FENSTERMACHER, Lowhill Township
12 men: all by oath—Michael BOBST, Christian SHNYDER (SCHNEIDER), Nicholas BACHMAN, Michael FENSTERMACHER, Jacob HANSS, Henry SHNYDER (Henrich SCHNEIDER), Paul BACHMAN, George BRAUCHER, Bastian WERLICH (Sebastian WERLIN), George Michael KUNTZ, Jacob HERBER, John WEISS

Estate of Samuel WERT, Weisenberg Township, 170 acres—report of inquest by Sheriff George GRAFF, Esq.:
widow
4 children: Peter, eldest son—accepted the land
others not named
sureties: Michael BOBST, Weisenberg Township, shop keeper, and John EBERT, same place
12 men: by oath—Mathias PROBST, Jacob MUMMY (MUME), John HAUBT, Samuel KISTLER, Philip FENSTERMACHER, Henry (Henrich) HARTMAN, David SANDER (XANDER), Jacob GANGWER, Nicholas BACHMAN, George ROUCH (ROW)
by affirmation—Friederich SEIBERLING, George CUSTARD

Estate of Dietrich SCHMETZER—request for citation against one administrator:
widow: Magdalena, administratrix
council: James BIDDLE, Esq.
administrator: Adam EDELMAN—had not made a final settlement and had two large sums belonging to the estate

**Court on 22 September 1790, continued:**

Estate of Melchior BARE, Macungie Township (had will; account exhibited in 1774)—request audit:

| | |
|---|---|
| executors: | Anthony STAHLER, Leonard STEININGER, Eve Elizabeth BARE |
| daughter: | Eve Elizabeth, wife of Jacob LINDEMAN, the petitioner, had not received share of estate; "it appears that a considerable sum of money remained in their hands [the executors] to be divided between widow and children...that part of said monies were received in Continental Currency and became lost to the said Heirs...." |
| auditors: | John ROMIG, Macungie Township, George KRIEBEL, Upper Milford Township, James GILL, same place, shop keeper |

Estate of Jacob PAULUS, Bethlehem Township—request inquest:

| | |
|---|---|
| land: | 64 acre bounded by William Henry LAWALL, Philip FRANKENFIELD, Peter GIFFIN, Dewalt GRATHWOHL |
| widow: | Feronica |
| 5 children: | Michael, eldest son |
| | Salome, wife of Philip MANN, Jr. |
| | Elizabeth, wife of Peter MANN |
| | Ann Mary, wife of George KOCH |
| | Barbara |

Estate of Christian FISHER, Upper Milford Township, innholder (had will)—request audit:

| | |
|---|---|
| petitioners: | Godfried KNAUSS and Jacob SHREIVER, guardians for 3 minor children |
| executors: | Christian FISHER and John Adam SHULER—settled the administration account without the knowledge of the guardians |
| auditors: | Peter KOHLER, Peter EALER, Esquires, Whitehall Township, and John ROMIG, Macungie Township |

Estate of Samuel CASEBIER, Mt. Bethel Township—request sale, auditors appointed:

| | |
|---|---|
| land: | 25 acres bounded by Thomas BOWMAN, Alexander CAMPELL, River Delaware |
| administrators: | Elisha BARTON and George NEWTON |
| auditors: | Benjamin DEPUE, Esquire, Joseph MARTIN, John McCALLUM |

New guardian for 2 minor children of Thomas RUCKMAN, Lower Mt. Bethel Township:

| | |
|---|---|
| widow: | Elizabeth |
| 2 children: | Rachel |
| | Mary |
| guardian: | former—Samuel REA, Lower Mt. Bethel Township |
| | new—Joseph MARTIN, Lower Mt. Bethel Township |

**Court on 23 September 1790**
**Justices, the Esquires: Peter RHOADS, Peter KOHLER, William HENRY, George BREINIG, Jacob ABEL, William WILLS, John SHAW**

Estate of Martin EILERT, Lowhill Township—request inquest:

| | |
|---|---|
| land: | 115 acres warrant land in Whitehall Township bounded by Peter DESHER and others |
| widow: | Christina, now wife of Frederick MEYER |
| 7 children: | Henry, eldest son |
| | Christopher |
| | Eve Elizabeth, wife of Peter FENSTERMACHER |
| | Joseph |
| | Christina, wife of Christian FENSTERMACHER |
| | Peter |
| | Catharine, wife of Daniel FENSTERMACHER |

**Court on 12 October 1790 Held at Town of Northampton**
**Justices, the Esquires: Peter RHOADS, Peter KOHLER, George BREINIG**

Guardian for Dorothea, over age 14, minor daughter of Daniel SHNEIDER, Whitehall Township:
guardian: Peter BURKHALTER, Jr., Whitehall Township

Guardian for Philip, over age 14, minor son of Christian RUTH:
guardian: George Frederick KNOUSS, Whitehall Township

**Court on 23 November 1790**
**Justices, the Esquires: William CRAIG, Thomas HARTMAN, Jacob ABEL**

Estate of George DOOTT, Macungie Township, 6 tracts—request inquest:

| | |
|---|---|
| land: | 1) 141 acres in Macungie Township bounded by Nicholas KLOTZ, Daniel TURNEY, Daniel SCHWARTZ, George SYDER |
| | 2-4) three tracts totaling 75 acres in Upper Milford Township bounded by Frederick KRATZER, Adam WEEDER, Jacob MOORE |
| | 5) 40 acres in Upper Milford Twp. bounded by Andrew GEERING, Jacob KNOWS |
| | 6) 320 acres in Salisbury Township bounded by Peter EALER, Lawrence KLEIN, Peter BOGER, John FETTER |
| widow | |
| 14 children: | George, eldest son |
| | Christina, wife of Adam WEEDER |
| | Catharine, wife of George REINHART |
| | Christian |
| | Margareth, wife of Henry WETZEL |
| | Henry |
| | David |
| | Magdalena |
| | John |
| | Daniel |
| | Joseph |
| | Solomon |
| | Elizabeth |
| | Eve |

**Court on 20 December 1790**
**Justices, the Esquires: William HENRY, Peter KOHLER, Thomas HARTMAN, Jacob ABEL, John SHAW**

Estate of Casper RUMAGE—motion of Robert TRAILL, Esq. for audit:
daughter: Mary, wife of Jacob SHAFFER
auditors: John SHAW and Lewis STACKER, Esquires, and John HUSTON

**Court on 21 December 1790**
**Justices, the Esquires: William HENRY, Peter KOHLER, Thomas HARTMAN, John SHAW**

Guardians for 2 minor children of Aaron HILLMAN, died about 13 years ago, Lower Smithfield Township (were other children):
widow: Judith, now wife of Mr. KLOTZHAM
2 children: Aaron, over age 14
Joseph, under age 14
guardian: for both children—Derrick VAN VLEET, Lower Smithfield Township

**Court on 22 December 1790**
**Justices, the Esquires: William HENRY, Peter KOHLER, Jacob HORNER**

Estate of Jacob PAULUS, Bethlehem Township, 64 acres—report of inquest by the late Sheriff George GRAFF:
widow
5 children: Michael, eldest son—accepted the land
others not named
sureties: John CLAUSS, Conrad KOCHER, Bethlehem Township
12 men:by oath—Henry LAWALL, Mathias GRESS, Michael KOHLER (KOEHLER), Jacob BEESACKER (BIESECHER), Conrad KOCHER, George HERTZEL (HEARTZEL), John (Hannes) UNANGST
by affirmation—Peter GIFFIN, Michael SCHURTZ (SCHORTZ), Frederick BOYER (BEYER), Leonard BEIDELMAN (BEYDELMAN), John KLOUS (Johannes CLAUSS)

Estate of Michael STRIEBY, 224 acres deeded land—report of inquest by the late Sheriff George GRAFF, Esq.:
11 children: Jacob, eldest son—accepted the land
others not named
sureties: Michael BOBST, Weisenberg Township, shop keeper, and Daniel SHNYDER, Lynn Township
12 men:by oath—Michael OHL, Philip MOSER, Burkhard (Borckhard) MOSER, Jacob OSWALD, Charles HORNBERGER, Adam GERMAN, Daniel SHNYDER, John SMITH (Johannes SCHMITT), Philip SITTER, Jacob WERTMAN, Philip Jacob PETER
by affirmation—Andrew STROUB (Andreas STRAUB)

Estate of Michael ENDRESS—request for attachment against one executor:
executor: George SEIDER, who "hath been guilty of a contempt in refusing to execute a Bond...."
on oath of: Philip WALTER

Estate of Melchior BARE (had will)—on motion of Samuel SITGREAVES, Esq., the auditors' report was set aside and not confirmed

**Court on 22 December 1790**

**Justices, the Esquires, now present: William HENRY, Peter KOHLER, Jacob HORNER**

Estate of Martin EILERT, Whitehall Township, 115 acres warrant—inquest report by late Sheriff George GRAFF, Esq.:

widow
7 children: Henry, eldest son—declined the land
Christopher, 2nd son—accepted the land (others not named)
sureties: Michael BOBST, Weisenberg Twp., shop keeper, and John WEBER, Heidelberg Twp.
12 men: by oath—Jacob MICKLY (MÜCHLY), Lowrence (Lorentz) RUCH, John (Johannes) ROTH, Melchior BEAR (Melcher BÄR), Adam SHEYERER (SHEYER), Peter TRAXEL (DRAXEL), Peter KERN, Peter MOYER (MEYER), Nicholas MOYER (Nicklas MEYER), Daniel TRAXLER (TRAXEL), Yost MAYER (MEYER)
by affirmation—Christian PARCH (BERTSCH)

**Court on 24 December 1790**
**Justices, the Esquires: William HENRY, Peter KOHLER, Thomas HARTMAN, Lewis STACKER**

Estate of Jacob BRAUCHER, Weisenberg Township—return of sale:

land: 75 acres 42 perches bounded by Paul PAULY, Lorentz HOLBIG, George KRAMLICH, Henry MESER
administrators: George BRAUCHER and Valentine GRAMLICH
sold to: Christian BRAUCHER, Weisenberg Township

Estate of John REINSCHMIT, Heidelberg Township—request inquest:

land: 118 acres warrant land adjoining Simon WEHR, Jacob HARTMAN, Jacob GROESEL, Andrew SENDEL, Andrew ROW
widow: Ann Mary
11 children, 5 are minors:
John, eldest son
Jacob
Samuel
Simon
Henry
Leonard
Mary
Juliana, wife of John Adam SMITH
Eve, wife of John KUNTZ
Elizabeth, wife of George HOLDER
Catharine, wife of Jacob ROW

Guardians for 5 minor children of George DUTT, "died some short time since," Macungie Township (all under age 14) (were other children):

widow: Magdalena
5 children: Daniel
Joseph
Solomon
Elizabeth
Eve
guardian: for all 5 children—Martin RITTER, Salisbury Township, innholder, and Philip WALTER, Milford Township

**Court on 24 December 1790, continued:**

Estate of Ferdinand WERTZ, Upper Milford Township—request inquest:

land: 114 acres bounded by Valentine KEISER, Rudolph LARASH, Isaac JARRET, Frederick REISE

widow

4 children: John, eldest son
Elizabeth, wife of Jacob BORTS
Mary, wife of John KAMMERER
Eve

**Court on 24 December 1790**
**Justices, the Esquires, now present: William HENRY, Thomas HARTMAN, Lewis STACHER**

Estate of Christian FISHER, Upper Milford Township—auditors' report:

executors: Christian FISHER and Adam SHULLER—owed funds to the estate

**Court on 24 December 1790**
**Justices, the Esquires, now present: William HENRY, Peter KOHLER, Thomas HARTMAN, Lewis STACHER, Jacob HORNER, John SHAW, William WILLS, Enoch BEER**

Estate of George DOOTT—report on inquest by Sheriff Jonas HARTZEL, Esq., on motion of Samuel SITGREAVES, Esq. was set aside; a new writ was ordered for next March

**Court on 15 February 1791**
**Justices, the Esquires: Enoch BEER, Jacob ABEL, John SHAW**

Estate of Dietrich SCHMETZER—request audit "in the neighborhood of the Petitioner (he being very aged)....":

petitioner: Adam EDELMAN, Lower Saucon Township, by attorney Robert TRAILL, Esq. (Adam could not attend due to sickness)

widow: Magdalena, also a petitioner

children

auditors: John BEYL, Esq., Felix LYNN, "practitioner in Physick," John BEYER, blacksmith, all of Lower Saucon Township

Estate of Henry RUMFELD—motion of Robert TRAILL, Esq., for citation against John RUMFELD, eldest son of deceased, to appear next March and declare whether or not he would accept the land as valued

**Court on 24 February 1791**

**Justices, the Esquires: Lewis STACHER, Thomas HARTMAN, Jacob ABEL**

Estate of John George MILLER, Macungie Township, 2 tracts—request inquest:

land: 1) 30 acres 37 perches warranted land bounded by Baltzer FRITZ, Leonard HEICHEL, Michael BASTIAN, Jacob STEPHEN
2) 7 acres 32 perches, part of Thousand Acre Tract, bounded by Jacob SHMEYER, Jacob MOHR, public road leading to Philadelphia, Peter MILLER, the late Frederick HAINTZ

widow: since deceased

6 children: George, eldest son
Barbara, wife of Jacob ECKEL
Margaret, wife of Frederick KAMERER
Catharine
Borgy
Frederick

**Court on 21 March 1791**

**Justices, the Esquires: William HENRY, Thomas HARTMAN, Christopher WAGNER, George BREINIG, Ludwig STÄHLER, Enoch BEER, Jacob ABEL, John SHAW, William WILLS**

Estate of John REINSCHMIT, Heidelberg Township, 118 acres—inquest report by Sheriff Jonas HARTZELL:

widow

11 children: John, eldest son—declined
Jacob, 2nd son—declined
Samuel, 3rd son—accepted the land
others not named

sureties: Christian SCHNEIDER, Heidelberg Township, and George SCHUMACHER, Weisenberg Township

12 men:by oath and affirmation—Jacob HATMAN (HARTMAN), Simon GEORGE, John (Johannes) HARTMAN, George HOLEBACH (HOLLENBACH), Christian SNYDER (SCHNEIDER), Samuel SNYDER (SCHNEIDER), Philip (Fielb) WEHR, John (Hannes) EVERT, Tobias EVERT, Christian SMITH (SCHMITT), Lenhard (Leonhard) MILLER, George SHOEMACKER (SCHUMACHER)

Estate of John George MILLER, Macungie Township, 2 tracts, 30 acres 37 perches and 7 acres 132 perches—report of inquest by Sheriff Jonas HARTZELL, Esq.:

6 children: George, eldest son—accepted the land
others not named

sureties: Peter EALER, Esq., Whitehall Township, and Jeremiah TREXLER, Macungie Township, innholder

12 men:all by oath—Andrew EISENHART (Andreas EISENHARD), Godfried DEFENDERFFER (DIEFENDERFFER), Jacob STEPHY (Johan Jacob STEFAN), Michael KEHME (KÄHM), Philip WESKO (WESCO), John SHERRED (JARETT), Philip SMYER (Phillib SCHMEIER), Peter MILLER, Jacob SMYER (SCHMEYER), Cornelius HUESE (JUSS), Jacob HERMAN, Berned HENICH (Leonard HENIG)

**Court on 21 March 1791, continued:**

Estate of George DOOTT, Macungie Township, 587 acres total in Macungie, Salisbury, and Upper Milford Townships—report of inquest by Sheriff Jonas HARTZELL, Esq.:

widow
14 children: George, eldest son—accepted the land
others not named
sureties: Jacob HEIL, Upper Milford Township , and George GLUCK, Whitehall Township
attorney: Mr. TRAILL, Esq.
12 men:by oath and affirmation—James GILL, John KNOWS (Johannes KNAUSS), Henry (Hennrrick) KEMERER, Andrew (Andreas) KECK, George GLÜCK, Michael KÄHM, Jacob LIBSHBORGER (LEIBERSPERGER), George SEIDER, Frederick ROMICH (ROMIG), Henry (Henrich) RITTER, Elias WEAVER (WEBER), George OTT

Guardians for 4 minor children of Anthony DECK, Forks Township:

petitioner: Michael KRESS, Williams Township, grandfather of the children
widow: Catharine, daughter of the petitioner
4 children: Michael, over age 14...............................guardian: Jacob DECK, Nazareth Township
Jacob, over age 14..................................guardian: John ODENWELDER, Forks Twp.
George Henry, under age 14
Anthony, under age 14
guardians: for younger 2 children—Jacob DECK and John ODENWELDER

Estate of Ferdinand WERTZ, Upper Milford Township, 117 acres—report of inquest by Sheriff Jonas HARTZELL, Esq.:

widow
4 children: John, eldest son—accepted the land
others not named
sureties: Nicholas HITTEL and George HAMAN, Upper Milford Township
12 men:by oath and affirmation—John WETZELL, Lenhard (Leonard) SCHLOUCH, David STROUSE (STRAUSS), Michael STERNER, George HAMAN, Adam DESH (DESCH), George REISE (REISS), Philip WESCO, Rudolph LARASH (LORASCH), Mathias WESCO, Jacob LINTEMAN (LINDERMAN), Valentine KEISER

Guardian for Ann Mary, under age 14, minor child of George GILBERT, Penn Township (were other children):

widow: Susanna
guardian: Daniel OSWALD, Lynn Township

Estate of Peter ECKENROTH, died about 2 years ago, Lynn Township—request audit:

petitioner: Christian, one son, on behalf of brothers and sisters
widow: Elizabeth, died before she had wholly administered the estate
administrator: George HERMANY, administrator de Bonis Non
auditors: Daniel OSWALD, John PROBST, Burkhard MOSER, all of Lynn Township

Estate of Casper ERB, Moore Township (had will)—request audit:

petitioner: David BLACKLEY, Allen Township, hatter, husband of Elizabeth ERB, one daughter of deceased
administrators: Lawrence ERB and Michael ERB
auditors: George PALMER, Esq., Paul FLICK, Moore Township, John HAYS, Allen Township

**Court on 21 March 1791, continued:**

Estate of George GILBERT, Penn Township, 2 tracts—request inquest:

| | |
|---|---|
| land: | 1) 255 acres bounded by Leonard ZIMMERMAN, Daniel ERRO, George HUNT, Valentine PROBST |
| | 2) 140 acres woodland bounded by Valentine PROBST, Martin PROBST, Michael STEIN |
| widow: | Susanna |
| 7 children: | George, eldest son |
| | Magdalena, wife of John Dieder BEEBELHEIN |
| | Catharine |
| | Jacob |
| | Philip |
| | Elizabeth |
| | Mary |

**Court on 27 March 1791**
**Justices, the Esquires: present as yesterday**

Estate of Jacob TRAUB, died about 15 years ago, Upper Milford Township—request inquest:

| | |
|---|---|
| land: | 61 acres bounded by George REINERT, Stephen DALMAN, Jacob SCHIFFER, and others |
| widow: | Eve Elizabeth |
| 4 children: | Jacob, eldest son |
| | George |
| | Elizabeth, wife of Jost BORGER |
| | Catharine, wife of Christopher BASTIAN |

**Court on 22 March 1791**
**Justices, the Esquires, now present: William HENRY, Christopher WAGNER, George BREINIG**

Guardian for George ROSS, over age 14, minor son of Lawrence ROSS, left legacies by both his father's and grandfather's estates:

| | |
|---|---|
| guardian: | George REEG, Heidelberg Township |

**Court on 22 March 1791**
**Justices, the Esquires, now present: William HENRY, Christopher WAGNER, George BREINIG Ludwig STÄHLER**

George SEIDER brought before the court by attachment and to remain in custody of the sheriff until he complied with the court order of last December

**Court on 22 March 1791**

**Justices, the Esquires, now present: William HENRY, Thomas HARTMAN, William WILLS, Lewis STACHER, Jacob ABEL, George BREINIG, John SHAW, Ludwick STÄHLER**

Estate of Peter REEG, died some short time ago, Heidelberg Township—request inquest:

| | |
|---|---|
| land: | 150 acres bounded by Henry HEFFLEFINGER, Jacob RITTENHOUSE, Peter SIGFRIED, Peter ANDREAS, Charles ROSS |
| widow: | Elizabeth |
| 5 children: | George, eldest son |
| | Eve, wife of Andrew FOX |
| | Mary, wife of George SHENEBERGER |
| | Barbara, wife of Peter KUNTZ |
| | Christina, wife of John SHUMACHER |
| 1 grandchild: | the child of daughter Valpory, long since deceased, late wife of Lorentz ROSS |

**Court on 23 March 1791**
**Justices, the Esquires: William HENRY, Enoch BEER, Ludwig STÄHLER**

New guardian for Daniel, now over age 14, minor son of Frederick SMITH, Lower Saucon Township:

| | |
|---|---|
| guardian: | former—Philip BAHL, Lower Saucon Township, declined the guardianship |
| | new—David MERSH, Lehigh Township |

**Court on 23 March 1791**
**Justices, the Esquires, now present: William HENRY, Thomas HARTMAN, Christopher WAGNER, George BREINIG, Lewis STACHER, Ludwig STÄHLER, Jacob ABEL, William WILLS**

Guardian for Peter, minor son of Martin EILERT, Lowhill Township:

| | |
|---|---|
| guardian: | Jacob HORNER, Esq. |

Estate of Peter CONRAD, Hamilton Township, 5 tracts (last 4 listed are contiguous)—request inquest:

| | |
|---|---|
| land: | 1) 93 acres warranted land bounded by Nicholas MICHAEL, Christopher KELLER, Philip BERGSTROESSER |
| | 2) 160 acres patented land |
| | 3) 15 acres patented land |
| | 4) 40 acres warranted land |
| | 5) 47 acres warranted land, these last 4 tracts bounded by Ludwig HELLER, Michael BUTZ, Christopher KELLER, John STORM, Henry ULRICH |
| widow: | Feronica |
| 13 children: | George Peter, eldest son |
| | Susanna, wife of Jacob FRANTZ |
| | Elizabeth, wife of Jacob MERWEIN |
| | Louisa, wife of John SCHNEIDER |
| | Margaret |
| | Christina |
| | John Melchior |
| | Henry |
| | John |
| | Sarah |
| | Catharine |
| | Joseph |
| | Jacob |

**Court on 23 March 1791, continued:**

Estate of Peter EVERHARD, Upper Milford Township—new surety:
eldest son: Conrad, had accepted the land—now one surety declined
surety: former—George RUCH, declined
new—Daniel DUBBS, Upper Milford Township

New guardian for 2 minor children of Thomas RUCHMAN, Mt. Bethel Township:
2 children: Susanna
Isabel
guardian: former—Samuel MILLER, Mt. Bethel Township, intended to move "from the parts"
new—David AYERS, Mt. Bethel Township

Estate of Henry RUMFELD, Upper Saucon Township—report of inquest by Sheriff George GRAFF, Esq.:
10 children: John, eldest son—now present and accepted the land
others not named
sureties: Michael SMITH, Bethlehem Township, Jacob BITTENBENDER, Easton Township, wheelwright
12 men: by oath—Daniel COOPER
by affirmation—Peter KNEPPLY, Abraham SEYDER (SEIDER), George Adam WEAVER (WEBER), Andrew (Andreas) EARDMAN (ERDMAN), Peter FOX (FUCHS), John NEWCOMER, John GEISSINGER, George BACHMAN, John BACHMAN, Joseph BACHMAN, Abraham GEISSINGER

Estate of Dietrich SCHMETZER, Lower Saucon Township—auditors' report:
administrators: Adam EDELMAN and Magdalena SCHMETZER

Guardians for 2 minor children of William McCARTY (both under age 14):
administrator: Hugh HORNER, Allen Township
2 children: Margaret
John
guardian: for both children—Joseph HORNER, Allen Township

**Court on 24 March 1791**
**Justices, the Esquires: George BREINIG, Jacob HORNER, Ludwig STAHLER**

Estate of Michael STRIEBY, Lynn Township—new sureties:
eldest son: Jacob—had accepted the land
sureties: former—Michael BOBST and Daniel SHNYDER, have since declined
new—John SMITH and John Adam CREITZ, Lynn Township

**Court on 25 March 1791**
**Justices, the Esquires: William HENRY, Thomas HARTMAN, Jacob ABEL**

Guardian for 2 minor children of Daniel SHNYDER, Whitehall Township (both under age 14):
petitioner: Stephen BALLIET, Esq.
2 children: Peter
David
guardian: Peter BURKHALTER, Whitehall Township

**Court on 25 March 1791, continued:**

Estate of Michael ENDRESS, Upper Milford Township—request audit:

| | |
|---|---|
| executors: | George SEYDER, the petitioner, Jacob STAHL |
| auditors: | James GILL, of Emmaus, George KRIEBEL, Upper Milford, George Adam BLANK, Salisbury Township |

Estate of Henry RUMFELD—request distribution of funds:

| | |
|---|---|
| petitioner: | John RUMFELD, one administrator |
| administrator: | Casper RUMFELD, other administrator |

Estate of Moritz BISCHOFF, Easton, clockmaker—request sale; auditors appointed:

| | |
|---|---|
| land: | tenement and lot in Easton on North side of great square, front 40' by depth 120' |
| widow: | Christina, administratrix |
| auditors: | John HERSTER, Peter SHNYDER, Jacob WYGAND, Borough of Easton |

Estate of Thomas RUCHMAN, Lower Mt. Bethel Township—motion of Samuel SITGREAVES, Esq. of behalf of the widow requesting audit:

| | |
|---|---|
| widow: | Elizabeth |
| auditors: | Samuel REA, William McFARREN, Joseph MARTIN, Lower Mt. Bethel Township |

**Court on 31 March 1791**
**Justices, the Esquires: Thomas HARTMAN, Lewis STACHER, Jacob ABEL**

Guardians for 7 minor children of Philip BUCHECKER, died some short time since, Upper Saucon Township (all under age 14) (were other children):

| | |
|---|---|
| petitioner: | Philip, eldest son |
| 7 children: | Magdalena |
| | Henry |
| | Jacob |
| | Daniel |
| | Eve |
| | Susanna |
| | "and a male infant the youngest on whom no name is yet confer'd" |
| guardians: | for all 7 minor children—Henry WEAVER, Upper Saucon Township, and Daniel SCHWARTZ, Upper Milford Township |

Guardian for Magdalena, under age 14, minor children of Henry MÄSER, Weisenberg Township:

| | |
|---|---|
| widow: | Barbara, now wife of Mr. KOFER |
| guardian: | John Adam BEAR |

**Court on 1 April 1791**
**Justices, the Esquires: Thomas HARTMAN, William CRAIG, Jacob ABEL**

Estate of Jacob BEAR, Allen Township (had will)—complaint against Jacob BEAR, a son of deceased; request audit:

| | |
|---|---|
| petitioner: | Felty SHOWALTER, who was left a sum of money by the will of Jacob BEAR—he accused Jacob BEAR, the son, of eluding the intentions of the will; he did not keep the executors informed of certain issues |
| executors: | Christian BEAR and David MILLER |
| auditors: | William HENRY, Peter RHOADS, Simon DREISBACH, Esquires |

**Court on 22 April 1791**

**Justices, the Esquires: William CRAIG, Thomas HARTMAN, Jacob ABEL**

Estate of Peter TISE, Upper Milford Township—request audit:

| | |
|---|---|
| petitioner: | Philip STAHL, husband of Salome TISE, one daughter of deceased |
| administrator: | Peter TISE, a son |
| auditors: | Christian HECKEWELDER, merchant, Joseph HORSEFIELD, gentleman, John HASSE, gentleman, all of Bethlehem Township |

**Court on 2 May 1791**
**Justices, the Esquires: William HENRY, Christopher WAGNER, Lewis STACHER, Jacob ABEL**

Estate of Peter TISE, Upper Milford Township—referring to 22 April entry:
auditors were reappointed and were ordered to report next 16 May

**Court on 2 May 1791**
**Justices, the Esquires, now present: William HENRY, Christopher WAGNER, Jacob ABEL**

Estate of Moritz BISHOFF, Easton, clock maker—auditors' report; permission to sell:

| | |
|---|---|
| widow: | Christina, administratrix |

Estates of Aaron DEPUE, Esq., and Chemima, his wife, both deceased sometime ago, Lower Smithfield Township—request inquest:

| | |
|---|---|
| father's land: | 60 acres patented land bounded by Jacob STROWD, now or late of Robert LEVERS, Esq., the late Godfrey VOELCKER, James DINGMAN |
| mother's land: | 115 acres warranted land bounded by Ulrich HAUSER, Thomas WRIGHT, and son Aaron DEPUE |
| 7 children: | Aaron, eldest son |
| | Samuel |
| | Elizabeth |
| | Sarah, wife of William OVERFIELD |
| | Jean, wife of Cornelius SHOEMAKER |
| | Rachel |
| | Susanna |

Jean ROSEBRUGH, widow of Rev. John ROSEBRUGH, Allen Township, died at about age 55 in 1777—request for further support was granted

**Court on 16 May 1791**
**Justices, the Esquires: Thomas HARTMAN, Christopher WAGNER, Jacob ABEL**

Estate of Peter TISE, Sr.—auditors' report; three evidences were brought to court that they had frequently heard Peter say that his son should have the land for 600 pounds, 200 for himself and 400 for the other heirs, 4 sisters:

| | |
|---|---|
| children: | Peter, Jr |
| | Elizabeth, wife of Ulrich LUTZ |
| | Margareth, wife of Mathew GREULICH |
| | Catherine, wife of Abraham STAHL |
| | Salome, wife of Philip STAHL |
| fees paid to: | Adam STAHLNECKER for expenses in defending |

**Court on 16 May 1791, continued:**

Estate of Thomas RUCKMAN—auditors' report:
widow: Elizabeth
8 minor children
administrators: William RUCKMAN and John JACOBY

Estate of Samuel CASEBIER (CASEBEER)—auditors' report; permission to sell:
administrators: Elisha BARTON and George NEWTON

**Court on 20 June 1791**
**Justices, the Esquires: William HENRY, George BREINIG, Jacob HORNER**

Estate of Peter CONRAD, Esq., Hamilton Township, 5 tracts, one woodland, total of 355 acres—report of inquest by Sheriff Jonas HARTZELL, Esq.:
widow
13 children: George Peter, eldest son—accepted the land
sureties: Henry HAUSSEN, John SCHNYDER, Hamilton Township, both blacksmiths
12 men:all by oath—Nicholas MICHAEL (MICHAL), Peter OBERSHIMER, Melchert BOSERT, Adam STECHER, Christopher KELLER, George GOWER, Lorence KUNKEL (Lorentz KUNCKEL), George SETZER, Casper METZGER, Jacob KELLER, Bathel SHIVELY (SCHEIBLE), Jacob SORVER (SORBER)

Estate of George GILBERT, Penn Township, 2 tracts, 255 acres and 140 acres—report of inquest by Sheriff Jonas HARTZELL, Esq.:
widow
7 children: George, eldest son—accepted the land
others not named
sureties: Jacob OSWALD, Lynn Township, joiner, and Leonard ZIMMERMAN, Penn Township
12 men:by oath and affirmation—Jacob OSWALD, Philip MOSER, Henry PROBST (Henrich BROBST), Andrew FELLER (Andreas FÖLLER), John EVERET, Daniel OSWALD, Jacob WARTMAN, Jacob SANDER, Leonard ZIMERMAN, George HANT, Michael HAPES (HABBES), John ZENER (Hannes ZEHNER)

**Court on 21 June 1791**
**Justices, the Esquires: William HENRY, George BREINIG, Christopher WAGNER, Jacob HORNER, William WILLS**

Guardians for 3 minor children of Michael STRIEBY, Lynn Township (were other children):
petitioner: Jacob STRIEBY, eldest son
3 children: John, over age 14....................................guardian: John MOSER, Whitehall Township
Adam, under age 14................................guardian: Peter BECHLER, Whitehall Twp.
Catharine, under age 14 ..........................guardian: Peter BECHLER, Whitehall Twp.

**Court on 21 June 1791**
**Justices, the Esquires, now present: William HENRY, Christopher WAGNER, Jacob HORNER, Enoch BEER**

Guardian for Joseph, over age 14, minor child of Jacob MUSSELMAN, Allen Township (were other children):
guardian: Christian MUSSELMAN, Upper Milford Township

**Court on 22 June 1791**
**Justices, the Esquires: William HENRY, George BREINIG, Christopher WAGNER, Jacob HORNER, Lodowick STÄHLER, William WILLS, Ezekiel SCHOONOVER**

Estate of Jacob TRAUB, Upper Milford Township, 51 acres—report of inquest by Sheriff Jonas HARTZELL:
widow
4 children: Jacob, eldest son—accepted the land
others not named
sureties: George HAMAN, David HEIMBACH, Upper Milford Township
12 men:all by oath—Samuel SNYDER (Simon SCHNEYDER), Daniel STOUFFER (STAUFER), David HEIMBACH, Henry HERTZEL, Peter STALLER (STÄHLER), Henry (Henrich) HERTZEL, Jr., Stephen DALMAN (Stäffen DALLMAN), Adam SHIFFER (SCHÖFFER), Wendel WEAND (WIAND), Jacob SHIFFER (SCHÖFFER), Stophel MOORE (Stoffel MOHR), William MOORE

Estate of Aaron DEPUE, Esq., 60 acres, and his wife Chemima, 115 acres, Lower Smithfield Township—report of inquest by Sheriff Jonas HARTZELL, Esq.:
8 children: Aaron. eldest son—accepted the land
others not named
sureties: Jacob STROWD, Esq., and John HUSTON, both of Lower Smithfield Township
12 men:all by oath—Daniel SHOEMAKER, Michael SLY (SLEY), Henry HOUSER (Henrich HAUSER), Richard SHAW, Peter FRIEDRICH (FRIDRICH), Ulrich HOUSER (HAUSER), John BROWN (Johannes BRAUN), Benjamin SCOONHOVER (SCHOONHOVER), Richard TILBERY (VAN FILBURY), Joseph MONTANYE, John FISH, David DILLS (DILS)

**Court on 22 June 1791**
**Justices, the Esquires, now present: William HENRY, Christopher WAGNER, George BREINIG, Jacob HORNER, Ludowick STÄHLER**

Guardians for 4 minor children of Samuel RALSTON, Allen Township (had will) (were other children):
executors: John RALSTON and Robert BROWN, Esq.
4 children: Gabriel, over age 14................................guardian: John RALSTON, Esq.
(not present, handled by his attorney Robert BROWN)
Sarah, over age 14..................................guardian: John HAYS, Sr., Allen Twp.
Isaac, under age 14.................................guardian: John McNAIR, Sr., Allen Twp.
Lettice, under age 14..............................guardian: John McNAIR, Sr., Allen Twp.

Guardians for 5 minor grandchildren of George HOFFMAN, Whitehall Township (all under age 14):
petitioner: Andrew RUPP, husband of Ann Mary, one daughter of the deceased
5 grandchildren, children of Ann Mary:
Andrew RUPP
Susanna RUPP
Solomon RUPP
John RUPP
Mary RUPP
guardian: for all 5 children—George RUPP, Sr., Macungie Township

**Court on 23 June 1791**
**Justices, the Esquires: William HENRY and associates**

Estate of Thomas RUCKMAN—motion of Samuel SITGREAVES, Esq. requesting an attachment issued against administrator to compel compliance with court order:

| | |
|---|---|
| widow: | Elizabeth |
| administrators: | William RUCKMAN and John JACOBY—had refused to comply |

**Court on 23 June 1791**
**Justices, the Esquires, now present: William HENRY, George BREINIG, Ludowick STÄHLER**

Estate of George FRANK, Allen Township (had will)—request audit:

| | |
|---|---|
| petition by: | widow's attorney, Thomas HARTMAN, Esq. |
| widow: | Ann Mary |
| only child: | George Adam |
| administrator: | George KOCH |
| auditors: | John YOUNGBERG of Nazareth, merchant, Jacob EYERLY, Jr., Esq., Nazareth, John MULHALLON, Esq., Nazareth Township |

Estate of Moritz BISHOFF—return of sale:

| | |
|---|---|
| administrator: | Christina BISHOFF |
| sold to: | Christian WINTER, Easton, clockmaker |

**Court on 24 June 1791**
**Justices, the Esquires: William HENRY, George BREINIG, Lewis STACHER, Thomas HARTMAN, Jacob ABEL, William WILLS**

Estate of Peter REEG—report of inquest by Sheriff Jonas HARTZELL, Esq., kept under advisement:

| | |
|---|---|
| eldest son: | George—did not attend |

Guardians for 7 minor children of John IHRIE, Mt. Bethel Township (all under age 14):

| | |
|---|---|
| petitioner: | Conrad IHRIE, Sr., father of deceased |
| 7 children: | Elizabeth |
| | Mary |
| | Catharine |
| | Sarah |
| | Conrad |
| | John |
| | Susanna |
| guardian: | for all 7 children—grandfather, Conrad IHRIE, and John ARNDT, Esq. |

## Court on 6 August 1791
## Justices, the Esquires: Thomas HARTMAN, Christopher WAGNER, Jacob ABEL

New guardians for minor children of Philip BUCHECKER, Upper Saucon Township; because, "it being such a number of years before the younger of said children shall...be entitled to chose a guardian...that the petitioner is uneasy at the said...SCHWARTZ, partly... on account of his living at too great a distance from the said children, and more especially as she is very apprehensive that his circumstances might...in time prove injurious to the estate...of such minor children if left for such a number of years in his hands.":

| | |
|---|---|
| widow: | Margareth, the petitioner |
| children: | Magdalena |
| | Henry |
| | Jacob |
| | Daniel |
| | Eve |
| | Susanna |
| | Peter |
| guardians: | former—Henry WEAVER and Daniel SCHWARTZ |
| | new—Henry WEAVER and Adam ROMIG, Upper Saucon Township, miller |

## Court on 12 August 1791
## Justices, the Esquires: William CRAIG, Thomas HARTMAN, Jacob ABEL

Estate of Esther DELYON, widow, tenement and lot in Easton—request sale; permission given:

| | |
|---|---|
| land: | south side of Northampton Street, on east the Reformed German Parsonage, on south a 20' alley, on west by lot of heirs of Lewis GORDON, front 55' by depth 220', #170 |
| administrator: | Myer HART |

## Court on 21 September 1791
## Justices, the Esquires: Peter RHOADS and David WAGENER

Guardians for 4 minor children of George HOFFMAN, Whitehall Township (were other children):

| | | |
|---|---|---|
| widow: | Ann Mary | |
| 4 children: | Henry, over age 14 | guardian: Henry KOCH, Macungie Twp. |
| | Christian, over age 14 | guardian: Jacob HAMAN, Whitehall Twp. |
| | Magdalena, under age 14 | guardian: Nicholas LITZENBERGER, Macungie Twp. |
| | Catharina, under age 14 | guardian: Peter GUTH, Whitehall Twp. |

Guardian for John, now over age 14, one minor child of Philip SCHUCK, Lynn Township (were other children):

| | |
|---|---|
| guardian: | Philip MOSER, Lynn Township |

Estate of Henry NEFF, Heidelberg Township, several contiguous tracts—request inquest:

| | |
|---|---|
| land: | 372 acres bounded by Jacob BRANDSTETTER, John RUMBEL, George LINTZ, Jacob MISSEMER, Ulrich NEFF, Frantz MISSEMER, Michael MISEMER |
| widow: | Catharine, now wife of Jacob OSWALD |
| 7 children: | Jacob, eldest son |
| | Henry |
| | Catharine |
| | John |
| | Margaret |
| | Peter |
| | Elizabeth, wife of Philip SHANTZ |

**Court on 24 September 1791**
**Justices, the Esquires: Jacob RUSH, Peter RHOADS, William HENRY, David WAGENER**

Estate of Esther DELYON—return of sale:
administrator: Myer HART
sold to: Abigail DELYON, City of Philadelphia, spinster

Estate of Michael ENDRESS—auditors' report; legacies were left to the children of Frederick HAINES, dec'd.:
executors: George SYDER, present, and Jacob STAHL, "being absent and having had due notice to attend"
daughter: Johanna, deceased, late wife of Frederick HAINES

Estate of George BERLIP, Chestnuthill Township—request sale; auditors appointed:
administrators: Elizabeth BERLIP and John MEIXSELL
land: 150 acres bounded by John MEIXSELL, Valentine MECKER, Jacob FRANCE
auditors: Lewis STACHER, Esq., Jacob HELLER, innholder, both of Plainfield Township, and Thomas McCARTY, Hamilton Township

**Court on 24 October 1791**
**Justices, the Esquires: William HENRY and David WAGENER**

New guardian for 2 minor children of Thomas RUCHMAN, Mt. Bethel Township:
widow: Elizabeth
3 children: John
Thomas
guardian: former—James DEPUE, "lately departed this life"
new—Peter BUTZ, [ blank ] Mt. Bethel Township

**Court on 20 December 1791**
**Justices, the Esquires: Jacob RUSH, Peter RHOADS, John MULHALLON, William HENRY**

Estate of Henry NEFF, Heidelberg Township, 7 contiguous tracts totaling 372 acres with mill on 150 acres—report of inquest by Sheriff Jonas HARTZELL, Esq.:
widow
7 children: Jacob, eldest son—accepted the land
others not named
sureties: Conrad NEFF and John SHEFFER, Weisenberg Township
12 men:by oath and affirmation—Henry HOFMAN, Christian SNYDER (SCHNEIDER), John HANDWERK, John EVRET (Hannes EBERT), Tobias EVERT (EBERT), Adam GERMAN, George LENTZ (CREUTZ), John RUMBEL (Johannes RUMPPEL), Jacob MANNS, Simon CREITZ, Dewalt PETER (PETTER), Philip PETER (Filib PETTER)

Guardians for 3 minor children of Thomas OWEN, Upper Saucon Township (all under age 14):
widow: Margaret
3 children: Owen
Hannah
Sarah
guardians: for all 3 children—Stephen TOOL and Christian KLEMMER, Upper Saucon Township

Estate of John GEORGE, died about 2 years ago, Lowhill Township—request inquest:

| | |
|---|---|
| land: | 200 acres bounded by Henry GEORGE, Lowrence GEORGE, Michael MOSER, Andrew KNERR, Casper KLOTZ |
| widow | |
| 9 children: | Peter, eldest son |
| | Christina |
| | Eve, wife of Peter STEEMMEL |
| | John |
| | Catherine |
| | Margaret |
| | Elizabeth |
| | Magdalena |
| | Susanna |

Estate of Thomas RUCKMAN, Lower Mt. Bethel Township—request audit:

| | |
|---|---|
| administrators: | William RUCKMAN, John JACOBIE |
| auditors: | Joseph MARTIN, Lower Mt. Bethel Township, gentleman, John HERSTER, Easton, Esq., John YOUNGBERG, Nazareth, merchant |

**Court on 21 December 1791**
**Justices, the Esquires: Jacob RUSH and William HENRY**

Guardian for minor children of John GEORGE, Lowhill Township (were other children):

| | |
|---|---|
| children: | John, over age 14; the remaining children are all under age 14: |
| | Catharine |
| | Margaret |
| | Elizabeth |
| | Magdalena |
| | Susanna |
| guardian: | for all 6 children—Andrew BUCHMAN, Lowhill Township |

Estate of George GILBERT, Penn Township—petition for approval of new sureties:

| | |
|---|---|
| eldest son: | George—accepted the land last June |
| sureties: | former—Jacob OSWALD and Leonard ZIMERMAN, both declined |
| | new—George GORT and Jacob SCHWARTZ, Macungie Township |

Estate of Henry YOUNG, Plainfield Township, deeded land—request inquest:

| | |
|---|---|
| land: | 239 acres b/by Philip YENT, Valentine YENT, George BENDER, Philip KELLER |
| widow: | Mary |
| 11 children: | John, eldest son |
| | Elizabeth, wife of John CLAUSS |
| | Margaret, wife of Leonard ANDRE |
| | Rosina, wife of John BOWER |
| | Mary |
| | Catharine |
| | Susanna |
| | Magdalena |
| | Feronica |
| | George |
| | Henry |

**Court on 21 December 1791, continued:**

Estate of Frederick ATHERHOLD, Bedminster Township, Bucks County—request inquest:

| | |
|---|---|
| land: | 55 acres, gristmill and tract in Moore Township, bounded by Adam HECKMAN, Peter RUNDIS, George PALMER, Michael SCHWARTZ |
| widow: | Esther |
| 11 children: | Daniel, eldest son |
| | Mary, wife of Michael WEIERMAN |
| | Abraham |
| | Christian |
| | Frederick |
| | David |
| | Joseph |
| | Esther |
| | Samuel |
| | Ann |
| | Gabriel |

**Court on 24 December 1791**
**Justices, the Esquires: Jacob RUSH, Peter RHOADS, David WAGENER**

Estate of Casper ERB, Moore Township—auditors' report:

| | |
|---|---|
| administrators: | Lawrence ERB and Michael ERB |
| petitioners: | David BLACKLY, Allen Township, hatter, and his wife Elizabeth, one daughter of the deceased |
| legacy to: | Elizabeth HOY |
| heirs: | Lawrence ERB |
| | Michael ERB |
| | Margaret, wife of Philip DRUMM |
| | Elizabeth, wife of David BLAKLY |

**Court on 10 January 1792**
**Justices, the Esquires: Peter RHOADS, William HENRY, David WAGENOR**

Estate of Thomas RUCKMAN—auditors' report:

| | |
|---|---|
| auditors: | Joseph MARTIN, John HERSTER, John YOUNGBERG |

Estate of Thomas RUCKMAN—distribution:

| | |
|---|---|
| administrators: | William RUCHMAN, son of deceased, and John JACOBY |
| widow | |
| children | |

Estate of Frederick ATHERHOLD—report on inquest by Sheriff Jonas HARTZELL, kept under advisement:
parties concerned were absent

## Court on 26 March 1792
## Justices, the Esquires: Peter RHOADS, John MULHALLON, David WAGNER

Estate of Jacob KOENIG, Bethlehem Township—request inquest:

| | |
|---|---|
| land: | 200 acres, part of Dry Land Tract, bounded by George MICHAEL, Philip GROSS, George SCHNABEL, Thomas HARTMAN, Esq. |
| widow: | since deceased |
| 10 children: | Mathias, eldest son |
| | Jacob |
| | Margaret, wife of Philip RIESER |
| | Adam |
| | Magdalena, wife of Jacob BUSS |
| | John |
| | Elizabeth, wife of Jacob YOUNG |
| | Christina, wife of Christopher KOTZ |
| | Christopher |
| | John George |

## Court on 10 April 1792
## Justices, the Esquires: Jacob RUSH, Peter RHOADS, John MULHALLON, William HENRY

Guardian for Solomon, over age 14, one minor child of Christian BACHMAN, Lower Saucon Township, miller:

| | |
|---|---|
| guardian: | John BACHMAN, brother of the child |

Guardian for John, over age 14, one minor child of George DUTT, Macungie Township (were other children):

| | |
|---|---|
| guardian: | Christian DUTT, his brother |

Guardian for 3 minor children of Jacob FEYOCK, Plainfield Township (all under age 14):

| | |
|---|---|
| administrator: | Michael KNOWS |
| 3 children: | Michael |
| | David |
| | Elizabeth |
| guardian: | for all 3 children—Christian Frederick STEINMAN of Gnadenthal |

Estate of George BERLIP, Chestnuthill Township, 150 acres—auditors' report; permission to sell:

| | |
|---|---|
| administrators: | Elizabeth BERLIP and John MEIXSELL |

Estate of George REINER, Upper Milford Township—request inquest:

| | |
|---|---|
| land: | 65 acres bounded by Christian REINER, Henry HERTZELL, Jacob TRAUB, Stephen DALMAN, Wendel WYAND, Nicholas STÄHLER |
| widow: | Sibylla |
| 6 children: | George, eldest son |
| | Frederick |
| | Catharine |
| | Christian |
| | Peter |
| | Daniel |

**Court on 11 April 1792**
**Justices, the Esquires: not named**

Estate of Henry YOUNG, Plainfield Township, 209 acres—report of inquest by Sheriff Jonas HARTZELL:
11 children: John, eldest son—accepted the land
others not named
sureties: Lewis STACHER, Esq., and Conrad GERMANTON, both of Plainfield Township
12 men:all by oath—Jacob HELLER, Christopher ENGEL, Conrad GERMANTON, William FREEMAN, Michael REAB (REB), Abraham HELLER, Deter BOWER (Dietrich BAUER), George PIFFER (PEIFFER), Peter BENDER, Conrad KODER, Valentine YENT, Peter SHUCK

Estate of Jacob KOENIG, Bethlehem Township, 200 acres—report of inquest by Sheriff Jonas HARTZELL:
10 children: Mathias, eldest son—declined
Jacob, 2nd son—accepted the land
sureties: John BUSS, Sr., Bethlehem Township, and Peter KACHLEIN, Forks Township
12 men:all by oath—Mathias KRESS, Mathias KING (KOENIG), George GROSS, Barned ARNDT, Frederick SAYLOR (SEILER), Conrad GEORGE, Michael LAWALL, George SNABEL (SCHNABEL), Fridrich WAGENER (WAGNER), Conrad EDELMAN, Paul DURNBLESER (THURNBLÖSER), John SNYDER (Johannes SCHNEIDER)

New guardian for Susanna ERDMAN, now over age 14, minor granddaughter of Jacob BILDHOUSE, Upper Milford Township (her maternal grandfather):
her father: Jacob ERDMAN, Springfield Township, Bucks County
guardian: former—John OHLEWEIN, Upper Milford Township, appointed June 1784
new—Jacob ERDMAN, her father

Guardian for Nicholas BRANG, now over age 14, minor grandchild of George MEYER, died lately:
his father: George BRANG, also deceased
guardian: John SCHWEITZER, Bethlehem Township

Estate of George ENGEL, Plainfield Township, gristmill and 2 tracts—request audit:
administrators: Christopher ENGEL and Abraham SORBER (SORBA?)
land: 1) 243 acres with mill bounded by Henry ENGEL, William FREEMAN, and others
2) 55 acres bounded by George EBERT, Adam ENGLER, John ARNDT
auditors: Lewis STACHER, Esq., Jacob HELLER, innholder, Dietrich BOWER, all of Plainfield Township

Estate of Frederick ATHERHOLD, Moore Township, 55 acres with gristmill—report of inquest by Sheriff Jonas HARTZELL, Esq.:
widow
11 children: Daniel, eldest son—now present and accepted the land
others not named
sureties: Jacob BAER and Adam HECKMAN, Allen Township
12 men:by oath and affirmation—Henry STROUS (STRAUSS), Adam HECKMAN, Jacob ERB, Nicholas NEHLICH (NEHLIG), George REES (RIES), Henry PERSON (Henrich BIERSON), David MUSELMAN, Henry DRISBACH (Henrich DREISBACH), Michael SCHWARTZ, Ludwig KRATZER, Daniel SHECKLER (SCHÄCKLER), Andrew HOWER (Andreas HAUER)

**Court on 11 April 1792, continued:**

Jean ROSEBRUGH, widow of Rev. John ROSEBRUGH, Allen Township, died age 55 years in 1777—request for support under advisement since last 24 September:
court denied— "the prayer of the said Petitioner cannot in propriety be complied with"

**Court on 12 April 1792**
**Justices, the Esquires: Jacob RUSH, Peter RHOADS, David WAGONER**

Estate of John GEORGE, Lowhill Township, 208 acres—report of inquest by Sheriff Jonas HARTZELL, Esq.:
widow
9 children: Peter, eldest son—accepted the land
others not named
sureties: Philip FENSTERMACHER, Lowhill Township, Michael BOBST, Weisenberg Twp.
12 men:all by oath—John Lewis LUKE, John (Hannes) MOSER, Michael DEIBERT (DEIBER), Peter FRANTZ, David KUNTZ, George STERN, Jacob DORNER, Christian SMITH (SCHMIDT), John (Hannes) WUCHTER, Michael ACKER, Martin WUCHTER, Casper KLOTZ

Guardians for 6 minor children of Adam SORVER, Chestnuthill Township (were other children):
petitioner: Jacob SORVER, brother of deceased
6 children: Adam, over age 14................................guardian: his uncle, Jacob SORVER
Daniel, over age 14................................guardian: Philip CORELL, Forks Township
Philip, under age 14
Sarah, under age 14
Jacob, under age 14
Abraham, under age 14
guardian: for 4 younger children—Lewis STACKER, Esq., Plainfield Township

**Court on 13 April 1792**
**Justices, the Esquires: Jacob RUSH, Peter RHOADS, John MULHALLON, David WAGNER**

Guardian for 2 minor grandsons of Richard WALKER, Bucks County, Esq. (had will) (both under age 14):
2 grandsons: Richard
Thomas
guardian: John WALKER, their father

**Court on 9 May 1792**
**Justices, the Esquires: Peter RHOADS and David WAGNER**

Estate of George REINER, Upper Milford Township, 65 acre—report of inquest by Sheriff Jonas HARTZELL:
widow
6 children: George, eldest son—accepted the land
others not named
sureties: Stephen DALLMAN and David HEIMBACK, Upper Milford Township
12 men:by oath and affirmation—John SHIMER, Simon SHNYDER (SCHNEIDER), Stophel MOORE (MOHR), Nicholas HITTEL, David HEIMBACH, Peter STÄHLER (KÖHLER), Mathias (Mathes) KERN, William MOORE (MOHR), Wendel WIAND, Simon KEHLE (KELL), Jacob RODEBERGER (RODENBURGER), Daniel STAUFFER

**Court on 9 May 1792, continued:**

Estate of Henry NEFF, Heidelberg Township—request for new sureties to be accepted:
eldest son: Jacob NEFF—had accepted the land
sureties: former—Conrad NEFF and John SCHEFFER (John declined)
new—with Conrad, Christian CLAUSS, Lynn Township

**Court on 15 August 1792**
**Justices, the Esquires: Jacob RUSH, Peter RHOADS, William HENRY**

Guardians for 2 minor children of George GILBERT, Penn Township (both now over 14) (were other children):
widow: Susanna
2 children: Philip....................................................guardian: Bernhard FULWEILER, Sr., Lynn T.
Elizabeth ..............................................guardian: Jacob MANNS, Lynn Twp.

Estate of George GILBERT—request audit:
auditors: Mathias PROBST, Esq., Philip MOSER, Thomas EVERITT, all of Lynn Township

Estate of George Adam FRANK—motion of Joseph THOMAS, Esq. to set aside the auditors' report:
administrator: George KOCH
new auditors: John HERSTER, Esq., John BROTZMAN, gentleman of Easton, John McNAIR, Esq. of Allen Township

Estate of George ENGEL, Plainfield Township, grist mill, saw mill, 243 acres and 45 acres—auditors' report; permission to sell, reserving 30 acres with buildings where the widow now dwelled

Estate of Peter REEG, Heidelberg Township, 171 acres, 150 perches—report of inquest by Sheriff Jonas HARTZELL, Esq.:
widow
5 children: George, eldest son—accepted the land
others not named
sureties: Michael DEIBERT, Whitehall Township, blacksmith, and Charles ROSS, Heidelberg Township
12 men:all by oath—Michael DEIBERT (DEIBER), Peter ANDREW (ANDRES), John REAVER (Johannes REBER), Martin ANDREW, Anthony SHAFFER (Andon SCHAEFFER), Dewald SHAFFER (SCHAEFFER), Peter MUFFLEY, Frederick PIFFER (PEIFER), Peter SIEGFRIED, George HELFRECH (Jerg HELFRIG), Andrew YELE (Andreas JEHL), Henry STETTLER (Henrich STAETTLER)

**Court on 17 August 1792**
**Justices, the Esquires: Jacob RUSH, Peter RHOADS, John MULHALLON**

Jean ROSEBRUGH, widow of Rev. John ROSEBRUGH, Allen Township—a plea for more support:
attorney: Samuel SITGREAVES, Esq.
**5 small children, the eldest only 10 and the youngest only 1 when father was killed in January 1777
**reference to husbands service and her frequent applications for support
**she was still unmarried and her expenses had increased in raising the children
**court still rejected her request

**Court on 17 August 1792, continued:**

Estate of Conrad SHNYDER, Bethlehem Township—request for distribution:
petitioner: Peter WOLF, husband of Elizabeth, late widow of deceased—felt that his wife should receive 1/3 balance of estate after sale of property
petition was denied

Jean ROSEBRUGH, widow of Rev. John ROSEBRUGH—further plea for court to reconsider her petition:
court reconsidered and granted her ½ pay in right of her husband from 18 May 1791 to 18 May 1792

**Court on 12 November 1792**
**Justices, the Esquires: Jacob RUSH, Peter RHOADS, David WAGENER**

New guardian for David, now over age 14, minor son of Christian BACHMAN, Lower Saucon Township:
guardian: former—Charles Ludwig KOCH
new—Philip GEISSINGER, Upper Saucon Township

**Court on 13 November 1792**
**Justices, the Esquires: Peter RHOADS and David WAGENER**

Estate of George GILBERT, Penn Township—auditors' report:
administratrix: Susanna
funds paid to: Mary SIEGFRIED
funds owed to: Adam CREUTZ

Estate of George GILBERT, Penn Township—request for release of bonds from hands of clerk:
widow: Susanna
children: George, eldest son—had accepted the land
others not named

Estate of William BEYSEL, Nazareth Township—request inquest:
land: 250 acres, part of Dry Land Tract, bounded by Philip FAAS, Baltzer STÄHLY, Elias HUMMEL, Christian BROWN, Jacob WILHELM
widow: Margaret
5 children: Peter, eldest son
Anna Mary, wife of John BLUM
Elizabeth
Adam
John

**Court on 16 November 1792**
**Justices, the Esquires: Peter RHOADS and John MULHALLON**

Estate of Jacob KOENIG, Bethlehem Township—request for new sureties to be accepted:
son: Jacob—had accepted the land
sureties: former—John BUSS, Sr., Bethlehem Township and Peter KACHLEIN, Forks Township; both refused to enter bonds
new—George HARTZELL, Bethlehem Township, Paul THORNBLESER, John BUSS, Jr., Nazareth Township

**Court on 17 November 1792**
**Justices, the Esquires: Jacob RUSH and Peter RHOADS**

Estate of Peter GROSS, Allen Township—request inquest:

land: 168 acres, part of Dry Land Tract, bounded by Michael MEYER, John RALSTON, John HAYS, Moses HEMPHILL, Casper RITTER

widow: Ann Mary

9 children: Abraham, eldest son
Isaac
Elizabeth
Catharine, wife of John BARTHOLD
Mary
Barbara
Sarah
Susanna
Christina

Estate of John OBITZ, Plainfield Township—request audit:

administrators: Jacob EYERLY, Jr., and George HAHN

auditors: John YOUNGBERG, merchant, and Jacob CHRIST, hatter, both of Nazareth, and Jacob HELLER, Plainfield Township, innholder

Guardians for 5 minor children of John OBITZ, Plainfield Township (all under age 14):

administrators: Jacob EYERLY, Jr., and George HAHN

5 children: Elisabeth
Catharina
Margareth
George
Anna Maria

guardians: for all 5 children—Joseph LEVERING, Esq., and Jacob SCHMICK, saddler, both of Nazareth

Guardian for 2 minor children of William BEYSEL, Nazareth Township (both under age 14) (were other children):

petitioners: Adam STOCKER and Adam HUMMEL, friends

2 children: Adam
John

guardian: for both children—Christian BROWN, Nazareth Township

**Court on 15 January 1793**
**Justices, the Esquires: Jacob RUSH, John MULHALLON, William HENRY, David WAGENER**

Estate of Peter EBERHART, Upper Milford Township—request for citation against guardian of petitioner:

petitioner: Abraham, one son of deceased —feared that some of his estate would be lost

guardian: Peter SHNYDER, Rockhill Township, Bucks County—appointed 3 years ago, lately sold his estate; cited to give security for his trust in February

Estate of John OBITZ, Plainfield Township—auditors' report; administration account was just and true:

administrators: Jacob EYERLY, Jr., and George HAHN

**Court on 15 January 1793, continued:**

Guardian for Elizabeth MYER, under age 14, minor daughter of Eve MYER, deceased:
- petitioner: Peter TURNEY, next friend and uncle of child; brother of the deceased
- guardian: Jacob HAMMAN, Whitehall Township

**Court on 16 January 1793**
**Justices, the Esquires: Peter RHOADS, John MULHALLON, William HENRY, David WAGENER**

Estate of Peter GROSS, Allen Township, 168 acres—report of inquest by Sheriff Jonas HARTZELL, Esq.:
- widow
- 9 children: Abraham, eldest son—accepted the land
  others not named
- sureties: George EHRET, Allen Township, butcher, and Isaac GROSS, Forks Township
- 12 men:by oath and affirmation—Michael HUBER, Michael SHORTZ, Moses HEMPHILL, Casper RITTER, Barnet ARNDT, Jacob BALIET, George NEYHART (NEUHART), William DANIEL, Fridrick HERMAN, Michael MAYER (MEYER), Lanard FOGEL, Nicholas REMEL (RIMMEL)

Estate of William BEYSEL, Nazareth Township, 250 acres—report of inquest by Sheriff Jonas HARTZELL:
- widow
- 5 children: Peter, eldest son—accepted the land
  others not named
- sureties: Bernhard ARNDT and Philip FASS, both of Nazareth Township
- 12 men:by oath and affirmation—Mathias KING (KOENIG), Barnet ARNDT, George GROSS, John SENTEE, William JONSON (JONSOHN), Conrad ERNST, Nicholas KRAMER (KRAEMER), George READER (ROEDTER), John KEMERER (Johannes KEMMER), Conrad GEORGE, Fridrich KREIDLER (KREITTER), John HARTZELL

Guardians for 4 minor children of Charles LABAR, Upper Mt. Bethel Township (were other children):
- petitioner: William LABAR, brother of deceased
- 4 children: Daniel, over age 14.................................guardian: Christopher SMITH, Up. Mt. Bethel
  Sarah, under age 14
  William, under age 14
  Anna Mary, under age 14
- guardian: for younger 3 children—their uncle, William LABAR

Guardians for 4 minor children of Melchior BAER, Whitehall Township (all under age 14):
- petitioner: Peter GROSS, brother-in-law of deceased
- 4 children: Henry...................................................guardian: Daniel TRAXELL, Whitehall Twp.
  Catharine...............................................guardian: Peter LEHR, Whitehall Twp.
  Susanna................................................guardian: Lowrence NEWHARD, Whitehall T.
  Magdalena.............................................guardian: Jacob GUTH

Guardian for 3 minor children of Conrad NEIN, Macungie Township (were other children):
- petitioner: John NEIN, eldest son
- 3 children: Mary Barbara
  Christina
  Mary
- guardian: for all 3 children—George Frederick KNAUSS, Whitehall Township

**Court on 16 January 1793, continued:**

Estate of Conrad NEIN, Macungie Township—request inquest:

| | |
|---|---|
| land: | 216 acres bounded by George Frederick KUNTZ, George BREINER, Jacob STEFFAN, Jacob SHOEMAKER, and others |
| widow: | Elizabeth |
| 10 children: | John, eldest son |
| | Catharine, wife of Adam GRESSEL |
| | Elizabeth |
| | Conrad |
| | Susanna |
| | Christian |
| | Magdalena |
| | Mary Barbara |
| | Christina |
| | Mary |

Estate of Christian NAUMAN, Bethlehem Township—request inquest:

| | |
|---|---|
| land: | 65 acres, part of Dry Land Tract which was in Bethlehem Township but now in Nazareth Township, bounded by Mathias WEITKNECHT, John HUNTER, Christian SPENGLER, Casper RITTER |
| widow: | Albertina, now wife of Valentine DILLINGER |
| 6 children: | Peter, eldest son |
| | Michael |
| | Jacob |
| | Mary Elizabeth |
| | Christina |
| | Mary |

**Court on 17 January 1793**

**Justices, the Esquires: Jacob RUSH, Peter RHOADS, John MULHALLON, William HENRY, David WAGENER**

Estate of Frederick GUDEKUNST, Lower Smithfield Township, miller—request inquest:

| | |
|---|---|
| land: | lot and tenement in Town of Northampton, 60' front by 230' depth, west side of Lehigh Street, bounded by John MYER, Jacob MACKLEY |
| widow: | now wife of Abraham ALBERT |
| 6 children: | John, eldest son |
| | Adam |
| | Christina |
| | Susannah |
| | Frederick |
| | Solomon |

Estate of Henry SHNYDER, Borough of Easton—request inquest:

| | |
|---|---|
| land: | house and lot of 1/4 acres in Easton |
| children: | Peter, who has since died, intestate, under age 21 |
| | Henry |
| | Margaret, wife of John HERSTER, Esq. |
| | Elizabeth, wife of Christopher MEIXSELL |
| | Catharine |
| | Julianna |

**Court on 17 January 1793, continued:**

Guardian for 7 minor children of Peter CONRAD, Esq., Hamilton Township (were other children):

petitioner: George Peter, son

7 children: John Melchior, over age 14......................guardian: John Melchior BOSSERT, of same
Henry, over age 14 ..................................guardian: Henry HAUSER, of same
John, under age 14
Sarah, under age 14
Jacob, under age 14
Catharine, under age 14
Joseph, under age 14

guardians: for younger 5 children—John Melchior BOSSERT and Henry HAUSER

**Court on 18 February 1793**
**Justices, the Esquires: William HENRY, David WAGENER**

Estate of Peter EBERHARD—citation against guardian of one minor son of deceased was not answered; court issued an attachment against him directed to the sheriff of Bucks County for him to appear in March:

son: Abraham

guardian: Peter SHNYDER, Rockhill Township, Bucks County—he was to come into court and explain why he had not given security for his guardianship duties; he failed to appear

testimony by: Conrad EBERHARD—gave oath that he had delivered the citation

**Court on 12 March 1793**
**Justices, the Esquires: John MULHALLON and David WAGENER**

William Ennis COURTRIGHT, Lower Smithfield Township, a soldier requesting support:

In June 1781, William, then aged 36 years, was a private in a company of militia of Northampton County commanded by Cap. Henry SHOEMAKER, of the 5th Battalion commanded by Col. Jacob STROWD, in service of Pennsylvania. On the evening of June 18, he was taken prisoner by a party of hostile Indians; on June 19, in a re-encounter between the same Indians, he was retaken but wounded by the Indians and his right thigh broken by a ball. He was now a cripple, totally helpless and bedridden. Physicians' and surgeons' bills had consumed his property, which had "obliged him to throw himself upon the Justice and Humanity of his County."

The court granted William ½ pay plus rations from 19 June 1781

**Court on 9 April 1793**
**Justices, the Esquires: Jacob RUSH and associates**

Estate of Henry SHNYDER, Borough of Easton—report of inquest by Sheriff Jonas HARTZELL, Esq.:

widow

5 children: Henry, eldest son—accepted the land
others not named

sureties: John HERSTER, Esq., and William BARNET, tanner, both of Easton

12 men: by oath and affirmation—Abraham BACHMAN, Frederick BARTHOLD, Jacob WEYGAND, William RAUP, Christopher HERTZEL, Christian BIXLER, John YOUNG, Frederick GUIWINER (GEWINNER), Michael YOHE (JOHE), Jacob SICKMAN, Abraham BERLIN, Abraham SELLER

**Court on 9 April 1793, continued:**

Estate of Christian NAUMAN, Nazareth Township, 65 acres—report of inquest by Sheriff Jonas HARTZELL:
widow
6 children: Peter, eldest son—accepted the land
others not named
sureties: Leonard SCHWERTZER and Conrad KOCHER, Bethlehem Township
12 men:by oath and affirmation—Michael BAYER (BEYER), Mathias KING (KOENIG), George GROSS, Philip FAASE (FASS), Barned (Bernart) ARNDT, John HUNTER, John SENTEE, John HARTZELL, Nicholas KREMER (KRAEMER), Conrad FREY, Conrad GEORGE, Isaac HARTZELL

New guardian for Mathias, now over 14, one minor son of Jacob GROSS, Lower Saucon Township (had will):
guardian: former—John BOYER, Lower Saucon Township, appointed by will; declined to act
new—Jacob OBERLY, Lower Saucon Township

**Court on 10 April 1793**
**Justices, the Esquires: not named**

Guardian for Leonard, over age 14, one son of Charles LABAR, Upper Mt. Bethel Township:
guardian: Henry SHNYDER, Borough of Easton, saddler

**Court on 11 April 1793**
**Justices, the Esquires: not named**

Estate of Leonard KNECHT, Nazareth Township—request inquest:
land: 212 acres, part of Dry Land Tract, bounded by John RUTH, Christian BROWN, Nazareth Tract, Ulrich KNECHT
widow: Margareth
7 children: Adam, eldest son
Margareth, wife of Peter MASTER
Catharine, wife of Jacob ROMICH
Christina, wife of Adam HUMMEL
Glora, wife of Nicholas HEYL
Sarah, wife of George SCHÄFFER
Leonard

Guardian for 3 minor children of Henry YOUNG, Plainfield Township (all under age 14) (were other children):
petitioner: John, eldest son
3 children: Magdalena
Henry
Feronica
guardian: for all 3 children—Lewis STACHER, Esq., Plainfield Township

Jean ROSBRUGH, widow of Rev. John ROSBRUGH—request for further support:
again gave details of her husband's service and death; court granted her ½ pay and rations for one year

The following notation was recorded here concerning court sessions:
"The Judges of the Orphan's Court do ordain and establish that the Stated times for holding Orphan's Court be on the same days that the Court of Common Pleas and quarter sessions of the Peace shall be held within the County."

**Court on 12 April 1793**
**Justices, the Esquires: not named**

New guardian for 4 minor children of Adam SORVER, Chestnuthill Township:
- 4 children: Philip
  - Sarah
  - Jacob
  - Abraham
- guardian: former—Lewis STACHER, Esq., now resigned
  - new—Christopher KELLER, Hamilton Township

Request for new guardian for Abraham, one minor child of Peter EVERHARD, Upper Milford Township:
- guardian: former—Peter SHNYDER, Rockhill Township, Bucks County; Peter resigned and requested that a new guardian be appointed

Guardian for Abraham, over age 14, minor son of Peter EVERHARD, Upper Milford Township:
- guardian: Jacob KÖHLER, Upper Milford Township

Estate of Thomas McCRACKEN, Lower Mt. Bethel Township—request inquest:
- land: 159 acres bounded by Peter MANN, Elias DIETRICH, Joseph FOX, Hugh McCRACKEN, Robert FORSEMAN, David AYERS, Thomas SILLYMAN
- widow: Margaret
- 4 children: Hugh
  - Samuel
  - John
  - Margaret
- 4 grandchildren, children of the eldest son, Robert, deceased

Estate of George KNAUSS—request audit:
- administrators: George Frederick KNAUSS and Philip KNAUSS
- auditors: Peter EALER, George GRAFF, Peter KOHLER, Esquires

Guardian for John, under age 14, minor son of Adam DORN, Mt. Bethel Township (were other children):
- petitioner: Henry HAUSER, brother-in-law of deceased
- guardian: Ulrich HAUSSER, Lower Saucon Township, innholder

Estate of Conrad NEIN—report of inquest by Sheriff Jonas HARTZELL, Esq. held under advisement:
- parties concerned did not attend

Estate of Frederick GUTEKUNST—report of inquest by Sheriff Jonas HARTZELL, Esq. held under advisement:
- parties concerned did not attend

## Court on 13 April 1793
## Justices, the Esquires: not named

Guardian for Christina, under age 14, minor daughter of Peter GROSS, Allen Township (were other children):
- petitioner: John BARTHOLD, husband of another daughter
- guardian: George EHRET, Allen Township, butcher

## Court on 12 August 1793
## Justices, the Esquires: Peter RHOADS and David WAGONER

Estate of Conrad NEIN, Macungie Township, 216 acres—report of inquest by Sheriff Jonas HARTZELL, Esq.:
widow
10 children: John, eldest son—accepted the land
others not named
sureties: Henry BORTZ and George Frederick KUNTZ, Macungie Township, yeoman
12 men:all by oath—Henry (Henrich) BORTZ, Philip KNOUSE, Philip KUNTZ, Fridrick METZGER, Jacob SHANTZ, Nicholas LETZENBERGER (Nickles LIETZENBERGER), Michel HISKEY (HISGE), Adam SMITH (SCHMITT), George BREINER, Henry (Henrich) KOCH, George RUPE (RUPP), Nicholas KRAMER (Nicklas GRAMMER)

Guardians for 4 minor children of Henry FAUST, Allen Township (all under age 14) (were other children):
widow: Catharine
4 children: Abraham.................................................guardian: Henry BEYL, of same
John.......................................................guardian: Henry BEYL, of same
Catherine................................................guardian: Christian SCHWARTZ, of same
Elizabeth ..............................................guardian: Christian SCHWARTZ, of same

**Court on 14 August 1793**
**Justices, the Esquires: Jacob RUSH, Peter RHOADS, William HENRY, John MULHALLON**

Estate of Theobald KUNTZ, Penn Township—request audit:
administrator: Michael HAPPES
land: 180 or 200 acres adjoining Michael HAPPES, Jacob SWARTZ, Andrew OHL, & others
auditors: Jacob WEISS and Nicholas KERN, Esquires of Towamensing Township, and Nathan WARNER, Penn Township

Estate of Conrad NEIN, Macungie Township—request audit:
administrators: Elizabeth NEIN and John NEIN
auditors: George BREINIG, Esquire, Peter EALER, Esquire, and George Frederick KNAUSE

Estate of George Adam FRANCK (had will)—motion by John ROSS, Esq., to appoint auditors:
executor: George KOCH
auditors: Henry SPERING, Esq., Robert TRAILL, Esq., and Peter SHNYDER, tanner, all of Borough of Easton

**Court on 14 August 1793**
**Justices, the Esquires, now present: William HENRY, John MULHALLON**

Estate of Leonard KNECHT, Nazareth Township, 212 acres plus a small tract of 2 ½ acres bought from RUTH—report of inquest by Sheriff Jonas HARTZELL, Esq.:
widow
7 children: Adam, eldest son—accepted the land
sureties: Leonard KNECHT and Adam HUMMEL, Nazareth Township, yeomen
12 men:by oath—Thomas HARTMAN, Esq., Conrad (Conrat) BEST, Philip FAASE (FASS), Christian BROWN (BRAUN), Peter REASER (RIESER), Ludwig WILHELM, John ERET (Johannes EHERETT), William JONSON (JANSON)
by affirmation—Jacob EYERLY, Esq., Philip MICHEL, Conrad ERNST, Isaac GROSS

**Court on 16 August 1793**
**Justices, the Esquires: Peter RHOADS and William HENRY**

Guardian for minor children of Abraham ABEL, Upper Mt. Bethel Township (both under age 14):
widow: Catharine
children: John
Sarah
guardian: for both children—Jacob BECK, of same

Estate of Frederick GUTEKUNST, Town of Northampton, lot—report of inquest by Sheriff Jonas HARTZELL:
widow
6 children: John, eldest son—accepted the land
others not named
sureties: Peter HAUCK, cordwainer, and Michael KUNTZ, joiner, both of Town of Northampton
12 men:by oath and affirmation—John MURPHEY, John KEIPER, Felix GREESOMER (GRIESEMER), Andrew GANGWERE (GANGWER), George FRIDRICK (FREDERICKS), Adam HALLER, John MILLER, Richard STEINE, Abraham RINKER, John MOORE (MOHRE), Peter KEIPER, Jacob MICKLY (MÜCHLY)

Guardian for Carolina Sophia REICHELT, age 9 years, minor granddaughter of John Gottl. REICHELT of Herrnhut, Upper Lusatia, Germany (had will):
Carolina Sophia was the only child of Charles Gottlieb REICHELT and his wife Mary Sophia. She was left a legacy by her grandfather. Her father Charles died when living in the Danish West India Islands. After his death, her mother Mary Sophia took Carolina and moved to Bethlehem, PA. There, her mother remarried, to a minister of the Church of the United Brethren named Abraham REINECKE. Abraham was now a minister serving in Lancaster, PA. The couple left Carolina in the School at Bethlehem.
guardian: Hans Christian VON SCHWEINIZ, Bethlehem, gentleman

**Court on 16 August 1793**
**Justices, the Esquires, now present: Jacob RUSH and Peter RHOADS**

Estate of Thomas McCRACKEN, Lower Mt. Bethel Township, 159 acres—report of inquest by Sheriff Jonas HARTZELL, Esq.:
widow
4 children: Hugh, eldest surviving son—accepted the land
Robert, eldest son, deceased (also, Robert's eldest son was Thomas)
others not named
sureties: Joseph MARTIN, Esq., and John SMITH, yeoman, both of Lower Mt. Bethel Twp.
12 men:by oath and affirmation—David AYERS, Peter BUTZ, John NELSON (NEILSON), Michael NEY, Ephrim (Ephraim) McCOLLUM, Isaac COLP (KULP), Elias DIETRICH, John SMITH, Valentine MILLER (MÜLLER), Henry WEAVER, Joseph FOX, William McWICKER (McVICKER)

**Court on 25 September 1793**
**Justices, the Esquires: Peter RHOADS and John MULHALLON**

Estate of Conrad NEIN—auditors' report followed by request to distribute balance:
administrators: Elizabeth NEIN and John NEIN, eldest son
eldest son: John—accepted the land

**Court on 25 September 1793, continued:**

Guardian for 5 minor children of Henry BEST, Lehigh Township (all under age 14) (were other children):

| | |
|---|---|
| petitioner: | Frederick KUNTZ, brother-in-law of deceased |
| 5 children: | Hannah |
| | Catharine |
| | Jacob |
| | Susannah |
| | Mary |
| guardians: | for all 5 children—John SAGER and George KUNTZ, Lehigh Township |

**Court on 15 October 1793**
**Justices, the Esquires: John MULHALLON and David WAGENER**

Estate of James DURHAM, Upper Mt. Bethel Township—request inquest:

| | |
|---|---|
| land: | 160 acres of warranted land bounded by John RODROCK, William LABAR, William SHURLOCK, Robert FORSMAN |
| widow: | Eve |
| 10 children: | Luke, eldest son |
| | James |
| | John, the petitioner |
| | Elizabeth, wife of Jeremia JOHNSON |
| | Edward |
| | Isaac |
| | Sarah |
| | Joseph |
| | Catherine |
| | Jeremia |

**Court on 30 October 1793**
**Justices, the Esquires: John MULHALLON and David WAGENER**

Estate of Conrad CRUMBACH, Town of Northampton (had will)—request audit:

| | |
|---|---|
| petitioner: | Lewis WALKER, husband of Eve, one grandchild and legatee of Conrad CRUMBACH |
| executors: | George Henry CRUMBACH and George GRAFF |
| auditors: | Jacob EYERLY, Jr., James GILL, Jonas HARTZELL, Esquires |

**Court on 11 November 1793**
**Justices, the Esquires: Jacob RUSH, Peter RHOADS, William HENRY, David WAGENER**

Guardian for 3 minor children of Samuel KAUFFMAN, Lower Saucon Township (were other children):

| | |
|---|---|
| petitioner: | Jacob KAUFFMAN, son of deceased |
| widow | |
| 3 children: | Catharine, over age 14 |
| | Abraham, under age 14 |
| | Jonathan, under age 14 |
| guardian: | for all 3 children—John BEYL, of same |

New guardian for Jacob RUTH, now over age 14, one son of Christian RUTH, Macungie Township:

| | |
|---|---|
| guardian: | former—Valentine SHÄFFER, appointed in 1782 |
| | new—Michael SCHMEYER, Macungie Township |

**Court on 14 November 1793**
**Justices, the Esquires: William HENRY and David WAGENER**

Estate of Theobald KUNTZ, Penn Township, 180 to 200 acres—auditors' report; permission to sell:
administrator: Michael HAPPES

Estate of Theobald FAHRINGER, Lehigh Township—return of sale:

| | |
|---|---|
| land: | part of real estate bounded by Moses BEER, John BEER, and Joseph PETTY |
| administrator: | Herman RUPP |
| sold to: | Jacob KESTER |

Estate of John YOUNG, Bethlehem Township—request inquest:

| | |
|---|---|
| land: | 83 acres, 36 perches in Plainfield Township that was surveyed to Christian SHICK, sold to Myer HART, who then granted it to YOUNG, bounded by land now or late of William RITCHE, Andreas KLEIN, Peter SEIB, and vacant land |
| widow: | now deceased |
| 5 children: | Abraham, eldest son |
| | Barbara, wife of John ESHELMAN |
| | Elizabeth, wife of George KIEFFER |
| | Mary, wife of Jacob HOFFMAN |
| | Magdalena, wife of Henry LANDES |

Estate of Henry MILLER, Macungie Township—return of sale:

| | |
|---|---|
| land: | 2 acres in Millerstown, Macungie Township, bounded by Christian FISHER and Michael SCHÄFFER |
| administrators: | Frederick MARTIN and Catharine RAWN (late MILLER) |
| sold to: | George SEIDER on November 1788 (court accepted the sale) |

Estate of George KNAUSS—auditors' report; need for new auditors to be appointed:

| | |
|---|---|
| administrators: | George Frederick KNAUSS and Philip KNAUSS |
| auditors: | one of former auditors, Peter KOHLER, Esq., is now deceased |
| | new—James GILL, Esq., to serve with the others, Peter EALER and George GRAFF |

**Court on 15 November 1793**
**Justices, the Esquires: Peter RHOADS and David WAGENER**

Guardians for 4 minor children of Frederick STUBEN, Salisbury Township (were other children):

| | |
|---|---|
| widow: | Catharine, the petitioner |
| 4 children: | Frederick, over age 14............................guardian: Adam BITSCH, Lower Saucon T. |
| | John, over age 14 |
| | John George, under age 14 |
| | Christina, under age 14 |
| guardian: | for younger 3 children—Philip BAHL, Esq. |

Estate of George Adam FRANK, Allen Township—auditors' report (report listed over 30 men):

| | |
|---|---|
| administrator: | George KOCH |
| widow: | Ann Mary |
| auditors: | Robert TRAILL, Peter SHNYDER, Henry SHERING |

**Court on 14 January 1794**
**Justices, the Esquires: Jacob RUSH, Peter RHOADS, William HENRY**

Guardian for Susannah, over 14, one daughter of Simon GAUER, Lehigh Township (were other children):
guardian: John RIELBERND, Chestnuthill Township

Estate of John YOUNG, Plainfield Township—report of inquest by Sheriff John CRAIG, Esq.:
5 children: Abraham, eldest son—accepted the land
others not named
sureties: Abraham BERLIN, Easton, blacksmith, and Adam HAUK, Plainfield Township
12 men:by oath—William CRAIG, Esq., Frederick BARTHOLD, John SHOOK, Adam YOHE, Jacob TITUS, George SHÄFFER, George SOPER (SOBER), Adam HAWK (HAUK), Jonas ANDREW (ANDRE)
by affirmation—Jacob PAINTER (BENDER), David MILLER, Henry MILLER

**Court on 16 January 1794**
**Justices, the Esquires: Jacob RUSH, Peter RHOADS, John MULHALLON, William HENRY, David WAGENER**

Estate of Simon GAUER, Lehigh Township—request audit:
petitioners: John RIELBERND husband of Catherine, one daughter of deceased, and a guardian to Susanna, one minor child of deceased
administrator: John DIETER
auditors: John SHAW, Esq. and John HUSTON of Hamilton Township, and Jacob HELLER, Plainfield Township, Esquire

Estate of William WILLS, Lower Smithfield Township—request sale; auditors appointed:
land: 300 acres on both sides of Marshall's Creek bounded by other land of William WILLS, now sold by Sheriff to [blank] and land of Christian EILENBERGER and others
administrator: Daniel SHOEMAKER
auditors: Nicholas DEPUE, Esq., Philip SHRAWDER, gentleman, and Isaac HUMPHREYS, gentleman, all of Lower Smithfield Township

Estate of John STERNER, Allen Township—request inquest:
land: part of Dry Land Tract, 150 acres bounded by land now or late of Thomas KIDD, George KORTZ, Peter DESHLER, Nicholas REMEL
widow: Margaret
6 children: John, eldest son
Elizabeth, wife of Benjamin ROBERTSON
Jacob
Abraham
Margaret
Joseph

Guardian for Abraham, over age 14, who "hath laboured in this County for near five years," minor son of William WALTON, died about 11 years ago, Bucks County (were other children):
guardian: Bernhard ARNDT, Nazareth Township

**Court on 17 January 1794**
**Justices, the Esquires: Peter RHOADS, William HENRY, David WAGNER**

Estate of James DURHAM, Upper Mt. Bethel Township—report on inquest by Sheriff John CRAIG, Esq.:
widow
10 children: Luke, eldest son—again, did not appear
John, 2nd son—accepted the land
others not named
sureties: Anthony KRATZER, Lower Saucon Township, John RIEGEL, Lower Mt. Bethel Township
12 men: by oath—Hugh FORSMAN, Esq., John HUTCHINSON, Adam SHOOK (SCHUG), Thomas MOOR (MOORE), William LANDERS, Alexander FORSMAN, Joseph FORSMAN, John FREES, Thomas SILLYMAN, Jr., Adam UTT
by affirmation—John ROADROCK (Johannes ROTHROCK), Jacob GEISSINGER

**Court on 31 March 1794**
**Justices, the Esquires: John MULHALLON and David WAGNER**

Guardian for Mary, under age 14, only child of Leonard ANDRE, Jr., Plainfield Township:
widow: Margaret, petitioner
guardian: John Adam ANDRE, Plainfield Township

**Court on 15 April 1794**
**Justices, the Esquires: Peter RHOADS and William HENRY**

New guardian for Mary, now over age 14, one minor daughter of Philip Jacob OVERBECK, Springfield Township, Bucks County (Mary "hath for several years past lived with some of her relatives in this County"):
guardian: former—Philip HERPEL, Bucks County, appointed by the Orphan's Court in Bucks County
new—George SCHÄFFER, Macungie Township

Guardians for 3 minor children of George KERN, Upper Milford Township (were other children):
3 children: George, over age 14................................guardian: George SEIDER, Up. Milford T.
Elizabeth, over age 14............................guardian: George SEIDER
John, under age 14.................................guardian: Ludwig STÄHLER, of same

Estate of Simon GAUER—auditors' report:
administrator: John DIETER—was found to be indebted to the heirs
auditors: John SHAW, John HUSTON, Jacob HELLER

Estate of William WILLS, Esq., Lower Smithfield Township, 300 acres—auditors' report gives list of over 25 men; permission to sell:
administrator: Daniel SHOEMAKER

**Court on 16 April 1794**
**Justices, the Esquires: Jacob RUSH, Peter RHOADS, William HENRY**

New guardian for John and Christian, both now over age 14, minor sons of Joseph STOUT, Plainfield Township:
guardian: former—Christian STOUT, appoint in 1778, about to remove from the neighborhood
new—Dietrich BAUER, Plainfield Township

**Court on 16 April 1794, continued:**

Estate of Henry FAUST, Allen Township—request inquest:

land: 193 acres patented land on River Lehigh bounded by the river and Christian FENSTERMACHER, Peter BEYSEL, the late Wendel HAUER
widow: Catharine
7 children: Philip, eldest son
John George
Michael
Abraham
John
Catharine
Elizabeth

Estate of Peter CONRAD, Esq., Hamilton Township—request audit:
administrators: Feronica CONRAD and Peter CONRAD
auditors: John HUSTON, Hamilton Township, John YOUNGBERG, Joseph LEVERING, Esq., Nazareth Township

Estate of Mordecai MORGAN—request audit:
administrators: Sarah MORGAN and Jacob STROWD
auditors: Nicholas DEPUE, Esq., Daniel SHOEMAKER, Philip SHRAWDER, Lower Smithfield Township

**Court on 17 April 1794**
**Justices, the Esquires: Peter RHOADS and William HENRY**

Guardian for 3 minor grandchildren of John LODENMACHER, Lower Saucon Township (had will):
petitioner: Michael ROTH, Springfield Township, Bucks County, husband of Mary (now also deceased), a daughter of the deceased
3 grandchildren, children of Mary, deceased, and Michael ROTH:
Catherine ROTH, over age 14
Michael ROTH, over age 14
John ROTH, under age 14
guardian: for all 3 children—Henry FUNK, Springfield Township, Bucks County

Estate of John STERNER, Allen Township, 150 acres—report of inquest by Sheriff John CRAIG, Esq.:
widow
6 children: John, eldest son—accepted the land
others not named
sureties: William SMITH and George EHRET, Allen Township
12 men:by oath—Peter DESHLER, Benjamin KIDD, James CARR (KERR), Michael BEAVER (Migael BIEBER), Charles HAASLY (Karl HESLE), George (Jorg) EHRET, William SMITH, Joseph LARASH (Joseb LAROSCH), Nicholas REMEL (RIMMEL), Valentine WALTMAN, Henry (Henrich) FATZINGER
by affirmation—Peter BEYSEL (BEISEL)

**Court on 17 April 1794**
**Justices, the Esquires, now present: John MULHALLON and David WAGENER**

Jean ROSBRUGH, widow of Rev. John ROSBRUGH—request for further support:

**petitioner repeated the history of her husband's service in the militia and his death

**the court granted her ½ pay plus rations for one year, from 18 May 1793 to 18 May 1794

**Court on 15 May 1794**
**Justices, the Esquires: John MULHALLON and David WAGENER**

Guardians for 4 minor children of John SIEGFRIED (all under age 14) (were other children):

| | |
|---|---|
| widow: | Mary |
| 4 children: | Catherine |
| | Elizabeth |
| | Jacob |
| | Isaac |
| guardians: | for all 4 children—Philip Jacob SCHREIBER, Whitehall Township, and Abraham LEVAN, Allen Township |

Estate of John SMITH, died bout 4 years ago, Upper Milford Township—request citation against the administrators to compel them to exhibit an administration account:

| | |
|---|---|
| petitioner: | Michael SMITH, brother of the deceased |
| widow: | Elizabeth, administratrix, now wife of Peter LYNN |

**Court on 5 July 1794**
**Justices, the Esquires: John MULHALLON and David WAGENER**

Estate of John STEWART, formerly of Upper Smithfield Township, but lately of Tioga County, New York—request sale; auditors appointed:

| | |
|---|---|
| land: | 90 acres warranted land in Upper Smithfield Township, bounded by Thomas QUICK, Frederick VANDERMERK, and others, about ½ mile from the Delaware River |
| administratrix: | Ann ANSON |
| auditors: | Samuel SEELY, Esq., John BILLIS, Esq., and Simeon WESTFALL |

**Court on 15 August 1794**
**Justices, the Esquires: Peter RHOADS and David WAGNER**

Estate of Henry FAUST—an inquest by Sheriff John CRAIG, Esq. could not be made because the 12-man jury could not agree on the valuation and partition of the property; a new writ for inquest was issued.

Estate of Peter KACHLEIN, Esquire, Easton (had will)—request audit:

| | |
|---|---|
| petitioners: | Jacob KACHLEIN, one son of deceased, and Peter IHRIE, husband of Elizabeth, one daughter of deceased |
| executors: | Peter SHNYDER, John YOUNG, and Christopher HERTZEL |
| auditors: | Joseph HORSFIELD, Esquire of Bethlehem, Joseph LEVERING, Esquire of Nazareth, and Joseph JONES, Bethlehem Township |

Estate of George KNAUSS—auditors' report; auditors found a large balance in the estate:

| | |
|---|---|
| auditors: | Peter EALER, George GRAFF, James GILL |

**Court on 15 August 1794, continued:**

Estate of Nicholas HERMANY, Maxatany Township, Berks County—request inquest:

land: 900 acres at Blooming Grove, Northampton County, adjoining land now or late vacant, and Samuel SEELY which Sheriff Peter EALER, Esq., late sheriff, by deed on 19 September 1787 granted and sold to Nicholas HERMANY as the late estate of Jonas SEELY, Esq., deceased

no widow

13 children: Andrew, eldest son
Abraham
Daniel
Jacob
Isaac
Nicholas
Peter
Philip
Benjamin
Susannah, wife of Charles KRAUSS
Mary
Sarah
Esther, wife of Frederick GROSS

Estate of Mordecai MORGAN—auditors' report:
administrators: Sarah MORGAN and Jacob STROWD
child

**Court on 8 September 1794**
**Justices, the Esquires: John MULHALLON and David WAGONER**

Estate of Melchior HAY, died last August, William Township—request inquest:
land: 375 acres patented land bounded by Christian BEST, Michel KRESS, Conrad HESS, Peter LADIG, on Lehigh River
widow: Margaret
8 children: Peter, eldest son
Susanna, wife of Abraham HORN
Jacob
John
Melchior
Catharine
Charles
Henry

**Court on 8 September 1794, continued:**

Estate of Jacob SCHIEFFER, died last August, Upper Milford Township—request audit:

land: 77 acres warranted land bounded by Jacob TRAUB, Peter HERTZELL, Jacob GEHRY, Leonard FRIESSEMER, Casper HELPER
no widow
10 children: George*, eldest son — now or late a resident of Germany in Europe [*note: in January 1795, his brother Jacob corrected the court records, stating that the eldest son's name was Matthias, not George]
Jacob, 2nd son
Eve, wife of Henry HERTZEL
Jeremiah
Adam
Andreas
George
Henry
Catherine, wife of Jacob METZGER
John

**Court on 11 November 1794**
**Justices, the Esquires: Jacob RUSH, William HENRY, David WAGONER**

New guardians for 2 minor daughters of Peter WEISS, Weisenberg Township (both now over age 14):
2 daughters: Christina
Susanna
guardians: former—Andrew MILLER and George CUSTARD, appointed in 1789
new—for Christina: Christian SEYGERLING, Weisenberg Township
for Susanna: George CUSTARD, Lynn Township

**Court on 12 November 1794**
**Justices, the Esquires: Peter RHOADS and John MULHALLON**

Estate of Henry FAUST, Allen Township, 193 acres—report of inquest by Sheriff John CRAIG, Esq.:
widow
7 children: Philip, eldest son—accepted the land
others not named
sureties: Peter BEYSEL, Allen Township, George YUNT, Whitehall Township
12 men: by oath—Jacob SHRIVER (SHREIBER), John LERCH, Godfrey KNOUSS (Gottfried KNAUSS), Abraham MENSCH (MENCH), Conrad MARKS (MARCK), John BALLIET, Peter MEYER, John RHOADS (Johannes ROTH), Valentine WALTMAN, Daniel TRAXELL (DRAXEL), Conrad HAAS
by affirmation—Nicholas (Hannickel) HOWER

Guardians for 2 minor children of John SCHIEFFERSTEIN, Weisenberg Township:
petitioner: Baltzer FRITZ, step-father of children
2 children: Margaret, over age 14............................guardian: Nicholas LITZENBERGER, Macungie Twp.
Andrew, under age 14............................guardian: Henry KOCH, Macungie Twp.

**Court on 12 November 1794, continued:**

Guardians for 3 minor children of Melchior HAY, Williams Township (were other children):

widow: Margaret
3 children: Catherine, over age 14............................guardian: Daniel WAGONER, Easton, miller
Charles, under age 14............................guardian: Peter SHNYDER, of same, tanner
Henry, under age 14..............................guardian: Peter SHNYDER, of same

Estate of Melchior HAY, Williams Township, 75 acres, patented—report of inquest by Sheriff John CRAIG:
widow
8 children: Peter, eldest son—accepted the land (others not named)
sureties: William RAUB, Easton, gentleman, John SIMON, Easton, hatter
12 men:by oath—John RICHARDS, Philip WOODRINGER (Fillib WOTTRING), Jacob BROTZMAN, John REEL (Johannes RIEL), Joseph RICHARD, John YEAGRE (JEGER), John (Johannes) ODEWÄLDER, Conrad EDELMAN, Christian BIXLER, Christopher BITTENBINDER
by affirmation—Jacob WEYGANDT, Peter NUNGESSER

Guardian for Mary, under age 14, minor child & only child of Leonard OSTERSTOCK, Easton, cordwainer:
petitioner: Jacob GUTH, step-father of child
guardian: Robert TRAILL, Easton

Guardian for 3 minor children of Moritz BISHOFF, Easton (all under age 14):
petitioner: Henry SHNYDER, Easton, saddler, brother-in-law of deceased
3 children: John
Elizabeth
Peter
guardian: for all 3 children—John HERSTER, Easton, Esquire

Estate of Jacob SCHIEFFER—request by Sheriff John CRAIG, Esq. for new writ of inquest, because "want of health prevented me in person to execute the within writ."

**Court on 13 November 1794**
**Justices, the Esquires: Jacob RUSH, Peter RHOADS, John MULHALLON**

Estate of Nicholas HERMANY, Upper Saucon Township, 900 acres—report of inquest by Sheriff John CRAIG, Esq. (the sheriff charged fees for "traveling about 80 miles extraordinary"):
13 children: Andrew, eldest son—accepted the land
others not named
sureties: John CRAIG and Nicholas KERN, Jr., Esquires
12 men:all by oath—Samuel SEELY, Esquire, Cornelius COLE, John BRINK, Samuel WATTERS (WATERS), Henry BRINK, Wilhelmus VANGORDON, Jonathan BRINK, Elias VANAUKEN, Tobias HAANBECK, Cornelius DEWITT, Charles McNAIR, Jonathan VANGORDON

**Court on 14 November 1794**
**Justices, the Esquires: Peter RHOADS and David WAGENER**

Guardian for William MAJORS, over age 14, who had resided in the county since his father died, one minor child of William MAJORS, State of New Jersey (were other children):
guardian: Edward MAJOR, of [blank] Mt. Bethel Township

**Court on 14 November 1794, continued:**

Estate of Casper RUMMAGE—request audit:

petitioner: Jacob STROWD—had considerable claims of the estate
widow: Mary, now wife of Jacob SCHÄFFER, also deceased, intestate, (his administrator was Lewis RUMMAGE)
auditors: Nicholas DEPUE, John SHAW, Esq., Philip SHRAWDER, gentleman

**Court on 19 November 1794**
**Justices, the Esquires: John MULHALLON and David WAGENER**

Estate of Melchior HAY, Williams Township—request that new surety be accepted:
eldest son: Peter—had accepted the land
sureties: former—William RAUB, who declined to enter bonds, and John SIMON, Easton
new—to replace RAUB, John BEST, Williams Township

**Court on 5 January 1795**
**Justices, the Esquires: William HENRY and David WAGNER**

Estate of Conrad ROESLY, died last May, Lower Saucon Township, 3 tracts, total 237 3/4 acres—request inquest:
land: 1) 136 1/4 acres adjoining by Peter RAUTEPUSH, the late John MELCHIOR, and vacant land
2) 52 acres adjoining the first
3) 49 acres adjoining by Anthony LERCH, church land, the late Joseph FRY, Melchior EDINGER
widow: Magdalena
7 children: John, eldest son
Henry
Jacob
Conrad
Joseph
Catherine, wife of Philip WAGENER
Elizabeth, wife of Rev. John MANN

**Court on 13 January 1795**
**Justices, the Esquires: Peter RHOADS, William HENRY, John MULHALLON, David WAGNER**

Estate of Peter CONRAD, Esq., Hamilton Township—auditors report and distribution:
widow: Veronica
3 daughters: Susannah
Elizabeth
Lewisa
10 other children

Estate of John Philip FUCHS, Bethlehem Township—request inquest:
land: 150 acres, patented, bounded by the late Casper WISTAR, James HAMILTON, John Nicholas FUCHS, granted by deed on 1 September 1762 by Conrad FUCHS to the deceased

**Court on 14 January 1795**
**Justices, the Esquires: not named**

Estate of Conrad ROESLY—request for new writ of inquest by Sheriff John CRAIG for he "had not time to execute the same"

Estate of Jacob SCHEIFFER, Upper Milford Township, 77 acres—report of inquest by Sheriff John CRAIG:

10 children: eldest son, absent and residing in Germany
Jacob, 2nd son—accepted the land
others not named

sureties: Henry HERTZEL and John GEBEL, Salisbury Township

12 men:all by oath—Lewis STEHLER (Ludwig STAHLER), Christopher (Stofel) MOHR, Nicholas KLOTZ, Daniel SWARTZ, John FISHER, Berned FEGLI (Bernth FÖGLE), Simon SNYDER (SCHNEYDER), Nicholas HITTLE, Wendel WEANT (WIAND), William MOHR, Peter STEHLER (STÄHLER), George SYDER (SEYDER)

New guardian for 2 minor children of Melchior HAY:

2 children: Charles
Henry

guardian: former—Peter SHNYDER, Easton—appointed last November
new—for Charles: Peter SHNYDER (the same as former)
for Henry: Robert TRAILL, Esq., Easton

**Court on 15 January 1795**
**Justices, the Esquires: not named**

Estate of Henry FAUST, Allen Township—request audit:

administrators: Catherine FAUST and Philip FAUST

auditors: John HORN, George RHOADS, George SHRYVER, Town of Northampton

Estate of Michael GABEL, died last December, Heidelberg Township—request inquest:

land: 70 or 80 acres warranted land bounded by Peter HANDWERCK, Christian KRUM, John KRUM, Frantz MISEMER, which was part of land that Peter KERGER had conveyed to the deceased

widow: Margaret Elizabeth

8 children: Michael, eldest son
Dorothea, wife of Frederick NEFF
Catharine, wife of George Henry HEIMBACH
Christina, wife of Rudolph LAUCHNER
Margaret, wife of Henry SEYBERT
Barbara, wife of Jacob BENNINGER
Mary, wife of John HAUSKNECHT
Elizabeth

Estate of Jacob SCHIEFFER, Upper Milford Township—the petitioner, Jacob SCHIEFFER, 2nd son, in his last petition where he accepted the land, had mistakenly called his elder brother George. However, the elder brother's name was Mathias.

**Court on 15 January 1795, continued:**

Estate of Mordecai MORGAN, Lower Smithfield Township, 2 tracts—request sale:

land: total of 450 acres located 3 miles above STROWD's Mill on JONES's Creek, bounded by Jacob STROWD, John FULTON, late of John DRAKE, late of Robert LEVERS, Esquire, which were held by the deceased by warrant:
1) granted in name of the deceased on 20 January 1785
2) granted in name of John DRAKE on 14 August 1750
administrators: Sarah HOLLINGSHEAD (late MORGAN), and Jacob STROWD

Estate of William WILLS, Esq., Lower Smithfield Township, 300 acres—return of sale:
administrator: Daniel SHOEMAKER
sold to: Samuel SITGREAVES and Jacob STROWD

Estate of George ENGEL, Plainfield Township—return of sale (reserving for use of widow, 32 acres, 8 per.):
land: 243 acres bounded by Henry ENGEL, William FREEMAN, Jacob SHNYDER, William JANSON with a water gristmill, late part of the real estate of the deceased
administrators: Christopher ENGEL and Abraham SORVER—they did not succeed in selling the property until last September
sold to: James WILLIAMSON, Mt. Bethel Township

**Court on 2 February 1795**
**Justices, the Esquires: William HENRY and David WAGENER**

Estate of Peter SHILP, Allen Township (had will)—report that the administration account was exhibited in the presence of the 3 children of the deceased:
administrator: John ARNDT
widow: Christina, administratrix, now wife of Casper RITTER
3 children: Peter
Conrad
Elizabeth

Estate of Noah LEE, Lower Smithfield Township—request inquest:
land: 200 acres, patented land, on Brodhead Creek, bounded by Jacob STROWD, John BOYS, late of Robert LEVERS, William LONG
widow: Rhoda
4 children: Ebenezer, eldest son
Mercy
John
Joseph
3 grandchildren, children of Jesse, who died before his father:
Hannah
Mary
Jesse

**Court on 2 March 1795**
**Justices, the Esquires: John MULHALLON and David WAGENER**

Guardian for Susanna, over age 14, one child of Jacob MUSSELMAN, Allen Township (were other children):
guardian: Jacob HIESTAND, Allen Township

**Court on 2 March 1795, continued:**

Guardians for 3 minor children of Paul MILLER, Moore Township (all under age 14):

petitioner: John BERTHOLD, friend
3 children: John
Dorothea
Paul
guardians: for all 3 children—John MILLER and Henry STRAUSS

Estate of Samuel RALSTON, died 10 January 1795, Allen Township, 100 acres—request sale:
administrator: James RALSTON
widow: Lettice
child: "left one son to survive him"

**Court on 25 March 1795**
**Justices, the Esquires: Peter RHOADS and William HENRY**

Guardian for Veronica, over age 14, one child of Jacob MUSSELMAN, Allen Township (were other children):
guardian: Jacob HIESTAND, Allen Township

Estate of Baltzer STEEL, Mt. Bethel Township—request inquest:
land: 40 ½ acres, warranted land in Plainfield Township, bounded all around by John HUTCHESON
attorney: John HUTCHESON, Mt. Bethel Township
widow: now deceased
6 children: John, eldest son
Eve, wife of John ABEL
Peter
Andrew
Adam
Baltzer

**Court on 14 April 1795**
**Justices, the Esquires: Peter RHOADS and associates**

Guardians of 5 minor children of Casper STERNER, Whitehall Township (all under age 14) (were other children):
5 children: Adam, over age 14.................................guardian: George RHOADS, Town of Northampton
remaining 4 children all under age 14:
John......................................................guardian: Conrad MARCH, Whitehall Tp.
Catharine...............................................guardian: Conrad MARCH, Whitehall Tp.
Daniel...................................................guardian: Abraham STERNER, Whitehall Tp.
Peter.....................................................guardian: Abraham STERNER, Whitehall Tp.

Estate of Henry FAUST, Allen Township—auditors' report stated that there was a balance due the estate; request distribution:
administrators: Catharine FAUST and Philip FAUST
widow
son: Philip—accepted the land

**Court on 14 April 1795, continued:**

Guardians for 3 minor children of Jacob HERMAN, Macungie Township (all under age 14):

petitioner: Frederick HERMAN, brother of deceased
3 children: Jacob
Sarah
John
guardians: for all 3 children—George Frederick KNAUSS and Peter EALER, Esquire, Whitehall Township

Guardians for 4 minor children of Adam DESHLER, Whitehall Township:
petitioner: George SCHREIVER, brother-in-law of deceased
4 children: Susanna, over age 14............................guardian: John BÄRE, Whitehall Twp.
Catharine, under age 14
Sarah, under age 14
Elizabeth, under age 14
guardians: for younger 3 children—Jacob SHRIVER and John BALLIET

Estate of Conrad ROESLY, Lower Saucon Township, 3 tracts totaling 237 acres—report of inquest by Sheriff John CRAIG, Esq.:
widow
7 children: John, eldest son—accepted the land
others not named
sureties: Anthony LERCH, Esq., and William BECKER, blacksmith, Lower Saucon Township
12 men: by oath—Anthony LERCH, Esq., John REEL (Johannes RIEL), Jacob CHRISTMAN, Philip LUTZ, William McHOSE, Nicholas KLINE (KLEIN), Christian RUCH, John MOYER, Jr. (Johannes MEYER), Abraham TRANSUE (DRANSU), Henry OHL, Jacob FEHR (FAIR)
by affirmation—Henry SOCKREIDER (SACKREITER)

New guardian for Christian, now over age 14, one child of George DUTT, Macungie Township (were other children):
guardian: former—appointed in 1790, Martin RITTER and Philip WALTER
new—Peter KÖHLER, Macungie Township

Estate of Michael GABEL—concerning the writ of inquest to be taken by Sheriff John CRAIG, Esq.; on motion of Samuel SITGREAVES, Esq., that the writ be quashed & declared void; eldest son Michael to pay all costs

Estate of Mordecai MORGAN—motion of Thomas ROSS, Esq. that cause be shown why sale of the real estate should not be set aside:
administrators: Sarah HOLLINGSHEAD and Jacob STROWD

**Court on 16 April 1795**
**Justices, the Esquires: not named**

Estate of Theobald KUNTZ, Penn Township, 180 or 200 acres—return of sale:
administrator: Michael HABBER
sold to: Christian SCHNEIDER

**Court on 16 April 1795, continued:**

Estate of Noah LEE, Lower Smithfield Township, 200 acres—report of inquest by Sheriff John CRAIG:

widow
4 children: Ebenezer, eldest living son—declined the land
John, next son in seniority—accepted the land
Jesse, eldest son, deceased, died before his father (leaving 3 children: Jesse, Hanna, and Mary)
other 2 living children not named
sureties: Jacob STROWD, Esq., and John FISH, both of Lower Smithfield Township
12 men:all by oath—John STARBIRD, Gerret BRODHEAD, Jacob STROWD, John BROWN (Johannes BRAUN), James DINGMAN, Joseph MANTAYNE, Richard (Derck) VAN TILBURY, John HUSTON, John RANSBURY, Francis GUILTNER (Frantz GÜLLNER), Daniel KOONS, Laurence KUNKLE

Estate of Henry MÄSER, died about 10 years ago, Weisenberg Township—request inquest:
land: 100 acres, warranted land, bounded by and adjoining John Adam BÄR, Christian BRAUCHER, Lowrence HOLBIG, Jacob BÄR, Christian KROMILIG
attorney: John Adam BÄR
widow: Elizabeth Barbara, now wife of George KOSER
3 children: Conrad, eldest son
Henry
Magdalena

Estate of Christian RUTH, died "considerable time ago," Macungie Township—request inquest:
land: 150 acres bounded by Michael SCHMEIER, Conrad MEITZLER, Ludwig MECKEL, Philip RUTH, Henry MEITZLER
widow: Ann Mary, now wife of Michael MECKEL
5 children: Christian, eldest son
Elizabeth, wife of Christian DUTT
Catherine, wife of George LÖSSIG
Philip
Jacob

Estate of Philip FUCHS—the writ for inquest by Sheriff John CRAIG, Esq. which was set aside on the motion of Samuel SITGREAVES, Esq., was reissued and was to be returned next August, the cost of which was to be paid out of the estate

Estate of Baltzer STEEL, Plainfield Township, 40 acres—report of inquest by Sheriff John CRAIG, Esq.:
6 children: John, eldest son, by his attorney, John HUTCHESON, accepted the land
others not named
sureties: John HUTCHESON, James HUTCHSEON, Lower Mt. Bethel Township, and Thomas SILLYMAN, Forks Township, Esquire
12 men:all by oath—Thomas SILLYMAN, Samuel REA, Adam WAGENER, Jacob YOUNG, Adam SANDT, Thomas SILLYMAN, Jr., Michael GLOSS (CLOSS), Nathaniel BRITTON (BRITTAIN), James MILLER, John SANDT (SEND), David BEIDELMAN, Michael SANDT

Estate of Samuel RALSTON, Allen Township, 100 acre—return of sale:
administrators: Lettice RALSTON and James RALSTON
sold to: Nicholas ESH

**Court on 16 April 1795, continued:**

Estate of Peter KNEPPLEY, Upper Saucon Township, 3 contiguous tracts plus 1 other—request inquest:

land: 1) 85 ½ acres bounded by Baltzer BEYL, Michael SEYDER, Henry BACHMAN, Jacob MORRY, John NEWCOMER; granted to Peter by patent 27 February 1767
2) adjoining 1st and 3rd tracts, 36 acres 8 perches, bounded by Henry BRUNNER, Peter SWABS, Jacob MORRY, Peter KNEPPLEY; granted to Peter by Jacob MORRY by deed 8 March 1760
3) adjoining 1st and 2nd tracts, 6 acres 56 perches, bounded by Peter KNEPPLEY and the Great Road to Philadelphia; granted to Peter by patent 26 February 1767
4) in Salisbury Township, 18 acres, 33 perches, bounded by John TOOL, William MORRY, late of Baltzer BEYL, and vacant land

widow: Christina

7 children: Mathias, eldest son
Melchior
Peter
John
Jacob
Esther
Mary

**Court on 17 April 1795**
**Justices, the Esquires: not named**

Guardian for Charles, over age 14, who is with some of his friends in this county, minor son and only child of Charles COOPER, some time a citizen of Philadelphia but late of Charles Town, South Carolina:

petitioner: Daniel COOPER, brother of deceased
guardian: Daniel COOPER, his uncle, the petitioner

Estate of George KERN, died "considerable time ago," Upper Milford Township—request inquest:

land: 50 acres, patented land, bounded by Mathias KERN, Christopher MOHR, Nicholas HITTEL, Adam LECHNER

no widow

5 children: Frederick, eldest son
Elizabeth
John George
Abraham
John

**Court on 28 April 1795**
**Justices, the Esquires: John MULHALLON and David WAGENER**

Jean ROSEBRUGH, widow of Rev. John ROSEBRUGH—request for further support (repeats the background of her situation):

petitioner: James RALSTON, her nephew
court granted another year of ½ pay plus rations

**Court on 28 April 1795, continued:**

Estate of Samuel MUSICK, died about 15 years ago, Whitehall Township—request inquest:

| | |
|---|---|
| land: | 150 acres, warranted land, bounded by Lowrence GOOD, the late Casper WISTAR, Leonard STEININGER |
| widow: | Dorothea, now wife of Andrew KNOEDLER |
| 8 children: | Samuel, eldest son—found to be insane and was appointed commissioners |
| | Margaret, wife of George GRAMLICH |
| | David |
| | Elizabeth, wife of John FLEXER |
| | Anthony |
| | Barbara |
| | Catharine |
| | Salome |

**Court on 29 April 1795**
**Justices, the Esquires: not named**

Estate of John OLWINE, Chester County—heirs requested that the 7 men they named view & divide the estate:

| | |
|---|---|
| land: | in both Chester County and Northampton County (50 acres) |
| widow: | Elizabeth |
| 8 children: | Abraham, eldest son |
| | Mary, wife of Casper RODES |
| | Elizabeth, wife of Peter HARTMAN |
| | Catherine, widow of Mr. RODES, deceased |
| | Jacob |
| | Margaret, by her guardian John RALSTON |
| | Sarah, by her guardian John RALSTON |
| | John, by his guardian George DEERY |
| 7 men: | John SHIMER, Esq., Philip WALTER, John ORT, Jacob KEALER, Jacob STAHLNECKER, Anthony STEHLER, Henry LAROSS |

**Court on 25 June 1795**
**Justices, the Esquires: Peter RHOADS and John MULHALLON**

Estate of Melchior HAY, Williams Township—request for new inquest; the petitioners felt the valuation made was too low and they presented several objection:

| | |
|---|---|
| petitioners: | David SAYLOR and his wife Catharine, daughter of deceased |
| | Peter SHNYDER, guardian for Charles HAY, son of deceased |
| | Robert TRAILL, guardian for Henry HAY, son of deceased |
| motion of: | T. ROSS, Esq.—the petition will be considered by the court during the next term when the petitioners can shew cause why it should be set aside |

Guardian for 2 minor children of William LATTIMORE, Allen Township (both under age 14):

| | |
|---|---|
| petitioner: | William LATTIMORE, cousin of the deceased |
| 2 children: | John |
| | Elizabeth |
| guardian: | for both children—John HAYS, Allen Township |

**Court on 25 June 1795, continued:**

Guardians for 3 minor grandchildren of Casper DOLL (had will which left them a legacy):

| | |
|---|---|
| petitioner: | Christopher ENGEL, Easton, father of the children |
| executors: | Lewis STACHER and John YOUNG |
| 3 children: | Henry ENGEL, over age 14....................guardian: his father, Christopher ENGEL |
| | Susanna ENGEL, under age 14...............guardian: Peter SHNYDER, Easton |
| | John ENGEL, under age 14.....................guardian: Peter SHNYDER, Easton |

**Court on 11 August 1795**
**Justices, the Esquires: Jacob RUSH, Peter RHOADS, William HENRY**

Estate of Melchior HAY, William Township—in reference to petition of last June for a new writ of inquest to be issued:

| | |
|---|---|
| motion of: | Samuel SITGREAVES, Esq.—the petitioners may appeal to the Supreme Court of Pennsylvania during the September term 1795 |

**End of Volume E**

## APPENDIX A

### Townships Appearing in Northampton County Orphans Court Records Many Are Now Located in Other Counties of Pennsylvania

**(Note: the dates given below represent the first time the townships' names appeared in these records and not the years in which they were formed as townships.)**

| Township Name | First Appeared in Orphans Court | Present-day County (when formed) | Comments |
|---|---|---|---|
| Allen | 1758 | Northampton | originally in Bucks County |
| Bethlehem | 1759 | Northampton | originally in Bucks County |
| Chestnuthill | 1775 | Monroe (1836) | |
| Delaware | 1770 | Northumberland (1772) | |
| Easton (as twp.?) | 1791 | City of Easton in Northampton | perhaps an error in record |
| Forks | 1767 | Northampton | |
| Hamilton | 1764 | Monroe (1836) | |
| Heidelberg | 1761 | Lehigh (1812) | |
| Lehigh | 1761 | Northampton | |
| Lower Mt. Bethel | 1790 | Northampton | |
| Lower Saucon | 1759 | Northampton | |
| Lower Smithfield | 1754 | Smithfield Twp., Monroe (1836) | originally in Bucks County |
| Lowhill | 1761 | Lehigh (1812) | |
| Lynn | 1761 | Lehigh (1812) | |
| Macungie | 1761 | Upper and Lower Macungie Twp., Lehigh (1812) | |
| Milford | 1753 | Upper and Lower Milford Twp., Lehigh (1812) | |
| Moore | 1767 | Northampton | |
| Mt. Bethel | 1762 | Upper and Lower Mt. Bethel Twp., Northampton | |
| Nazareth | 1789 | Upper and Lower Nazareth Twp., Northampton | |
| Penn | 1775 | East Penn, Carbon (1843) | |
| Plainfield | 1761 | Northampton | |
| Salisbury | 1762 | Lehigh (1812) | |
| Towamensing | 1762 | Carbon (1843) | |
| Upper Milford | 1761 | Lehigh (1812) | |
| Upper Saucon | 1753 | Lehigh (1812) | |
| Upper Smithfield | 1766 | Smithfield Twp. Monroe (1836) | |
| Weisenberg | 1761 | Lehigh (1812) | |
| Whitehall | 1758 | Lehigh (1812) | |
| Williams | 1758 | Northampton | originally in Bucks County |

## APPENDIX B

### Localities Mentioned in the Orphans Court Records Outside of Northampton County with the Names of Those who Lived or Owned Property in Those Areas

| Locality | Name | Date First Mentioned in the Records |
|---|---|---|
| **Europe:** | | |
| England | Thomas MACHENESS | 1781 |
| general area | Peter Paul BADER (an estate there) | 1784 |
| Germany | Charles BEETCH (died there) | 1774 |
| Germany | Thomas SCHAFF (legacy there) | 1759 |
| Germany | Matthias SCHEIFFER | 1794 |
| Germany, Frankfort | Anna Maria OTTO (an estate there) | 1759 |
| Germany, Herrnhut, Upper Lusatia | John Gottlieb REICHELT | 1793 |
| Hamburgh in Europe | John George SHOEMACHER | 1784 |
| **West India:** | | |
| Danish West India Islands | Charles Gottlieb REICHELT | 1793 |
| Jamaica | Peter Paul BADER (died there) | 1784 |
| **States outside of Pennsylvania:** | | |
| Carolina Province | Jacob BARE | 1767 |
| New Jersey | William MAJORS | 1794 |
| New Jersey, Hunterdon Tp. | Moore FURMAN | 1787 |
| New Jersey, Hunterdon Tp. | Jonas PETTIT | 1787 |
| New Jersey, Walpack Tp., Sussex Co. | Harman COAL | 1777 |
| New York | William SMITH | 1788 |
| New York, Tioga Co. | John STEWART | 1794 |
| South Carolina, Charles Town | Charles COOPER | 1795 |
| Virginia, Frederickstown | Jacob STEINER | 1783 |
| **Counties in Pennsylvania:** | | |
| Berks, Albany Tp. | Michael BROBST | 1771 |
| Berks, Maxatany Tp. | Nicholas HERMANY | 1794 |
| Berks, Robeson Tp. | Adam BETZ | 1762 |
| Bucks | Christian BUSE | 1778 |
| Bucks | Philip HERPEL | 1794 |
| Bucks | Moses MARSHALL | 1775 |
| Bucks | Richard WALKER | 1792 |
| Bucks | William WALTON | 1794 |
| Bucks, Bedminster Tp. | Frederick ATHERHOLD | 1791 |
| Bucks, Lower Milford Tp. | Michael BISCHOFF (land adj. Northampton) | 1789 |
| Bucks, Rockhill Tp. | Peter SHNYDER | 1790 |
| Bucks, Springfield Tp. | Jacob ERDMAN | 1781/1792 |
| Bucks, Springfield Tp. | Michael FABEYON | 1786 |
| Bucks, Springfield Tp. | Abraham FUNCK | 1783/1789 |
| Bucks, Springfield Tp. | Henry FUNK | 1794 |
| Bucks, Springfield Tp. | Peter GRUVER | 1783 |
| Bucks, Springfield Tp. | Philip Jacob OVERBECK | 1794 |
| Bucks, Springfield Tp. | Michael ROTH | 1794 |

**APPENDIX B: Counties in Pennsylvania, continued:**

| | | |
|---|---|---|
| Bucks, Southampton Tp. | Joseph LONGSTRETH | 1785 |
| Chester | John OLWINE | 1795 |
| Cumberland, Shawonese | Peter CORSA | 1784 |
| Cumberland, West Pennsborough Tp. | James BROWN | 1782 |
| Fayette | William NICHOL | 1786 |
| Lancaster | Abraham REINECKE | 1793 |
| Montgomery, Mooreland Tp. | Abraham DUFFIELD | 1785 |
| Montgomery, North Wales Tp. | Isaac SUMMONY | 1786 |
| Montgomery, Upper Hanover Tp. | Jacob GARY | 1785 |
| Northumberland | Dewald PEELMAN | 1786 |
| Philadelphia | Enoch ARMITAGE | 1766 |
| Philadelphia | Elisabeth GILBERT | 1783 |
| Philadelphia | Balzer LOHR | 1761 |
| Philadelphia | John RUSH | 1771 |
| Philadelphia | Jacob SHEAVER | 1755 |
| Philadelphia, Byberry Tp. | Jacob COMLY | 1784 |
| Philadelphia, City of | Thomas AFFLECK | 1783 |
| Philadelphia, City of | Charles COOPER | 1795 |
| Philadelphia, City of | Abigail DELYON | 1791 |
| Philadelphia, City of | William GRINDING | 1778 |
| Philadelphia, City of | Melchior STEINER | 1783 |
| Philadelphia, Solford Tp. | Conrad WORMON | 1772 |
| Philadelphia, Lower Salford Tp. | John Isaac KLEIN | 1785 |
| Philadelphia, Upper Hanover Tp. | Michael ZIMMERMAN, the elder | 1762 |

**INDEX OF THE JUSTICES OF THE ORPHANS COURT**
**(These names will not appear in the general index unless directly concerned with an estate.)**

## INDEX OF OTHER COURT OFFICERS

**(These names do not appear in the general index unless directly concerned with an estate.)**

## GENERAL INDEX

Every name listed in the abstracts is indexed here except officers of the court (indexed elsewhere). Because of the inconsistency of spelling in the Orphans Court records, many names, though representing the same person or family, were spelled in many variations. Often, the spellings are quite similar, perhaps spelled with one "m" in one reference and with two "m's" in another, or "Miller" then later, "Muller." An attempt has been made to group similar names together in this index, though many have probably been missed. Also, to reduce the task of typing this index, the author has generalized some spellings of first names listed under one surname when several variations appeared in the records (e.g. "Catherine," "Catharine," or "Catherina" might all be listed simply as "Catherine" under a specific surname). When both the maiden name and married name of a woman is known, she is listed under both surnames.

*~A~*

***~C~***

*~E~*

## ~*F*~

***~G~***

***~K~***

*~L~*

***~Mc~***

***~O~***

***~P~***

*~Q~*



*~R~*

## *~U~*

~X~



~*Y*~

## ~Z~